Leading Learning/Learning Leading: A Retrospective on a Life's Work

Internationally recognized for his writing on educational leadership, and the ethics of educational leadership, Robert J. Starratt brings together a thoughtfully crafted selection of his writing, representing key aspects of his life and work, leading to his current thinking on the convergence of school leadership, the professional ethics of educators, and the integrity of the teaching-learning process.

This retrospective reveals Starratt's enduring work as probing the foundational intelligibility of the teaching-learning process and its connection to human development of both students and teachers. It exhibits his efforts to focus the leadership of the teaching-learning process on a combination of cognitive insight into the intelligibility of the world, affective dwelling in the particulars of that intelligibility, and the responsibilities one's relationships with the particular might suggest.

A new introduction contextualises Starratt's work against key developments in the field. The unique collection of chapters develop various themes, from human resource development to the complexity of curriculum change and from ethical analysis of school organizational structures to the complex dramas in students' personal lives and in the classroom. The book chronicles Starratt's contributions to the field and his role as a leading scholar, who has played a key part in the development of leadership and ethics in education over the course of his career.

Leading Learning/Learning Leading will be of global interest to education leaders and researchers engaged in the field of educational leadership and ethical education.

Robert J. Starratt is Emeritus Professor of Education at The Lynch School of Education, Boston College, USA.

World Library of Educationalists series

In the **World Library of Educationalists** series, international experts compile career-long collections of what they judge to be their finest pieces – extracts from books, key articles, salient research findings, major theoretical and practical contributions – so the world can read them in a single manageable volume. Readers will be able to follow the themes and strands and see how their work contributes to the development of the field.

A full list of titles in this series is available at: www.routledge.com.
Recently published titles:

Dysconscious Racism, Afrocentric Praxis, and Education for Human Freedom: Through the Years I Keep on Toiling
The selected works of Joyce E. King
Joyce E. King

A Developing Discourse in Music Education
The selected works of Keith Swanwick
Keith Swanwick

Struggles for Equity in Education
The selected works of Mel Ainscow
Mel Ainscow

Faith, Mission and Challenge in Catholic Education
The selected works of Gerald Grace
Gerald Grace

Towards a Convergence Between Science and Environmental Education
The selected works of Justin Dillon
Justin Dillon

From Practice to Praxis: A reflexive turn
The selected works of Susan Groundwater-Smith
Susan Groundwater-Smith

Learning, Development and Education: From learning theory to education and practice
The selected works of Knud Illeris
Knud Illeris

(Post)Critical Methodologies: The Science Possible After the Critiques
The selected works of Patti Lather
Patti Lather

Education, Ethnicity, Society and Global Change in Asia
The selected works of Gerard A. Postiglione
Gerard A. Postiglione

Leading Learning/Learning Leading: A Retrospective on a Life's Work
The selected works of Robert J. Starratt
Robert J. Starratt

Leading Learning/Learning Leading: A Retrospective on a Life's Work

The Selected Works of Robert J. Starratt

Robert J. Starratt

LONDON AND NEW YORK

First published 2017
by Routledge
2 Park Square, Milton Park, Abingdon, Oxon OX14 4RN

and by Routledge
711 Third Avenue, New York, NY 10017

Routledge is an imprint of the Taylor & Francis Group, an informa business

© 2017 Robert J. Starratt

The right of Robert J. Starratt to be identified as author of this work has been asserted by him in accordance with sections 77 and 78 of the Copyright, Designs and Patents Act 1988.

All rights reserved. No part of this book may be reprinted or reproduced or utilised in any form or by any electronic, mechanical, or other means, now known or hereafter invented, including photocopying and recording, or in any information storage or retrieval system, without permission in writing from the publishers.

Trademark notice: Product or corporate names may be trademarks or registered trademarks, and are used only for identification and explanation without intent to infringe.

British Library Cataloguing in Publication Data
A catalogue record for this book is available from the British Library

Library of Congress Cataloging in Publication Data
A catalog record for this book has been requested

ISBN: 978-1-138-03693-2 (hbk)
ISBN: 978-1-315-17819-6 (ebk)

Typeset in Sabon and Futura
by Florence Production Ltd, Stoodleigh, Devon, UK

To Edythe Starratt
Wise Mother
Inquisitive Learner
The Real Deal

Contents

1	Introduction	1
2	Knowing at the level of sympathy	16
3	The drama of schooling/the schooling of drama	26
4	The challenging world of educational leadership	38
5	Cultivating a perspective on learning	58
6	Building an ethical school	78
7	Working within the geography of human development	93
8	Foundational qualities of an ethical person	112
9	The moral dimension of human resource development	125
10	The ethics of teaching	138
11	Cultivating a mature community	154
12	The complexity of ethical living and learning	169
	Index	173

CHAPTER ONE

Introduction

The title of this book attempts to capture my life's work as an educator. Summaries of "one's life work" are, however, inescapably autobiographical interpretations of the author's better moments in a journey also marked, as well, by less than heroic mistakes and self-serving rationalizations. Leadership is a complex process, often enlightened by early failures and imperfect successes. Leading a *learning process* in the setting of a school is particularly challenging, due to the multiple—student, parent, teacher, school committee, and state authority—understandings/opinions of what constitutes genuine learning and the pedagogical process that promotes the integrity of learning.

The process of leading learning involved, at least in my case, a gradual unfolding of a more focused understanding of what learning involves, and how one's leadership, often indirectly mediated by multiple, other supportive variables—student personal motivation, parental constant encouragement, teachers' creative pedagogical initiatives, school district generous budgetary funding, etc., that promote quality learning of both teachers and students. The composing of a summary of "one's life work" as an educator is fraught with the temptation to self-promotion and appropriation of credit for the success of school improvement initiatives, with hardly a mention of the hard work of so many engaged members of the school internal and external community.

The leadership of learning will always be negotiated, as well, within a larger context of random historical variables, such as the variable potential for political mobilization of supportive human and financial resources; shifts in available technology; emerging policy initiatives concerning the rights of various underserved student populations; shifts in attitudes concerning environmental challenges—to mention some recent historical changes that currently require new leadership responses to long neglected challenges to the education of generations of citizens.

With these cautionary observations about the limited power of individual school leaders in their efforts to promote the integrity of quality learning in schools, I will nonetheless stress throughout the chapters of this book the *potential* to make an enormous difference in the lives of teachers and students at the individual school level. In selecting exemplary chapters in this book, I have chosen those that reflect this strong belief in the leadership potential of school principals as they collaborate with other educational professionals in the school to effect an environment of significant learning for the human development of the learners in their charge.

The gradual articulation of my ideas about leading learning has been fed by an expansive reading agenda of the works of many scholarly giants, as well as by experiential learning opportunities derived from practical involvements as a teacher, school principal, university professor, and a variety of consulting opportunities. In other words, my writing in education reflects a life-long learning trajectory that continues, fortunately, into the present.

At the outset, it is important for me to remember that I am composing this retrospective, not so much to have readers agree with what I have to say, but in the hope that some or all of the chapters will speak to readers about *their own* core beliefs and values as educators, and engage them in a dialogue between the text and the realities of their work as educators. The goal of the book is insightful dialogue about the possibilities of one's leadership, not discipleship.

I've chosen to begin the retrospective with a brief recounting of four periods in my journey to the present. The recounting will reveal at least some of the more obvious contextual and specific influences on my work as an educator. Those four periods refer to 1) roughly the first 25 years of my life; 2) the 1960s; 3) the early 1970s into the later 1980s; 4) from the late 1980s into the present. Within each period, the reader may find some clues to what and why I have written what I have.

The first twenty-five years: Learning how to "become educated" without a mind

I was born in 1935 into the world as the youngest of five children in a financially challenged, but humanly rich home environment. America was emerging from the depths of the Great Depression and was soon to be drawn into the Second World War. My early life-world—the affective, interpersonal world of family and relatives, of friends and enemies—mirrored the self-centered focus of most children around forging one's own way of becoming a somebody (Becker, 1971). Mine was a working-class world supported and constrained by parents, siblings, cousins, aunts and uncles, as well as school teachers and school chums and neighborhood life. That life-world was my intimate personal world that formed the base of my identity. Fortunately, our parents patiently negotiated the daily pulls and pushes of each one of the five of us in our individual efforts to assert those identities. Nevertheless, I was gradually socialized into the world of white, Anglo-Saxon, masculine, competitive, capitalistic culture and Roman Catholic religiosity during my childhood and adolescence. Looking back now, I might characterize my life-world then as a relatively conventional, Norman Rockwell kind of world.

I attended the parish grammar school from kindergarten through eighth grade. Those grammar school years were fairly mindless years. The happiest hours of my day were those hours after the last class ended. The happiest day of the year was the day we began our summer holiday. I do recall fondly our occasional class visits to the town library across the street from our school where the librarian would read us stories about the adventures of youngsters our own age. Another positive thing I remember was the various exercises of diagramming sentences in the eighth grade, when I began to understand, through the classroom exercises, the "parts of speech"—how adverbs went with verbs, and adjectives went with nouns, how an independent clause differed from a dependent clause, what an active-voice verb looked like and what a passive-voice verb looked like. The subjunctive verb usage gave me some initial trouble, but I finally crossed that threshold of intelligibility. The major negative thing I learned in grammar school was that, outside of diagramming sentences, school was something to be endured. It had next to no connection with my life outside of the school day.

As graduation from St. Mary's grammar school approached, I was convinced that if I went to the public high school where many of my friends were going, I would probably end up in jail. I had heard from an older fellow from the neighborhood that the Jesuit high school about twenty miles or so up the road—the one he was attending—was a good school, so I pestered my mother to let me try for a scholarship to go there. I took the test for a scholarship but—given my elementary school experience—did not do well enough for the scholarship. Undeterred, I asked my mother to make an appointment with the principal to see whether I could get a work-scholarship that would cover the one hundred dollar yearly tuition that my parents could not afford. Somehow, Father Kennedy, the Jesuit principal was impressed with my eagerness to attend the school, so he took a chance and offered me a work scholarship—working with the maintenance crew for an hour after school, and working in the school cafeteria to cover my lunch expenses. This was to be the first experience of a lifetime series of gratuitous occasions that set my life on a path I never would have predicted. I took advantage of the opportunity, despite the challenges involved. Fortunately, I found an upper classman at the Jesuit school who was driving to the school from my neighborhood and arranged for the morning transportation to the school. For the afternoon return, I hitch-hiked my way back home. In the ensuing summers of odd jobs, I was able to earn enough money to pay for my own tuition at the school, and to cover the cost of a student-commuter train ticket to and from the school.

However, I found the school curriculum at the Jesuit school as similarly divorced from my out-of-school world as I had at St. Mary's. Because my mother told me I could not play sports at school unless I earned at least Second Honors (a grade average in the eighties), I did my best to comply. I managed to memorize enough of the textbook material to pass the quizzes and tests with at least a grade of eighty. As had been the case at St. Mary's, I learned to give enough right answers, though I rarely, if ever, understood why they were the right answers.

In the spring semester of my ninth grade, I joined the school track team, thus beginning a four-year participation in that sport and a lifetime addiction to running. The following year I also joined the football team. Athletics became the most important thing in my life. I still treasure the many happy memories from those years with my team mates. Also, I now have the arthritic condition of cranky knees to thank for that addiction to sports.

In the summer of 1953, after graduating from high school with a superficial acquaintance with the academic curriculum and with a vague adolescent idealism, I said goodbye to my buddies and girlfriends and entered the religious community known as the Jesuits. Though now separated from my family, I entered a larger family that continued to provide the security of that life world, even though the monastic life style of the seminary seemed awkwardly obsolete and wedded to a medieval vision of how the world functioned.

Involvement in the academic program of the first seven seminary years was, for me, relatively inconsequential. However, midway through my third seminary year,

I had a teacher who rescued me from my drifting indifference to formal studies. He regularly assigned a weekend essay on any topic we wanted to write about. In the following week he would select one of the essays for a dramatic reading. One day in class he chose to read my essay and to comment favorably on it. After class he took me aside and told me that I had a gift for writing, and that he looked forward to reading more of my essays. I was thunderstruck. No teacher before had ever complimented me for any academic achievement. His encouragement communicated to me that I had a mind and creative potential and that I should put it to good use. Most of my classmates in the seminary had been honor students in high school, and had developed an appetite for reading good literature. Some even enjoyed conversing in Latin and French. I was a captive of the contrary attitude of those classmates of mine who excelled in various athletic endeavors, namely, that success in academics was a sign of effeminacy. But now I began to work on my writing. I began to read Shakespeare on the sly and got hooked on his language and the depth of feeling his characters evoked in me. I realized I was miles behind most of my classmates in my intellectual development. That realization motivated me to initially embrace the journey into good literature and historical studies.

However, much of this involvement was on my own. During the subsequent three years of studying philosophy, I spent more time developing my jump shot in basketball than in any serious engagement with the regimen of scholastic philosophy. The lecture-driven pedagogy and the prepackaged curriculum of scholastic philosophy—resuscitated in post-war Europe and presented in seminary textbooks composed in Latin, whose orthodoxy was guaranteed by an *Imprimatur* granted by a Vatican official—expected more or less memorized responses to exams in Latin. We seminarians organized informal study groups that passed around semester exams from recent years and prepared answers to the exam questions taken from our lecture notes. It was a closed system inherited from the scholastic synthesis of the late middle ages that rewarded memorization of someone else's answers to someone else's questions.

Only once during those seven years did I become genuinely intellectually involved throughout one course, and that was in a survey course in existential philosophy in the last semester of the last year of my philosophy studies. Those philosophers spoke to me about issues that impinged on how I was deciding to live my life. Due to that course, I ended up reading most of the works of Albert Camus, who became a kind of "patron saint" in my personal community of saints. There were also occasional controversial books pirated and passed around among classmates. One of my favorites was *The Divine Milieu* by Teilhard de Chardin, a French anthropologist and a Jesuit priest who had been "silenced" by Rome for his writings about evolution and cosmology. I struggled with his earlier work, *The Phenomenon of Man*, but kept on reading it over the next several years until I was able to connect the depth of that book with other scientific authors on evolution and cosmology. During those years occasional elective courses in English and American literature opened up a reading agenda that began in curiosity but matured into a lasting influence on my own writing.

After earning a Bachelor and Masters degree in Philosophy, granted through the seminary's academic links with Boston College, I was eager to enter the world of teaching, despite the fact that I would be called upon to teach subjects that I was woefully unprepared for—ninth grade Algebra and twelfth grade English Literature. After my first year of teaching, I came to appreciate the wisdom of the adage: "If you want to really learn a subject, try teaching it."

A life narrative: The 1960s

The tumultuous decade of the 1960s occasioned an awakening to the dramatic challenges and adventures of the larger world of national and global realities. During that decade, I taught for two idyllic years in a Jesuit boarding school in the Berkshire Mountains of Western Massachussetts. During the course of two years there, I began to explore what was educationally possible even in a dysfunctional school environment. During the ensuing years of the 1960s, I completed a Masters degree at the Harvard Graduate School of Education, a seminary Masters in Theology, and a Doctorate in Educational Administration at the University of Illinois.

Needless to say, the larger world of that decade forcefully disrupted the relative complacency of my life up till then. I, as many of my contemporaries, had to evaluate the shortcomings of our own prior education, as well as the new ideas and trends in education. The election of John Kennedy as President; the founding of the Peace Corps; the confrontation between the US and Russia in Cuba; the rebellion against the Vietnam War; the energy behind the Civil Rights struggle; the continuing emergence of the Women's Rights struggle; the War on Poverty; the opening of the Catholic Church to the modern world in the Second Vatican Council, and its more radical expression in the emergence of liberation theology; the landing of humans on the moon; the emergence of the youth rebellion in music, art, life styles, and politics—all this called for reassessing our certainties during a decade when I was actively a student in three universities that were themselves caught up in responding to these controversial interruptions in the staid universe they traditionally occupied. Needless to say, the 1960s were a time of intense intellectual growth for me. That growth was stimulated by my exposure, for most of that decade, to graduate studies during this time of social and intellectual ferment. Much of that growth, however, involved questioning the disconnect between the curriculum of the academy and the curriculum of living an authentic life.

The Sergiovanni connection

My career as a scholar of educational practice began and continued under the collaborative relationship with an outstanding scholar and human being, Tom Sergiovanni. When I started my full-time studies in the doctoral program at the University of Illinois in the summer of 1967, Tom had just arrived as a novice professor from the University of Rochester. I had enrolled that summer in his course in instructional supervision, after which he invited me to serve as his research assistant. He was just at the beginning of his career as a prolific scholar and writer in education, so I was kept busy assisting in his research projects, hauling boxes of surveys, for example, on the job-satisfaction of teachers, to the computing center on campus and returning with boxes of printout pages of statistical analysis. He also had me busy reading journals in the University's huge library collection to search for other pertinent research on organizational effectiveness.

Since we were close enough in age, we developed a mutually supportive relationship that enabled an easy flow of ideas. Toward the end of the fall semester, Tom invited me to work with him on a textbook dealing with instructional supervision. He had become aware of my interest in curriculum theory and pedagogy, and suggested that I could write the chapters that would deal with supervisory issues in those areas, and he would focus more on the organizational dynamics of schools that promoted more effective supervision of teachers. The title of the book was: *Emerging Patterns of Supervision: Human Perspectives*. Tom's rich background in the research on the dynamics of organizations enabled him to apply that research to the way administrators and teachers might work more collaboratively in the many ways the schools organized and structured the work of the school, especially in the supervision of instruction. Tom focused on the supervisors' ability to surface and support the human talent and professional inventiveness of teachers within a positive school culture that valued the dignity and potential of everyone in the school. He wanted to encourage supervisors to emphasize that their work was involved with a *human* development of teachers' talent, rather than fixation on the impersonal, bureaucratic rating sheets of teachers' behaviors. My contribution to the book would be chapters that dealt with foundational issues such as the supervisor's educational platform (something like an abbreviated educational philosophy), the teacher and supervisor's work on curriculum concerns, the who, what, and why of teacher evaluation, the supervisor's leadership style, supervisory activity as moral activity, and so forth. Given my dissatisfaction with my earlier education, my chapters tended to exhibit a more critical edge toward the status quo of the schooling process. McGraw Hill publishing company responded positively to our book prospectus and thus began a publication in 1971 that has gone through nine editions, the latest published in 2013, a few months after Tom departed to teach supervision to the angels.

Electing to take that first course with Tom was another one of those chance decisions that was to deeply affect my life and career as an educator. It led to a forty-four year collaborative agenda that deeply influenced my scholarly writing in education and, due to the demands of keeping the book current, sustained it over all the editions of those years. That attention to the *human exchange* in the educational and learning process was to remain a core focus embedded in both Tom's and my other writings over the years. Looking back, I am extremely grateful for Tom's support and encouragement. We continued over the years to find deep connections across our particular research interests. The initial theme of the human dimension in the complex work of supervision continued to be a central focus of the various revisions and editions of the book. My focus on human development has matured under the inspiration of the writings of Erik Erikson, and received its fullest expression in one of my most recent books, *Refocusing School Leadership: Foregrounding Human Development Throughout the Work of the School* (Routledge, 2011).

Knowing at the level of sympathy: The dissertation

The choice of a dissertation study involved a major turning point in my life's work. I had been "going to school" for approximately thirty years. During those years I had learned how to survive as a student by studying how to give correct answers to be found in textbooks and curriculum units and expressed in response to teachers' questions in class and in quizzes, and in other assessments of my "learning." I then learned how to be a high school teacher of algebra and literature by "covering the material" in the textbook and curriculum outline, and testing the students' learning of that material in the same way I had been taught. In university courses, I learned how to succeed as a student, again by giving correct answers to professors' questions. I would occasionally ask questions in class, but rarely encountered responses beyond the familiar, "Well, what do you think?"

Tom Sergiovanni was an exception. My questions in his class brought an attempt to engage in some kind of genuine dialogical pursuit. That dialogue often led to further dialogue outside of class. With other professors, it usually became clear that the professor preferred to move forward with the lecture or the material in the text. That kind of passive learning enabled me to survive the undergraduate years, earn a Masters degree in Philosophy, a Masters degree in Education, a Masters degree in Theology, and to complete the course work toward a Doctorate in education.

At that point, I had had enough. That was when I began to realize what my life's work in education would involve. I decided that my doctoral dissertation would attempt to fashion a theory of learning that addressed a deeper, more complex curriculum and learning agenda. By and large, my dissertation committee provided encouraging, general feedback, but their research concerns were different than mine. They simply gave me more or less free reign to let the study progress however it might. In any event, the work on the dissertation proved immensely satisfying. I believed that I now had a clearer sense of a learning theory that would form the cornerstone of my leadership of a high school.

While I was working with Tom on the supervision book, I was also attempting to articulate the focus of my dissertation study—a critical review of developments in curriculum theory at that time, and an attempt to bring those developments into a richer synthesis that integrated the cognitive dimensions of curriculum and learning theory with the aesthetic, expressive, and performative dimensions of learning theory.

I was reading broadly in philosophy, aesthetics, epistemology, cognitive theory, and literature. Some examples of those readings included the following: Jerome Bruner, *The Process of Education* (Cambridge, MA: Harvard University Press, 1960); Jerome Bruner, *Toward a Theory of Instruction* (Cambridge, MA: Belknapp Press, 1966); Ernst Cassirer, *An Introduction to a Philosophy of Human Culture* (New Haven: Yale University Press, 1962); John Dewey, *Democracy and Education* (New York: Macmillan, 1916); John Dewey, *Art and Experience* (New York: Capricorn Books, 1958); Iredell Jenkins, *Art and the Human Enterprise* (Cambridge, MA: Harvard University Press, 1958); Susanne K. Langer, *Mind: An Essay on Human Feeling* (Baltimore: Johns Hopkins University Press, 1967); Albert W. Levi, *Philosophy and the Modern World* (Bloomington, Indiana: Indiana University Press, 1959); John Macmurray, *Reason and Emotion* (London: Faber, 1935); John Macmurray, *Persons in Relation* (New York: Harper & Brothers, 1961); Alexis de Toqueville, *Democracy in America*, trans. George Lawrence, ed. J. P. Mayer (New York: Doubleday, Anchor Books, 1969); Michael Polanyi, *Personal Knowledge: Towards a Post Critical Philosophy* (New York: Harper Torchbooks, 1965); Michael Polanyi, *The Tacit Dimension* (New York: Doubleday & Company, 1966);

Michael Polanyi, "The Creative Imagination", *Chemical and Engineering News* 44 (No.17, 1966): 85–93; Max Scheler, *The Nature of Sympathy* (London: Routledge & Kegan Paul, 1959); Alfred North Whitehead, *Process and Reality: An Essay in Cosmology* (NewYork: Macmillan, 1929); Alfred North Whitehead, *Adventures of Ideas* (NewYork: Macmillan, 1933); Alfred North Whitehead, *The Aims of Education and Other Essays* (New York: Free Press, 1967).

The philosophical breadth of those readings indicates the kind of search I was engaged in. Given the barren landscape of the education I was subjected to during thirty or so years of my life, those readings enabled me to begin to articulate what I felt was missing in my education. I was searching for a kind of teaching and learning that sought to connect the curriculum with the lived experience of learners, that encouraged a deeper dialogue with the intelligibility of the subject under study, and that called forth the significance and value of the human adventure with this particular segment of knowledge. During my encounter with these scholars, I was searching for a school curriculum and pedagogy that might connect my personal and professional life to the world, to reveal its beauty and tragedy, its demands and challenges, its connections to multiple understandings and perspectives that enabled me to engage the world in its complexity and breadth. Without knowing where an un-named and increasingly disappointed longing that had been growing during the first thirty or so years of my life was leading me, I was seeking a level of understanding in my studies that enabled me to take inside and to *feel* the significance of the knowledge those studies communicated. I wanted to know why it was important for me to study what I was studying; what was its value in my life and the lives of students. By and large, my teachers up till then had not communicated that kind of feeling towards what they were teaching. Their major concern seemed to be to "cover" the material in the textbook, without explaining why we should study "this stuff" in the first place. I wanted to find scholars who wrote about a deeper, more engaging kind of learning and teaching.

This immersion into an articulation of learning as sympathetic knowing, was to become one of the couplets that eventually became part of this book's title. If I were to lead as an educator, I had to articulate what that leadership was leading, namely a form of transformative learning that embodied a whole philosophy of education. Likewise, if I were to lead that kind of learning, I had to learn how to be a different kind of leader, one who was also continually learning himself how to engage with other educators in a common search for transformative pedagogies that more fully engaged with the transformation of young lives into more fully engaged learners.

In retrospect, one author who stands out as hugely influential on my thinking during those years was, and still is, Loren Eiseley. A friend from Boston introduced me to Eiseley's first book, *The Immense Journey* (1957) while I was just beginning my literature review for my dissertation. As I read further in his books, he quickly joined the list of my personal "patron saints" in my community of saints. His books, intended for a general audience interested in scientific and philosophical thinking, offered collections of reflective essays on the theories of evolution, on his experiences while conducting archaeological studies in the field, on the inventiveness and intelligence in nature, on the history of science and philosophy. Eiseley had a very personal, poetic, and probing writing style that spoke deeply to me. His written works exemplified the depth and felt meanings I wished I had experienced in my earlier education. They were books that implied a philosophy of learning and reflection on the implications of scientific knowledge. If someone were to ask me what I meant by "Knowing at the Level of Sympathy," I would tell him or her to read one of Eiseley's books. The dissertation provided me with a foundation that over many years has shaped and energized my research agenda around a broader epistemology that undergirds a more comprehensive curriculum and learning theory. The dissertation also grounded my educating practice of serving as the principal of two schools, and the development of university educational leadership programs and courses. So much of my writing, subsequent to the work involved in my dissertation, has flowed directly or indirectly from that breakthrough achievement.

The life narrative: 1969–1987

With a recently minted doctorate in educational administration, I was appointed in 1969 to the position of Principal of the Jesuit high school I had attended as an adolescent, some twenty years earlier. That was the beginning of my six-year immersion in the on-the-ground practice of educational leadership, a practice immersed within a context of multiple external and internal challenges facing all schools at that time. However, my doctoral studies and dissertation provided me a beginning foundation for articulating initiatives that I thought were called for in responding to the challenges embedded in the external social and cultural context, as well as in the internal culture of the school.

The work as principal plunged me into a six-year effort of school renewal in two rather different schools—first in a fairly traditional Jesuit college prep school in suburban Connecticut, followed by a more family-oriented school in Colorado. In both settings, I was involved in intense work with the teaching faculties in an effort to open up the curriculum to a more generous attention to the arts, to community service, to involvement of alumni in bringing a career-exploration-connection to the academic curriculum, to some forms of team-teaching across academic disciplines, and to a more qualitative evaluation and reporting of student learning. Those initiatives encountered various levels of resistance. By hindsight, I realize that I might have moved more slowly on some initiatives to allow members of the faculty opportunities to gain more self-confidence in adjusting to them. However, I viewed the situation as requiring a large mix of simultaneous initiatives that interacted with and reinforced one another. For example, some effort at team teaching reinforced exposure to interdisciplinary curriculum units that offered deeper and broader insights into the subject matter. Newly required art and drama courses opened up neglected areas for imagination and self-expression, and fed into some of the performative kinds of learning that opened the doors to adolescent expressions of identity. The scheduling of two-week, full-day, on- or off-campus mini-courses in January opened up opportunities in outdoor education, career exploration, more reflective group explorations of ideas, explorations in community service, as well as intensive on-campus remediation courses for ninth graders who were struggling in math and language. These initiatives encouraged the teaching faculty to team up and construct more creative pedagogies that increased more active student involvement in particular learning activities.

Finally, since in most schools the grading system is the tail that wags the dog, in both schools we adopted a qualitative report card system that provided personalized feedback *in prose* on specific student academic strengths, and on areas needing more particular attention. No numerical or letter grades were given until the final grade at the end of the year or the end of the semester course. That way, students who got a slow start in a course would not get penalized by averaging low grades with high grades. The periodic student evaluation reports identified specific areas of progress and areas needing greater effort, leaving open the possibility for students to move from underperforming status to an A or B grade that reflected their latest performance on evaluations at the end of the course. The reverse was also possible, namely, that the final grade might indicate a falling off of effort toward the end of the course, so that the A student could not coast along during the last weeks of the course.

There were other changes that attended to student-life purposes. Both schools served only male students, with, at best, a token female staff. When the opportunity arose, I intentionally hired female teachers and encouraged them not only to be creative in their academic pedagogy, but also—in the dominant male culture of the school—to oppose sexist stereotypes and jokes, and cultivate and model a greater sensitivity toward female issues when appropriate learning opportunities arose.

During those years, I learned about working with parents in more proactive, ongoing communication both to clarify what we were up to, and to listen to their concerns and suggestions. Given the turmoil going on in the larger world, the parents were also trying to absorb the changes, both academic and religious, going on in their children's education. Our parent-teacher nights tended to be rather lively, that is to say, contentiously probing. Some parents thought our initiatives were too radical; others thought they were overdue.

While involved in these controversial and demanding change efforts, I was invited to participate in a new research and development team of other principals of Jesuit high schools in the United States who would address the larger issues of school-wide initiatives in more organically coherent curriculum development planning. Another task of this team was to design a Masters program in school leadership for aspiring principals and presidents of Jesuit high schools, and to seek out a collaborative effort with one of the Jesuit universities in the United States that already had the resources to support this specific Masters program. This team worked under the direction of a new national board of directors of the recently formed Jesuit Secondary Education Association (JSEA).

My writings about educational leadership were in response to several felt needs: 1) the need for the supervision book to articulate a more detailed integration of the work of instructional supervision with a more specific, dynamic theory of the leadership of the supervisor; 2) given the development of the design of a Masters program for the preparation of principals of Jesuit high schools, the need to attach the work of the principal to a theory of visionary leadership that energized the principal's role as instructional leader; 3) the need of the field of educational leadership to balance the concentration on management concerns elaborated in the research of corporate leadership with a complementary focus on visionary or value/meaning focused leadership; 4) my personal need to articulate a theory of educational leadership that would ground my own exercise of leadership.

I had come to the realization that the leadership literature connected to education was more focused on transactional leadership derived from organizational management in the corporate world and measured by quantifiable productivity benchmarks, than on transformational leadership focused on value oriented growth measures of human beings. The educational leadership literature as well as the pedagogical process I had been exposed to at Harvard and the University of Illinois did not reflect a vision of learning I had in mind. I needed to articulate what that visionary leadership might look like. Without the clarity I now have of what my agenda involved, I took up a study of leadership that was more expressive of what I understood intuitively would be more transformational of the life of schools, a leadership focused on a rich learning agenda for young people. Thus, my scholarly agenda as a practicing principal *and* as a university professor is more appropriately entitled "leading learning/learning leading." That tends to capture the dynamic involved in educating leadership—one couplet necessarily requiring the other couplet.

An example might illustrate the dynamism of each couplet. Because the book, Supervision, Human Perspectives, had been well received, during my initial years as a principal I was invited to present a paper on my views of the challenges around curriculum theory at a conference organized by Bill Pinar and Madelaine Grumet, attended by a group of young scholars who identified themselves as "Curriculum Reconceptualists." The conference papers were exploring a variety of postmodern perspectives that were critical of the epistemology embedded in traditional school curriculum. I showed up at the conference wearing my clerical suit and presented my ideas on a fresh look at John Dewey. I realized right away that both my attire and my paper probably advertised my persona as an outlier at the conference. During the evening reception on the first night, I was confronted by an amply bearded participant in bib overalls smoking a joint who asked me what a (bleeping) Thomist had to offer this community of critical scholars. Despite the intended put-down, we had an interesting conversation. That conference and the subsequent publication of the papers presented therein introduced me to the lively community of scholars who were attempting to push beyond the traditional, overly rational constructs of school curriculum and its learning tasks and the evaluation of its learning outcomes—all framed in perspectives whose legitimacy was derived from modernist views dating back to Descartes's view of the individual knower's reliance on scientific knowledge derived from empirical studies. That conference opened up a significant reading journey that influenced much of my subsequent writing on leadership and ethics. I want to praise the significant influence Bill and Madelaine have had on the field of curriculum studies. I have followed their consistently insightful writing over the years. I differ, however, with many younger Reconceptualists on their sometimes overblown rhetoric and easy generalizations. I have intentionally attempted to be a bridge in my writing between the significance of their views and the limitations of the more traditional assumptions about the rationality and legitimacy of the school curriculum. My leading of learning in this instance certainly involved my (critical) learning of educational leadership's blind spots.

Another initiative that has influenced my writing involved professional development weekends designed to foster dialogue between Jesuit and lay staff on how they saw their work as an explicit ministry within the religious mission of the school. This initiative took on an international flavor as it spread to Catholic schools in Pacific Rim countries, Australia, and India and cultivated an express attention to the spirituality of teaching itself. Involvement in those discussions within the

Asian cultural and religious context stimulated some of my more ecumenical writing on spirituality in the integral practice of educating. Indeed, much of the practical work on the design and the leading of major changes in two high schools brought realistic perspectives on the supervision of instruction focus of some of my developing writings in that area. My work was deeply and inescapably involved in practicing what I was writing about and writing about what I was practicing. Again, for me, leadership in education involved learning leading as well as leading learning.

I enjoyed a sabbatical year in 1975-76 that included travel in South America to learn Spanish and to study some educational initiatives that incorporated various aspects of liberation theology. A few years before my time in South America I was fortunate to meet Paulo Freire, who was then lecturing at Harvard, and to immerse myself in his writings. I was therefore interested in seeing his ideas being implemented in various settings in Bolivia and Peru. His elaboration of an empowering pedagogy in literacy that nurtured a conscientious inquiry into lived experience—primarily among adult peasants and urban shanty-town communities—carried overtones, expressed in a different vocabulary, of my theory of sympathetic knowing as applied to the education of youth—those oppressed by poverty and racial and gender discrimination, and those in elite suburbs oppressed by multiple pressures from a hyperrationalized, competitive schooling experience. The larger political context of Bolivia and Peru at that time, both under military control, required a circumspect, basically listening presence in local communities there. While in Bolivia, I became aware that my letters to my parents in the US were being read before being resealed and sent on. I began to encourage my mother to send a friendly greeting at the beginning of her letters to those reading the mail. She enjoyed the game. Again, the learning of leadership of a critical educational process required a leading of a more personalized, emancipatory learning environment.

My return to the United States was followed by some months of pastoral ministry in an inner city parish in Chicago where I became familiar with communities of African Americans and Mexican Americans living in public housing in that part of Chicago. I was struck by the contrast between different experiences of poverty in Latin America and in the United States. Yet, in both contexts I witnessed the deep humanity of people who struggled to retain their dignity and sense of community while sustaining a life with many challenges. Living among the people in both contexts enabled a much valued understanding of how education was seen as providing the gateway to a better way of living. The learning experiences of that year were to influence my writing, especially on the moral character of learning as a foundational introduction to active membership in the worlds of culture, nature and society. The theme of learning for active membership in the world provided a nuancing of the meaning of leading that kind of learning.

In 1976 I moved on to Fordham University in New York City as a full-time member of the research and development team serving Jesuit high schools in the United States. As a member of that team I enjoyed a rich experience of exchanging ideas with my team members as we designed a specific Masters program for aspiring principals in Jesuit schools. We also mounted a three-year national effort to work on curriculum development with groups of principals and teachers in various regions of the country. That experience brought insights into the complexities of the change process and the need for sensitivity to the mix of various elements in each school culture. Again, this kind of learning influenced a different way of leading a learning process of educating communities.

During those years I also began a series of visits to Australia to speak at various meetings of Australian educators. Australia was at that time exploring a devolution of school leadership from state level inspectors to local school districts choosing their own headmasters who were now being prepared in university programs in school administration. Tom Sergiovanni had been initially invited to lead workshops for these aspiring principals, but prior commitments led to his recommending me as his fill-in. One visit led to further invitations in subsequent years. On those visits I was privileged to meet many extraordinary educators, some of whom became dear friends. Those visits inspired some of my best writing, which eventually made its way into an initial version of one of my better books, *Centering Educational Administration: Cultivating Meaning, Community, Responsibility* (2003).

During those years at Fordham, I also taught in Masters and Doctoral degree programs for public school educators in New York City and its surrounding suburbs. My writing during those years tended to focus on the role of leading a community of practitioners, about a rich exposure to learning theory, and about confronting ethical challenges in the operation of the schools, along with incisive forays into ethical theory. Again, learning about leadership in these urban schools involved innovative ways of approaching the schools' complex learning agenda. My graduate students—creative leaders in various urban settings—were teaching me as much as I was teaching them about what leadership in these schools implies.

A life journey: 1987 to the present

An event that influenced my writing during this period of my life was my departure from the Jesuit community and marriage to my wife, Ruth. While everything that preceded that change continued to influence my writing, I began to write to a broader audience. Much of my earlier writing was concerned with the renewal of Jesuit schools. Nevertheless, I believed that much of my previous writing could be applied to public and private schools, but in language and imagery that would suit that broader audience. That effort involved calling attention to the potentially close affiliation between spirituality, and a practice of ethical virtue. I continued to address Catholic school audiences within their familiar theological language, but my attention was increasingly drawn to a public school audience that was voicing many of my own concerns about a more transformative curriculum and pedagogy in their classrooms.

Inspired by the leadership of David Bickimer, who was building a community of alternative-school educators in New York City, we began a distinctive Masters program in Educational Leadership at Fordham that focused on preparing educators from a growing number of New York City alternative schools for the role of principal of those schools. These educators were already involved with initiatives that echoed many of the initiatives I had been engaged in while working within the Jesuit context. David taught within that program and encouraged me to hire other creative alternative school principals as adjuncts in the program. They lent a credibility and authenticity to the program. The colorful language of this community was probably more explicitly assertive about what I would have termed "transformative pedagogy," but I had no doubts about where their hearts were.

Their commitments were energized by an intuition of the moral character of authentic learning, about which I began to write a great deal.

Another opportunity that stimulated much of my writing during this period fell out of the sky with an invitation to join a community of international scholars that were exploring the ethical dimensions of educational leadership. Paul Begley, then at the University of Toronto and one of the founding leaders of that group, suggested that I attend their annual meeting and present a paper on my work in that area. My subsequent connection with that group of international scholars through their annual meetings encouraged much of my writing during this time around the application of ethical theory to the complex work of the school.

Professor Lyse Langlois of Laval University in Quebec was a member of this group, and her empirical research on the interactive ethical perspectives of Justice, Care, and Critique, in the decisions of administrators in Canada, helped to verify the relative strength of those interactive perspectives that I had emphasized in my earlier writing on the complementarity of those three ethics in administrative decision making.

Thanks to the focus of this group, in subsequent years I began to elaborate on the professional ethics of educational practice, namely the intentional promotion of *the moral good of learning* in the school's academic curriculum, and the critique of the harm visited upon large numbers of students in the school's failure to provide an adequate *opportunity to learn* the curriculum material they were being tested on in the state's accountability system of imposed tests on its curriculum standards. The failure to provide a genuine opportunity to learn continues to challenge how we lead a learning and assessment process that disadvantages large numbers of students and shifts them into punishing remedial programs that often guarantee continued failure.

Thanks to Andy Hargreaves' invitation to write a book on Ethical Leadership for a book series he was developing, I began to explore leadership virtues that would support a school's ethical focus on the opportunity-to-learn agenda. These writings led to invitations to present my views on the ethics of leadership to educators in Sweden, Ireland, Canada and Australia. In turn, those opportunities led to a fuller treatment of foundational perspectives on ethical education in the recent book, *Cultivating an Ethical School* (Routledge, 2012). That book incorporated more foundational material that emphasized the theoretical perspective of Erik Erikson on the human developmental cycle from infancy to mature adulthood, thereby enabling me to clarify the distinction between the pre-ethical years of young learners moving toward a more secure identity and the mature ethical years of adult intimacy and generativity. This distinction pointed to a more appropriate educational approach to supporting foundational dispositions upon which school-age young people can move toward a fuller ethical identity in young adulthood.

The later years in this stage of my writing have been devoted toward a more organic articulation of the relationship of the school's academic curriculum to membership in the worlds of culture, nature, and society. In turn, that articulation implied some attention to knowing at the level of feeling for what it means to be a member of these worlds, appreciating both the cognitive as well as the moral and aesthetic side of membership in the world. Underlying this level of understanding—the sympathetic appreciation of membership—is an ontology of relationality that grounds our understanding of how everything is related over space and time.

The articulation of this ontology helps to ground a philosophy of education that I have been tacitly and haphazardly struggling toward since I first went to school. Moreover, it has positioned me to continue to explore more explicit examples of this kind of connection of the school curriculum to the students' relational membership and participation in the worlds of culture, nature and society.

Taken in their totality, my books, book chapters and conference papers represent a progressive recycling of interacting core concerns. Each book reveals a re-positioning of those core concerns in different, complementary relationships with other or new concerns. Those concerns include: a concern for a transformed and transforming curriculum that demands transformed and transforming pedagogies and learning opportunities; a concern for transforming leadership that articulates a transforming vision that guides institutional expressions of that vision; a concern that recognizes the personal and communal dramas being enacted throughout the school and the need for constant improvisation of the script of those dramas; a concern for an explicit attention to the daily curriculum of community in which students learn life skills that facilitate living in community; a concern for ethical theory and practice that guides how young and mature adults negotiate the challenges of self-governing in an educating community; a concern for an explicit articulation of the human good promoted by every curriculum unit, as well as by the totality of the curriculum; a concern for the continuing human development of every member of the school community in all activities of the school.

Papers delivered at educational conferences and subsequently published in journals and book chapters tended to advance my thinking in one or more of those concerns. Multiple revisions of graduate courses in university programs also stimulated new insights into one or more of these concerns and their interaction with other concerns in subsequent books.

The review of my life journey should provide the reader with some clues as to the questions I was addressing in the various chapters of this retrospective. I included these excerpts from the larger body of my writings because I believe they illustrate—imperfectly, to be sure—the scholarly quest I have been on these many years. Looking back over the substance of my educational writing and speaking, one of the glaring defects I now detect, is the failure to more explicitly deal with issues of race in the schooling process. Given the present concern for a proactive attention to race in a world that is much more involved with social justice globally, I acknowledge that I still have much to learn and to respond to in the years that I have left. My hope is that the chapters of this book can nonetheless speak to many questions and concerns that readers of this book may bring to their own work and, in the process, help them to name their questions and concerns with greater precision and enlarge their convictions about the direction of their leadership.

References

Becker, E. (1971). *The birth and death of meaning* (second edition). New York: The Free Press.

Eiseley, L. (1957). *The immense journey.* New York: Vantage Books

CHAPTER TWO
▄▄▄▄▄▄▄▄

Knowing at the level of sympathy
A curriculum challenge

> The essence of education is that it be religious. . . . A religious education is an education which inculcates duty and reverence.
> —A. N. WHITEHEAD[1]

The public school curriculum seems to have moved to an extreme end of the spectrum, which includes several levels of imbalance, all reinforcing one another. Forces outside the curriculum field—some political, some technological, some financial, and some from management science—have influenced the movement to the extreme. These forces have called for a greater accountability from the schools, for quantifiable results that can be measured against quantifiable results from other states and nations, for management and evaluation systems driven by quantifiable objectives, for definitions of minimum competencies of basic skills, for measurable promotion and graduation requirements, and for a well-calibrated delivery system of instructional services.[2]

The movement has led to a focus on "student achievement" that seems to be equated with student learnings that really count, those measured on standardized tests. What standardized tests seem best equipped to measure are "skills": memory skills, vocabulary skills, sentence-attack skills, problem-solving skills, decoding skills, numeracy skills, and thinking skills. Curriculum and instructional protocols now emphasize the acquisition or mastery of skills.[3]

The recent research on school and classroom effectiveness has encouraged these developments in curriculum and instruction. While many original scholars who conducted the research hedged their conclusions with qualifying reservations, many commentators on the research have been less cautious.[4] With the clamor for school reform in most states, the rhetoric of effective instruction has induced states to target staff-development and inservice monies to workshops that train teachers in classroom effectiveness-teaching behaviors.[5] Supervisors and principals are encouraged or mandated to evaluate teachers according to these teaching protocols. Curriculum is to be tailored to instruction that leads to improved test scores. Teachers are encouraged, simply, to make the test the curriculum.

Fortunately, this picture of curriculum and instruction is selective. It describes a movement toward imbalance. It does not dwell on some of the commonsense, beneficial outcomes of direct instruction in skill mastery for children at particular stages in their development. Even more fortunately, some teachers can place the focus on skills, test scores, and the simplistic formulas for effective teaching in a larger perspective. While they resent self-serving administrative rhetoric about instructional leadership, they have enough sense to recognize the useful elements (which most of them had already incorporated into their teaching) and to retain their broad concern for other student learnings.[6]

The challenge before us is to restore the balance of the public school curriculum. This essay offers a perspective for constructing a balance. The perspective seeks to redress the fragmentation of knowledge into usable bits to pass exams. The perspective offers to enrich and deepen the quality of learning as well as point to its broader social implications. This perspective is *knowing at the level of sympathy*.

Sympathetic knowing

Knowing at the level of sympathy covers various acts of knowing. It is knowing that involves an appreciation of what is known. It is knowing that takes in the particularity of what is known in its fascinating individuality, including knowing the context, the landscape and history, and the connectedness of what is known to its spatial and temporal environment. It is knowing that consists of an intimate experience of the known and thus embraces its value and significance in its own right. It is relational knowing in which the known affects the knower while the knower dwells in the known. Although sympathetic knowing must be described by image and metaphor (the way we know most things), it is not some kind of exotic, mystical, parapsychological gymnastic. It is not a new epistemology or a new learning theory. With its endorsement from Whitehead, Dewey, Scheler, Reid, Langer, Polanyi, and Macmurray, it has a reputable pedigree.[7]

Without belaboring a lengthy theoretical foundation for this perspective, this essay attempts to address the curriculum implications of adopting a perspective of knowing at the level of sympathy. For the sake of simplicity, I focus on three aspects of sympathetic knowing as they might appear in a curriculum: sympathetic knowing as appreciation, sympathetic knowing as experiencing connectedness, and sympathetic knowing as experiencing social responsibility. Simple illustrations of curriculum ideas that would respond to the complex learning agenda implied in this perspective follow.

Sympathetic knowing as appreciation

We usually think of knowing as appreciation as part of aesthetics and art criticism. However, knowing as appreciation is involved in many human experiences beyond what is normally considered aesthetic experience. Understanding a math problem, building a model airplane, swimming, laughing at a joke, suffering an earache, and listening to a neighbor's story of a family tragedy can all involve knowing as appreciation. Jenkins maintains that all conscious activity is made up of three interpenetrating, functional components: the aesthetic, the affective, and the cognitive.[8] The aesthetic focuses on the particularity of things; the affective focuses on the importance of things for us, and the cognitive component focuses on the connectedness of things. These components of consciousness are always active simultaneously, though with relative degrees of intensity. Depending on a person's attitude toward the object, the purpose, interest, or concern at the time, one of the three components tends to dominate the experience.

In building a model airplane in a science course, students may focus on the cognitive component, looking at the abstract structural relationships between wing span, velocity, and weight. Or they might simultaneously focus on the plane's particular lines and symmetry, appreciating the visible, tangible sense of harmony and proportion. Similarly, they may feel proud they have built the plane, appreciating how it expresses their understanding of airplane technology. Knowing as appreciation involves all three aspects of the object: its value, particularity, and connectedness.

More formal aesthetic experiences tend to heighten our knowing as appreciation. As Jenkins says, "Art deepens our sympathy for the things and situations—for the human persons and problems—it presents."[9] By entering into the world presented by the artist, we see the world from the perspective of the objects and personalities he or she depicts, rather than from our own perspective. We grow to understand from the inside instead of judging from the outside and so are more prepared to accept them on their own terms.

Taught perhaps initially by experiences with art, students could similarly be led through units in the language arts and social studies curriculum to an appreciation of other people, other cultures, other moments in history on their own terms. The acquisition of factual information about the characters in *To Kill a Mockingbird*, for example, should be secondary to appreciating what the world looked and felt like to those characters. Students' easy indifference in memorizing the statistics of death by bubonic plague should be replaced with some appreciation of what it felt like to live in a European city where the plague was out of control.

Beneath that level of sympathetic knowing is, as Cassirer suggests, a need to discover and assert a fundamental and indelible solidarity of life that undergirds life's multiplicities.[10] Youngsters growing up in our fast-paced society, spending more time in huge enclosed shopping malls than in the outdoors with nature, whose contacts with synthetic artifacts are so removed from natural sources, whose contact with reality is largely mediated through television and popular music, indeed need to slow the pace, ask basic questions, get in touch with the larger rhythms and patterns of history, and discover their roots in collective memory.[11] For knowing as appreciation, curriculum materials are practically nonexistent, though some materials are present in black history and black cultural curriculum.

Sympathetic knowing as appreciation comes about by *indwelling*. As Polanyi suggests, all forms of knowing involve some form of indwelling. This tacit knowing is natural and automatically takes place without our thinking about it.[12] But it is possible to use indwelling intentionally by consciously savoring what we have learned, by looking at it intensely to drink in the hues, tones, shapes, and harmonies. Using indwelling intentionally is like tasting a good wine: Smell the aroma, sip a little at a time, roll it around in the mouth to activate all the taste buds, and linger on the total effect. Using indwelling intentionally is like returning to a favorite painting or rereading a favorite poem out loud. Some sports fans will run a television tape of an exceptional performance over and over. Repetition allows us to dwell inside the experience, to appreciate it for its own sake. Curriculum materials rarely encourage intentional indwelling with repeated returns to the material. Oddly enough, mathematics provides one of the few academic experiences of this kind of appreciation. Through many repetitions of similar mathematical problems, the student is drawn to dwell in the structural and logical uniformities of the mathematical operation.

Sympathetic knowing as experiencing connectedness

We do not need to read *The Closing of the American Mind* to be aware of the fragmentation of knowledge into disparate disciplines, with the consequent fragmentation of moral systems into a relativistic plurality of perspectives.[13] For the past 300 years or so, the medieval synthesis has been subjected to intense centrifugal forces.[14] When we add to the fragmentation of such a unified worldview the strong tradition of American individualism, so aptly described by de Tocqueville and subsequently charted by Bellah and his associates, we realize how even more difficult it is to maintain any sense of a larger network of relationships, other than strictly legal and utilitarian, that bonds people together in a meaningful community, or indeed to a meaningful universe.[15] Yet a curriculum driven by exclusively utilitarian and functional reasoning, which the schools seem to be accepting, cannot provide a sense of a meaningful community or of a meaningful universe. Therefore, a curriculum that promotes a sense of connectedness is so necessary to restore the balance.

The mathematical physicist turned philosopher, Alfred North Whitehead, points to the physical foundation for this sense of connectedness.[16] He demonstrates convincingly that a single fact in isolation is simply a fiction. In a world described by Newtonian atomic physics, isolated self-sufficient atoms are conceivable, as are isolated events, isolated causes, isolated persons, isolated communities. In a world described by relativity and field-theory physics, the universe is conceived as a huge field of energy in constant interaction and flux in which every particle is related to and affects every other particle in the field. Connectedness is the essence of all things of all types.

The modern physicist's worldview is reinforced by biological and environmental scientists. Within organisms are identifiable parts and systems, but they function in relation to the whole. Within discernible life environments are food chains and regenerative processes, all working to maintain the larger ecosystem. From the pollution of waterways and the destruction of the ozone layer by flurocarbons, we see the delicate ecological systems that sustain life on the planet. We now see that industrial choices made in what used to be the segmented economic sphere affect many other spheres of life.

Connectedness, likewise, is becoming more apparent in economics. Global money markets are affected by events in Ireland and Iran, in India and Japan. Not only are countries and the economic fortunes of their citizens affected by present world trade, they are perhaps affected even more by trading and speculation in futures, not simply futures in grain and raw materials, but futures in terms of industrial investment plans and projections.

A curriculum that continues to treat units of learning as isolated items to be mastered for exams, or for the exercise of a certain skill, distorts students' view of the world as it is and as it is in relation to them. This curriculum creates "school learning" that can cripple students' later participation in the real world.

Sympathetic knowing as experiencing connectedness can be approached at the macro as well as the micro level. Evidence from the natural and social sciences points toward the experience of connectedness at the macro level. An equally important facet of experiencing connectedness takes place on the micro level, the level of the person in the act of knowing something sympathetically. Knowing at the level of sympathy involves feeling, imagination, and intellect, all interpenetrated by memory. When knowers experience connectedness with what they are seeking to know, the experience becomes dialogic. But first, they must adopt an attitude of respect, trust, and caring toward what they are seeking. On the contrary, approaching the object of knowledge with the amateur's naive intention of using it for some other end could violate the integrity of the object and end up harming both the knower and the known (whether that be a person, historical fact, acetyline torch, or tax-return form).

The known object reveals itself in the act of being known. Sometimes knowing is just that—a revelation—as though the object being sought in the act of knowing says to the knower, if you want to know me, you have to dance with me. In the act of dancing, the knower becomes a partner, not dominating the dance, but learning to follow as well as to lead, attending to the intricacy of the steps and rhythms of the partner, recognizing that dancing is an expression both of the autonomy of the other and of the multiple levels of relationships that bind the dancers together.

Polanyi refers to this kind of indwelling as a contemplative union with the known.[17] The sympathetic grasp of the connectedness between the knower and known allows the knower to reach inside to the intimate particularity of the known and allows the object to flow into the knower's soul. Clearly, this language implies a rapture and a total fascination. Not all acts of sympathetic knowing reach such heights; in the course of most people's lives, it may happen occasionally. Still, the beginning efforts to know something sympathetically have this kind of experience as an ultimate goal. Although only partially reached in the ordinary act of knowing, the experience of connectedness immeasurably enriches the learning process.

At a more tacit level, the experience of connectedness between the knower and the known draws the knower into contact with life itself. To know sympathetically is to know the object standing out from nothingness, expressing its individuality as a special event, to use Whitehead's term, in the history of the universe, and therefore of transcendent value because that event will never be repeated in precisely that way.[18] Knowing that event sympathetically simultaneously teaches the knower how to be alive, to be somebody, to be a presence, irreplaceable, irrepeatable, standing out from the landscape singing one's own song. Experiencing connectedness to what is known enriches the knower's sense of life with the life communicated by the known. Thus, the contact is life-giving. As the knower experiences this connectedness with many forms of life over an extended time, the experience gradually blossoms into the knowledge, at least tacit, that he or she belongs to a universal unity that affirms individuality at the same time as it bonds to a community of life.

Depending on the age and cognitive development of the students involved, curriculum units could be more or less explicit about drawing attention to the larger unities that connect the smaller parts. Throughout the K-12 curriculum, various units could be designed to bring the learner to the experience of connectedness at the micro level. Most primary school teachers are adept at encouraging this fascination with nature and living creatures. Unfortunately, curriculum materials and the tests that dominate them encourage increasing detachment and disconnectedness as students progress through upper grades.

Although sometimes justified in the name of promoting scientific objectivity, this detachment appears to be done more to allow for the testing of massive numbers of youngsters whose personal connection to what they are learning is devalued.

Perhaps a dramatic analogy will bring the point home. Much of what goes on in schools may be classified as cognitive rape. Knowledge is presented as something to be possessed objectively, for our use and consumption. Students "learn their lessons" so they can answer questions, get grades, win awards, get promoted, or simply get the teacher off their backs. They are seldom encouraged to appreciate what they are studying in its own right, regardless of its utility. They hear little talk of the integrity of the objects of knowledge, such that their use cannot be indiscriminate, irresponsible, or illegal. What schools are encouraging is a kind of rape of the object of knowledge: The violator misses the meaning the act was supposed to have. The violation is horrifying because it takes an act of profound communion and turns it into an act of aggression. There should be a law against what goes on in schools.

Sympathetic knowing as experiencing social responsibility

In *Emile*, Rousseau employs a novel method of protecting Emile's chastity during his early adolescence. He suggests that through the study of history and biography, he can channel Emile's passion into compassion. The young adolescent by his natural instincts is moved toward friendship and caring. Rousseau would have him study human history, and various individual biographies, to learn how people bring calamity, misfortune, and suffering on themselves and others. He would encourage an imaginative identification with the human beings in their history to induce the knowledge that men are not naturally kings or lords or courtiers or rich men. All men are born naked and poor; all are subject to the miseries of life, to sorrows, ills, needs and pains of every kind. Finally, all are condemned to death. This is what truly belongs to every man. This is what no mortal is exempt from. Begin, therefore, by studying in human nature what is most inseparable from it. . . . offer the young man objects on which the expansive forces of his heart can act. . . . excite in him goodness, humanity, commiseration.[19]

Rousseau would have Emile read history and biography at the level of sympathy. He would have Emile understand that, despite the quest for transcendence and high ideals, people constantly overstep through pride and selfishness and bring disaster on themselves and others. Rather than fostering a morose or cynical attitude about life, this understanding should invite a more compassionate acceptance of human limitation. It should inspire a commitment to building a social and political system that serves the human family more equitably and compassionately.

A curriculum in today's schools that encouraged knowing at the level of sympathy would provide multiple learning experiences that promote cross-cultural understanding, acceptance, and respect, that challenge students to accept diversity and simultaneously to embrace the humanity of the person who is different. This appreciation of how other people have the same basic stories even though their customs differ provides the foundation for building a sense of community. It begins in the school itself, with students learning from one another, with community celebrations of ethnic traditions in music, poetry, meals, and cultural heroes. The curriculum would include field trips to museums and cultural centers where students could learn more about the artifacts and customs of different people. It might encourage partnerships with a school in another country so that students could exchange letters and projects and, where possible, could visit each other's schools. Such living experiences of a common humanity amidst diversity would facilitate a closer study through the print and visual media of other people, especially of those struggling for survival from disease, poverty, or injustice.

Students progressing through a curriculum of sympathetic learning move from knowing and appreciating fellow students in their own classroom, to sharing and celebrating their own cultural background and that of their fellows in the school, to appreciating several cultures different from those familiar in their own setting, to reflecting on and experiencing the sense of the human family, to having concern for those in distress. The curriculum tries to establish a foundation for a lived experience of community and then to build on that experience the more mature awareness of social responsibility for the well-being of community members.

Based on that foundation, curriculums in social studies could focus more intensely on how to improve a democratic social system. Students could get a taste for what discrimination or unemployment or homelessness feels like by studying human and civil rights cases and dramatizing and debating them in class. Knowing what it feels like to suffer social injustice can stimulate students to develop attitudes and activities that promote community building and social change.

The capstone to this curriculum includes exploring various forms of citizen involvement in community and public affairs. Recognizing that special interest politics will always have its place, students could learn political activities that serve the larger good of the community. They could debate episodes from current events in class simulations. Thus, students would develop an appreciation of the values and interests at stake in legal and political controversies. Beyond their fascination with the strategies and maneuvers of the players involved in the political game, students should be encouraged to weigh the consequences on the larger community when a small minority runs things to suit its own interests. This curriculum supports the fundamental theme that citizens in a democracy have to participate responsibly in their own self-governance. The curriculum attempts to provide the knowledge of how to participate in the political process, as well as in more informal influence groups; it also attempts to develop the feelings of caring and responsibility needed to motivate students to participate.

In a school that promotes social responsibility, other strands of the curriculum besides social studies promote sympathetic knowing. Science curriculums could include units posing realistic environmental problems that require scientific solutions. Beyond the scientific knowledge necessary to address the environmental problems are the public policy implications of using that scientific knowledge for the good of the whole community. These problems include the disposal of nuclear wastes, the effect of fertilizers and pesticides on food chains and underground water systems, in vitro experiments, protection of the habitats of endangered species, alternatives to flurocarbons, and the elimination of acid rain. Learning science to help deal with these problems connects school learning to the real world, to levels of meaning that go beyond purely scientific knowledge to the human import of using science. If students feel a sense of responsibility for their world, then learning science takes on a new meaning, if only to know enough to be able to vote intelligently on public policy issues related to the environment. Learning science from this perspective becomes an act of citizenship.

Although courses in anthropology, sociology, and economics tend to be reserved for the last few years of high school, and then as electives, they, too, could be recast to reflect a concern for social responsibility. Where the curriculum stimulates sympathetic knowing, the knowledge that a curriculum promotes goes beyond passively absorbing facts to actively exploring how to use the knowledge of the social sciences to promote community life. In societies that claim to be self-governing, the social sciences and curriculums built on them have to move beyond describing the way things are (and by implication, cannot otherwise be) to a concern for the way things might be if we explored other policy alternatives.

Ample positive reasons exist for redirecting the natural and social science curriculums away from an exclusive concentration on learning the right answers for standardized tests to a more balanced concern for learning fundamental problem-solving methodologies and basic information to help us appreciate our world and make it a better place for all the human family to prosper.

Conclusion

I have tried to address what is perceived as an imbalance in current thinking about curriculum in today's schools. I have added my voice to other voices concerned about the distortion of the curriculum caused by standardized testing. Rather than a wholesale abandonment of direct teaching or of curriculums promoting mastery of basic skills, we need an enlarged sense of the curriculum that leaves room for important learnings increasingly neglected in today's schools.

These neglected learnings include an appreciation of what is learned for its own sake, an understanding of the spatial and temporal fabric in which all individual units of knowledge are embedded, and the sense of social responsibility learning has traditionally communicated. Teaching the perspectives of sympathetic knowing would be relatively easy for most teachers. More than anything else, they would need some clear relief from the exclusive domination of standardized testing in the curriculum. With even a modest reduction, most teachers could (and many do) balance students' learning with a more expansive appreciation of and involvement with their world.

This essay is little more than a commentary on the pregnant quotation from Whitehead at the beginning. Perhaps the quotation bears repeating in its more ample expression in conclusion.

> The essence of education is that it be religious. Pray, what is religious education? A religious education is an education which inculcates duty and reverence. Duty arises from our potential control over the course of events. Where attainable knowledge could have changed the issue, ignorance has the guilt of vice. And the foundation of reverence is this perception, that the present holds within itself the complete sum of existence, backwards and forwards, that whole amplitude of time, which is eternity.[20]

Notes

1. Alfred North Whitehead, *The Aims of Education and Other Essays* (New York: Free Press, 1967), p. 14.
2. Commentators on recent school reform efforts include Gary N. McClosky, Eugene F. Provenzano, Jr., Marilyn M. Cohn, and Robert B. Kottkamp, *A Profession at Risk: Legislated Learning as a Disincentive to Teaching* (Washington, DC: Office of Educational Research and Improvement, 1987); Daniel L. Duke, "What Is the Nature of Educational Excellence and Should We Try to Measure It?" *Phi Delta Kappan* 66 (June 1985): 671–674; David N. Plank, "The Ayes of Texas: Rhetoric, Reality, and School Reform," *Politics of Education Bulletin* 13 (Summer 1986): 13–16; Arthur G. Wirth, "Contemporary Work and the Quality of Life," and Steven Tozer, "Elite Power and Democratic Ideals," in *Society as Educator in an Age of Transition*, ed. Kenneth D. Benne and Stephen Tozer, 86th Yearbook of the National Society for the Study of Education, Part II (Chicago: University of Chicago Press, 1987), pp. 54–87, 186–225.
3. Linda M. McNeil, *Contradictions of Control: School Structure and School Knowledge* (New York: Methuen/Routledge & Kegan Paul, 1986).
4. See the careful work of David A. Squires, William G. Huitt, and John K. Segars, *Effective Schools and Classrooms: A Research-Based Perspective* (Alexandria, VA: Association for Supervision and Curriculum Development, 1983).
5. Allan Odden and Beverly Anderson, "How Successful State Education Improvement Programs Work," *Phi Delta Kappan* 67 (April 1986): 582–585.
6. Linda M. McNeil, *Contradictions of Control: School Structure and School Knowledge* (New York: Methuen/Routledge & Kegan Paul, 1986).
7. See, for example, Alfred North Whitehead, *Process and Reality: An Essay in Cosmology* (New York: Macmillan, 1929); Alfred North Whitehead, *Adventures of Ideas* (New York: Macmillan, 1933); John Dewey, *Art as Experience* (New York: Capricorn Books, 1958); Max Scheler, *The Nature of Sympathy* (London: Routledge & Kegan Paul, 1959); Louis A Reid, "Feeling, Thinking, Knowing," *Proceedings of the Aristotelian Society* 77 (1976–77): 165–182; Susanne K. Langer, *Mind: An Essay on Human Feeling* (Baltimore: Johns Hopkins University Press, 1967); Michael Polanyi, *Personal Knowledge: Towards a Post-Critical Philosophy* (New York: Harper Torchbooks, 1965); Michael Polanyi, "The Creative Imagination," *Chemical and Engineering News* 44 (No. 17, 1966): 85–93; John Macmurray, *Reason and Emotion* (London: Faber, 1935); John Macmurray, *Persons in Relation* (New York: Harper & Brothers, 1961).
8. Iredell Jenkins, *Art and the Human Enterprise* (Cambridge, MA: Harvard University Press, 1958), pp. 17–19.
9. Ibid., p. 130.
10. Ernst Cassirer, *An Essay on Man: An Introduction to a Philosophy of Human Culture* (New Haven, CT: Yale University Press, 1962), p. 82.
11. At a recent conference at Harvard University Graduate School of Education, I was delighted to hear many of these ideas embedded in the thinking of Professor Don Oliver. See his book, *Education, Modernity, and Fractured Meaning* (Albany: State University of New York Press, 1989).
12. Michael Polanyi, *The Tacit Dimension* (New York: Doubleday & Company, 1966), p. 18.
13. Allan David Bloom, *The Closing of the American Mind* (New York: Simon & Schuster, 1987).
14. A fine historical perspective is provided by Ernest Becker in *The Structure of Evil* (New York: Free Press, 1968).
15. Alexis de Toqueville, *Democracy in America*, trans. George Lawrence, ed. J. P. Mayer (New York: Doubleday, Anchor Books, 1969); Robert N. Bellah, Richard Madsen, William M. Sullivan, Ann Swidler, and Steven M. Tipton, *Habits of the Heart* (New York: Harper & Row, 1985). For an incisive commentary on the importance of a sense of community for even minimum academic achievement, see James S. Coleman and

Thomas Hoffer, *Public and Private High Schools: The Impact of Communities* (New York: Basic Books, 1987).
16 An excellent summary of Whitehead's work can be found in Albert W. Levi, *Philosophy and the Modern World* (Bloomington: Indiana University Press, 1959), pp. 482–531.
17 Michael Polanyi, *The Tacit Dimension* (New York: Doubleday & Company, 1966), p. 18.
18 Alfred North Whitehead, *The Aims of Education and Other Essays* (New York: Free Press, 1967), pp. 146–147.
19 Jean-Jacques Rousseau, *Emile*, trans. Allan Bloom (New York: Basic Books, 1979), pp. 222–223.
20 Alfred North Whitehead, *The Aims of Education and Other Essays* (New York: Free Press, 1967), p. 14.

CHAPTER THREE

The drama of schooling/ the schooling of drama

The title of this book and of this chapter is vexing. On the one hand, it appears that schooling is the locus of the drama; then again, it appears that the drama being considered is much larger than schooling. What the bothersome juxtaposition of phrases is meant to convey is fundamentally what John Dewey proposed as a view of schooling, namely, that schooling was not a preparation for life, but that the schooling one experienced was an experience of life. As one experienced that life, one was also being schooled in living, and in the process of experimental knowing that led to the continuous transformation of experience upon which an authentically democratic society depended.[1]

Living in a democracy for Dewey meant living in a constant negotiation of meanings, values, plans of actions, evaluation of social and political strategies – learning what democracy in this particular situation might look like. In other words, living in a democracy involved the very same processes children were learning in school: inquiry, collaboration, scientific verification, experimentation, group debate and consensus building, correcting past misunderstandings through new transformations of experience. The hurly burly of social and political democracy would gradually be tamed by group discussion, rational argument and scientifically verified information. The taming process would always be incomplete, however, because, on the one hand, the information and intelligence available at a given time to address situations would always be incomplete, and on the other, the transformations attempted would always be limited and imperfect. In schools, youngsters would be exposed to the inherent pedagogy of this kind of democratic living by constantly building more adequate understandings of how nature, society and human beings 'work', and how they might 'work better'.

In our perspective, both individual and social life are dramatic. This means that individual lives and the life of communities, groups, societies mean something, are significant, count for something. What individuals do with their lives is important to the group, community and society in which they live. What choices groups, communities and societies make are weighted with significant consequences. That is to say, human life and social life are not simply matters to be explained by mathematical laws of physics and chemistry. Beyond those laws, there is a drama of human aspiration, longing, struggle, choice, adventure and creation. The drama involves the gamble of whether the individual and the community will achieve something heroic, something beautiful, something expressive of a transcendent quality inherent in the human spirit, or whether the individual or the community will, through some fatal flaw, pursue a course of action that is eventually destructive of the human meanings and purposes by which human life is dignified.

Drama as an art form reveals the interpenetration of the present with the past and the future.[2] As a form, the drama is never complete until it is over. While the drama is going on, the action is still unfolding toward a conclusion. The consequences of the actors' choices make all the actions that preceded them take on a particular significance. Either the actor is going to succeed or going to fail. We do not know until the final scene. That suspension of completion of each action builds in a tension to the present moment: will the course of action lead to the desired outcome, or is the actor stumbling blindly toward disaster? The actions and choices in the drama have an implied future, but we do not know that future until the end of the play. At the end of the play, the unity of the form comes together in a gestalt of insight, as we see in an instant the organic unfolding of the action towards its resolution. Drama implies a destiny in the process of being fulfilled. The action is dramatic precisely because it is filled with expectation, dread, hope, naiveté, questing – all of which point toward the future moment when the action realizes a completion.

When we leave the theater, we know that we, too, are involved in a lifetime of action which is leading toward a future. That future likewise confirms our choices as wise or foolish, prudent or deluded, significant or empty. The risk of living is that we are never sure that our choices will lead us to the end of the rainbow. We do not know whether the outcome will vindicate our labor, our risks, our questing, or whether the outcome will show us to have been misguided, blind or deceived. The intrinsic drama in our lives is that our present implies a destiny in the process of being fulfilled or frustrated. People who have no future have no way to ground their present or their past in meaning.

The drama of individual human life and of communal life involves choices. These choices are always limited by the knowledge humans possess at the time, as well as by their desires and imaginings. The choices involve questions of value and significance. Beneath the values and meanings involved in those choices lies an inarticulate worldview made up of assumptions about the way the world is and about the way the world should be. In other words, human action implies frames of understanding which give significance to the choices to act in one way rather than another. Even people we label as insane or criminal act for some reason. Though we accuse others of being 'unreasonable' we usually mean that they are not acting according to our understanding of what is appropriate or necessary.

While not the only source of knowledge, schools expressly deal with frames of understanding and with the tools for developing and expressing those frames of understanding. Using those frames of understanding, youngsters gradually move toward adulthood by experimenting with ways of creating themselves and governing themselves, with ways of creating social relationships and governing them. They not only learn the script of being an individual and the script for social life, they try them on for size and see whether they want to follow them. Furthermore, they learn the fundamental worldview that makes the script meaningful.

The larger social drama can be presented in school as relatively fixed, with the scripts relatively inflexible, and the worldview presented as ontologically exhaustive or ideologically perfect. Schools may also present the social drama more realistically as a world in the making, filled with uncertainties, fraught with dangers, yet open to marvellous possibilities – a place where history is made, not simply recorded by other people about other people. In such a drama there is a need for heroic players, for people to engage in the dramatic action of politics and science and art in order to create a new, a better world. This larger social drama is an arena of individual and communal fulfilment. That is to say, one can become involved in a larger drama that calls the individual to transcend narcissistic hedonism by means of a morally fulfilling engagement with the larger purposes of the community.

In one sense, the knowledge by which to engage in the social drama is already there. Developments in the human sciences, the natural sciences and the social sciences have provided both the knowledge and the tools for engaging in the social drama, for making history. Those very developments have also brought an awareness of the *limitations* of the tools and the knowledge of the human, natural and social sciences. They have also brought an awareness that the worldview one might construct with this knowledge is a human construct, a shaping of knowledge to serve human purposes, whether those purposes are emancipatory or controlling. This implies that the search for knowledge and understanding is itself a drama in which humans try to write a script by which the large social drama will be governed.

If knowledge itself is problematic, rather than given, so too are the forms by which the social drama is expressed. These are also seen to be human constructs, established to channel the dramatic action in a certain direction. Then the forms of the social drama are legitimate areas of study and evaluation in school, and legitimate areas of imagining alternatives and evaluating their consequences. With the powerful tool of computer simulation technology, such imagining of alternatives can generate quite specific scenarios.

If the social drama is in fact not fixed and predictable but evolving, dynamic, unpredictable, and if the worldview underlying the social drama is in fact a human construct serving identifiable human purposes, then schooling for responsible participation in that social drama should itself deal with the dramatic nature of knowledge, and the dramatic nature of constructing ameliorative forms for the drama. That approach to knowledge and intentional self governance applies both to the drama of individual life and the drama of social life.

Schooling is dramatic because the everyday lives of youngsters and adults in school is filled with small but significant challenges, victories, defeats, tensions and resolutions. There is drama inherent in a classroom debate; in the bloom of an insight into a law of thermodynamics; in the achievement of making the junior varsity soccer team; in being caught smoking in the boys' room; in negotiating a friendship over lunch; in passing final exams. Schooling is dramatic in a deeper sense, however, because the consequences of schooling are so critical both to the individual and to society. The schooling of the drama is dramatic in itself because the future of the drama depends upon the conduct of schooling. Even though we cannot read the future accurately, we can read the past well enough to avoid those scripts that lead to dead ends, or to the destruction of the social drama.

So that these mind-twisting general arguments might take on some semblance of practical meaning, we will explore three examples of dramatic learnings during the schooling years, learnings which simultaneously involve participation in the larger social drama. Those parts of the social drama touched upon here will include the world of friendships, the world of work and the world of citizenship. A brief summary of pre-school experiences and of the formal context of schooling will set the stage for the drama inherent in these three experiences. We will see, however, that these three elements of the larger social drama are deeply problematic and the schooling in them is indeed a highly contentious issue of social policy. The problematic nature of schooling in these areas simply reinforces the argument of this chapter, namely that the conduct of schooling holds dramatic significance for many players in the drama.

The basics of social behavior

As children emerge from infancy and then move toward early adolescence, they move from behavior that is relatively narcissistic, diffuse, undifferentiated toward behavior that is relatively other-attentive, focused, sequenced and purposeful. Through observation, imitation, play, interaction with peers, example and conditioning by parents, and direct instruction, children learn the basics of social behavior. They learn that certain behaviors are taboo in public, that certain words are vulgar and to be censored in public, that what is allowed in the playground is not allowed in church or the classroom. They learn conventional phrases that signify good manners or deference or respect. They learn how to follow a map, how to ride on a bus or train, how to carry on the business of grocery shopping, or gardening, or serving tea. In all these instances, youngsters are learning how to negotiate the circumstances of ordinary life, and while doing so to give a good performance. They are learning how to win the applause or approval of the audience.

They also are learning that not all social life is totally scripted. When they are with a friend, they can talk about topics they wouldn't discuss with parents or teachers. They can be a little crazy, letting down the normal social reserve, laughing at nonsensical conversations, giving reign to fantasy. With parents, especially mothers, children can often be more spontaneous, asking questions, wondering why things are thus and so, expressing their feelings of confusion, anger, loneliness. In games, children can experiment and improvise, even though their behavior is bounded by the rules of the game. They find times and places to 'be themselves'. There are many occasions, however, when they cannot be themselves, cannot say what they feel, or act spontaneously.

These differences enable them to distinguish between levels of the social drama. There are occasions when they experience the joy of feeling free to be themselves. There are other occasions when they experience being totally bound up in others' scripts. On still other occasions, they feel partly free to make up their own script and partly constrained to follow the script others are writing for them.

The formal school experience

When youngsters come to school, they experience being treated as a member of a group, as a person assigned a role, a school-defined role, namely that of being a pupil or a student. Schools have rules which everyone is supposed to follow, and lessons which everyone is supposed to learn. There are times for expressive activities, like singing or drawing or folk dancing, but the main part of the day is spent learning what adults have decided is important to learn. One of the hidden learnings contained in the initial experience of schooling is that one is 'owned', so to speak, by the school, and by the community which the school serves. One does not have the choice not to go to school, nor the choice not to learn a particular lesson. The adult world appears to possess the absolute right to demand that youngsters submit to the everyday demands of school. Even parents, who used to appear all powerful, can be called into the school and admonished about their child's failures.

Without being able to name it or understand it, a young child comes up against a force into whose hands he or she is placed which has the right to demand obedience, and which has the right to punish disobedience. Although normally not a terrifying experience, this initial encounter with the state communicates an absolute quality to the script one is told to learn in school. This is serious business, absolutely necessary, a definition of reality one cannot toy with.

In school one learns not only what's real, but the way things are supposed to be. If one refuses to accept the script, then one is excluded from normal places within society, cast out to the perimeter where only crazy or evil people live. The message communicated is 'You'd better go along with the program *or else*'. While later on youngsters tend to internalize the script being learned in school as, in fact, the way things are and the way things are supposed to be, there lingers still the faint trace of threat of being socially ostracized for nonconformity. Schooling for the social drama is indeed serious business.

Schooling and friendship

Schools provide youngsters with the experience of a large variety of people who are not of their own family, clan, or even ethnic group. They have to learn to deal with these others in limited time slots, to deal with them as members of groups, described in abstract categories (He's Italian; she's Irish; he's a musician, she's a scientist; she's really smart; she's only average.) They are people they spend some time with for certain purposes, unlike family members to whom they have almost total access. Through language conventions, they are able to communicate their thoughts and feelings, at least on a superficial level. They learn the subtle signs of acceptance or rejection in the choice of words others use with them, the tone of voice, the look in the eye.

Friendships grow through association with larger groups. One manages to get on a team, or to join a club, or be invited to associate with an organization. Sometimes these are connected with the school, sometimes not. Many of the basic skills and understandings necessary to begin a friendship have been learned and reinforced in the family. Schools take up what the family has begun, however, and refine and develop those basic learnings.

Friendship is negotiated through language. To be sure, friendship involves much more than language. Friendship grows, however, because two people can converse about things they have in common. Little children who do not have much of a command of language will express themselves to a friend with a hug and a smile, but the friendship will not develop very far until they can talk. Being able to talk to one another implies other elements in that drama of friendship. It implies speaking truthfully. It implies the ability to make promises and agreements.

It implies sharing stories about the day's events with one another, and through the stories, sharing the meanings and values embedded in the stories. Although making friends is not taught in school, teachers often deal with those ingredients which solidify friendships, ingredients such as loyalty, integrity, respect, honesty, keeping promises.[3]

Friendship is crucial to the experience of the social drama. If youngsters grew up with no friends, then their relationships with others would tend to be impersonal and distant. They would tend to converse with them in conventional, learned patterns, following scripts they had learned about what to say to this kind of person in these kinds of circumstances. Making a friend introduces a person to one of the more profound experiences of improvisation within the social drama. Since everyone is unique, there are few ground rules for making friends. What is extended as an invitation may be rejected as an intrusion. One has to proceed initially somewhat cautiously, attending to all the subtle cues of tone of voice, body language, eye contact, status distance, etc., in order to sense how one is being understood. Attempting to make a friend makes one vulnerable to rejection, ridicule, humiliation, until one gets the signals that one is accepted.

Once one is accepted as a friend, then a whole new world of possibilities opens up. Having a friend enables one to carry on those conversations one had with an imaginary friend or with oneself. It enables one to try out things the friend is interested in, engaging in new games, exploring fantasies, traveling together to explore uncharted areas of the neighborhood, learning how to get along with the friend's parents and siblings. It also gives form to the feeling of one's own importance, and provides an experience that one counts for something with someone else.

Sharing life with a friend introduces a youngster to an essential experience of the social drama, one that takes the youngster beyond the drama of the family into a drama of being with and, in a sense, belonging to someone else.[4] That experience is profoundly dramatic for it involves the risks of self exposure, the anxiety of vulnerability, the burden of loyalty, the pain of a quarrel, the excitement of doing something new together, the threat of intruders into that private world – in short, the experience of improvising a relationship that grounds one's essential humanity. Friendships allow a very important experience to develop, namely, the experience of discourse and the mutuality of linguistic exchange. With a friend one can explore ideas and perceptions and questions. In the course of discussing something, where the formulation of a perception is exchanged somewhat like a tennis ball being thrown back and forth in a game of 'catch', two friends can agree upon a linguistic definition of an experience, a formulation of a question, a metaphorical construct that captures a feeling. In the course of their discourse, youngsters learn how to create and share meaning. This facility at linguistic expression and refinement of meaning is a crucial element in the improvisation of the social drama.

Without being able to name it, youngsters understand that social life has several levels of relationships: some relationships are relatively superficial, where one learns to speak the lines that will get one through the episode with a minimum of bother; some are very secure and ordinary, taken for granted, as in family life; some are very special, as with a friend, for they engage one's whole person in a deeper exchange where one feels more fully alive.

In all forms of social life, however, one must have even a minimal sense of oneself as a subject, and as engaging with other subjects. A social life in which all human exchange was between persons who treated each other as objects appears frightening or monstrous. That is the kind of society in which everyone is categorized, reduced to an abstraction or a statistic; one makes up a percentage of the population who works in factories; one is a consumer or a producer, a member of the opposition or a member of the party. It is that kind of depersonalized society that makes a police state possible. In a police state there can be no free exchange between people because one is liable to be reported to the authorities for the slightest indiscretion. That kind of depersonalization allows the most deceitful forms of advertising to be justified on the grounds that it increases profits.

The experience of friendship teaches us to experience common humanity. Through the empathy we develop in friendship, we are able to place ourselves in the shoes of another person. Through the experience of friendship we have a sense of value. Being grounded in our own human value, and in understanding the value of another person, we can engage them in social life as a subject with other subjects, according them the respect and dignity and trust so necessary to keep social life humanly and morally fulfilling. In a highly competitive world, in an increasingly narcissistic world, however, this kind of human social life is problematic.[5] Although schools often encourage participation and teamwork, they rarely spend much time (some student counselors are exceptions) helping youngsters to come to terms with the demands of friendship.

Schooling in the script of work

As Dreeben illustrates, schooling prepares one for the world of work.[6] The routine of school teaches the script of being consistently on time, taking responsibility for doing one's own work, measuring up to certain levels of mastery, being self reliant and self sufficient, working on-schedule, meeting deadlines, working for rewards, obeying procedural rules and guidelines, delaying gratification, controlling elimination, displacing personal whimsy and impulse, accepting being treated impersonally, understanding the universal applicability of rules to people differing widely in talent and background, displacing physical gratification with symbolic rewards, seeking higher status differentiation through symbolic emblems and costumes, understanding the scientific basis behind the technology involved in one's work, accepting status differentials as based on merit, accepting the economic system which defines the conditions of work. All of these things we learn, or learn to a significant degree in school. That is not to say that we understand why things are the way they are. It simply means that we learn to accept the script as the definition of the way things are.

Many of these elements in the script of workers are learned indirectly and taught indirectly simply through the scripted routines present in the everyday life of the school. Schools as bureaucratic organizations do not differ that significantly from most other bureaucratically run organizations. Schools socialize youngsters into behaviors considered appropriate for most bureaucratic organizations.

If schools were to insist, however, on understanding the human significance of the social drama, they would of necessity teach the ability to improvise in one's work, to invent better solutions to problems on the job, to derive pride and satisfaction from knowing how one's work contributes to the welfare of others. In other words, where schools attend to the human purposes served by the scripts being learned, and encourage improvisation within the script in order to promote human purposes, then they will empower youngsters to enact the social drama of the world of work in self-renewing and humanly fulfilling ways.

Schooling in the scripts of citizenship

When it comes to schooling in citizenship, schools actually teach several scripts, many of which are at cross purposes with each other. These scripts reflect the ambivalence and tension between scripts in the social drama. As a citizen, one is expected to participate in a democratic process of government; one is supposed to support democracy as a cherished form of carrying on public school life. Yet there is a competing script of individualism in American life according to which we are supposed to be self-sufficient, entrepreneurs, independent, self-reliant. De Tocqueville identified this tension in the American character as early as the 1830s. He saw family life, religion and participation in local politics as those ingredients in the American character which would sustain a commitment to free and democratic institutions.[7] He also pointed, however, to a tendency toward individualism which would pull Americans away from participation in public life toward a concentration on private gain and personal privilege.

Recently Robert Bellah and his associates have studied this tension in the American character and found that individualism has grown to the point where it overshadows participation in the life of the local community or the nation.[8] What people seem to want is a cozy, secure and private place they can call their own where they can withdraw from the confusion, conflict and stress of public life and enjoy the satisfaction of a rich interpersonal life with loved ones and the comforts of even modest luxuries and recreational pursuits which modern technology affords. The satisfaction of making a contribution to the welfare of the community, or concern for less fortunate members of the community, or the structuring of a more equitable share of prosperity and access to opportunities into legal and political institutions, no longer holds the appeal or even the moral obligation to most contemporary Americans. Voting in local or national elections tends to define the civic responsibilities of many, but even that population seems to be shrinking.[9]

Schools communicate such contradictory scripts to youngsters. On the one hand students are urged to develop school spirit, to get involved in school activities, to discover the satisfaction of being part of a team, part of the school family. Similarly, they are encouraged to cherish 'our democratic way of life'. In social studies they are taught the differences between democratic and totalitarian forms of government. In civic courses they are encouraged to participate in political life, in debates over public policy, in national and local elections. In some schools, service clubs and volunteer student organizations are encouraged to assist the elderly, the handicapped, and the victims of natural disasters.

On the other hand, students are taught the script of competition. Achievement is an individual matter; one has to compete against one's peers for grades, for class rank, for acceptance to prestige universities. What is called teamwork in extra-curricular activities is called cheating in final exams. The ideology of individual merit and individual success tends to obliterate awareness of the social uses to which learning might be put. While the school promotes the bonding that comes from group activities, the real drama is the individual struggle for academic rewards. Grades and test scores are the currency that purchase access to the next levels of education, which in turn purchase access to the most lucrative jobs. The message preached in schools is that access to the good life, to the American dream is what schooling is all about. The bigger slices of that good life go to individuals who compete for the highest grades.[10]

Problems with the schooling of drama

Educators who wish to make schools more responsive to the challenges of schooling for the social drama confront disagreements among players in the social drama and scholars of the social drama about the kind of participation the schools ought to be preparing youngsters for. The National Commission on Excellence in Education believed that schools need to prepare youngsters for the life-long learning implied in the accelerated world of work and competitive international economics. The national drama to them was moving toward a bifurcation of the population, with a decreasing minority of highly educated experts making technical, economic and political decisions, and an increasing majority of poorly educated citizens incapable not only of participating in a highly competitive work place, but even more importantly of asking the right kinds of questions to guide social policy. Beyond all other desirable educational activities, preparation of youngsters to handle the cognitive demands of on-going relearning in the rapidly computerized workplace defined the script of schooling, defined schooling for the social drama.[11] Similar sentiments were voiced by another nationally prominent group.[12]

Others have criticized the rosy picture of the economy and the work place presented by those reports. Carnoy indicates that increased use of computers and robots in the work place may accelerate the bifurcation of the workforce, leaving the much larger majority of workers stuck in low paying service jobs such as maintenance, security, and secretarial jobs.[13] Furthermore, those jobs may not require the complex skills which the advocates of school reform are calling for. Hence, even if all American youth were to cooperate with the calls for reform and prepare themselves for the high tech workplace, there is simply not room at the top for more than a small percentage of them. Moreover, the middle-range of jobs will have shrunk, many of them replaced by computer networks.

Wirth cites the impact of high technology on the work force mentioned by Carnoy.[14] He goes further by raising questions about the political insensitivity of corporate America to the social disparities already plaguing the nation, and to the increasing cost to the environment of increased production and consumption which the new technologies will generate.

Beyond those critics one can cite more profound analyses of problematic elements in the social drama and schooling of the social drama. Feminists have criticized the domination of the culture, the economy, the government, the legal system, most forms of public organizational life and even language itself by male perspectives and values. They point to the school as an agency that has unwittingly lent itself to the perpetuation of women's subjugation.[15] An increasingly articulate community of scholars on the left have criticized the political and cultural hegemony of corporate America over the drama of social life and of schooling for that drama.

Earlier criticisms of the schools as simply reproducing the structures of domination one finds in society[16] have given way to more sophisticated analyses that utilize the works of European philosophers such as Horkheimer, Habermas, Foucault and Derrida.[17] Those philosophical frames of reference enable these critics to analyze power relationships, not only as they appear in economic and political forms, but as they are embedded in the very language we use. Beyond that, knowledge itself has become the coinage of power.

Hence schooling can express in the way it treats language and knowledge (as either a given or as a construct to be used for or against others) either an emancipatory or controlling mission. In other words schooling can continue the fiction that the script represents ontological reality, or it can present the script as a human construct which itself is problematic and therefore in need of reconstruction.

Redefining schooling as a drama

Whether one accepts the criticism of schooling from the right or from the left, it is clear that there is a new awareness that a nation's future is very much at stake in the way it conducts its schools. In a sense everyone would agree that the nation's future is being worked out now in its schools, not in a deterministic sense, but in terms of shaping the imagination of possibilities. From one perspective, the economic and human costs to be paid in the future are already present in the choices of thousands of youth to drop out of school. From another perspective, the political and human costs to be paid in the future are already present in the acceptance by teachers and parents of the political *status quo* as the best possibility for their children, and in their encouraging youngsters to master bodies of knowledge which communicate that view of reality present in the textbooks and curriculum guides being turned out under the influence of a male dominated, military–industrial complex.[18]

From an individual or from a communal point of view what happens in schools has a life-long effect on youngsters. Schooling is dramatic, not because a normal day in school is the potential subject of a Hollywood movie or an epic novel. Schooling is dramatic because the small choices youngsters make each day under the guidance of the choices teachers make cumulatively add up to life-long choices. Those choices, moreover, have social consequences. They have consequences for how communities will create or stifle more human social forms for their drama.

Those in-school choices have to do with being a somebody or a nobody, or perhaps a private somebody and a public nobody, or a public somebody and a private nobody. Youngsters can choose to remain passive, to allow their roles and their selves to be defined by the curriculum, the teacher, their peers, the school authorities, television, or the commodity culture. Or they can actively choose to engage in the drama as a somebody in their own right. They can ask why things mean only this or that or they can accept the textbook definition of what things mean. They can incorporate their personal meanings into the fabric of school knowledge, or be told that those personal meanings are to be kept to oneself.

Similarly, teachers can be active or passive players in the drama. They can teach science as outlined in the textbook, or they can teach the scientific material as it relates to current debates on environmental policies. They can teach history as outlined in the curriculum manual, or they can teach the history lesson as given in the textbook and go on to invite a restructuring of the historical sequence in the light of different choices the historical players might have made. Stories can be taught as independent pieces of literature, things out there to be used for entertainment (and memorized for getting grades), or they can be taught as versions of dramas of people like themselves.

Principals and others on the administrative staff are challenged to become engaged in the drama as well. How they manage and coordinate the drama definitely affects the drama for better or worse. They can treat it as a play almost totally scripted, or see it as always, every day, something to be made anew, where the drama of encouraging youngsters to reach out for a better expression of themselves, for a fresh understanding of their world, makes every day filled with dramatic possibilities.

In the chapters that follow, we will develop this theme. After first setting the drama in its organizational context, with its built-in tensions, we will consider how schools contribute to the formation of characters in the social drama and to the formation of a collective effort to carry on the drama. Subsequent chapters explore how teachers, administrators, parents and school board members can exercise leadership in playing and coaching and criticizing the drama of schooling.

Notes

1 See John Dewey (1961) *Democracy and Education*, New York, Macmillan; (1963) *Experience and Education*, New York, Collier Books. For an insightful commentary on the thought of John Dewey, see John J. McDermott's two volume work (1973) *The Philosophy of John Dewey*, New York, G. P. Putnam's Sons.
2 Susanne Langer cites the seldom recognized literary scholar, Charles Morgan, for the source of this observation on the incompleteness of the art form of drama, what he called the 'illusion of form'. See Morgan C. (1933) 'The nature of dramatic illusion', *The Transactions of the Royal Society of Literature*, Vol. 12; Langer, S. (1953) *Feeling and Form*, New York, Charles Scribner's Sons, pp. 306–325.
3 For an insightful and sensitive treatment of this aspect of schooling, see Parker Palmer (1983) *To Know As We Are Known*, San Francisco, Harper and Row.
4 John McMurray has underscored the necessity for personal relationships in all spheres of human life. See McMurray, J. (1961) *Persons in Relation*, London, Faber and Faber.
5 See Christopher Lash (1978) *The Culture of Narcissism*, New York, W. W. Norton; M. Scott Peck (1983) *People of the Lie*, New York, Simon and Schuster; Robert Bellah et al., (1986) *Habits of the Heart*, New York, Harper and Row.
6 Dreeben, R. (1968) *On What is Learned at School*, Reading, MA, Addison Wesley.
7 de Tocqueville, A. (1969) *Democracy in America*, in Lawrence, G. (Trans) and Mayer, J. (Ed.), New York, Doubleday Anchor Books.
8 Bellah, R. et al. (1985) *Habits of the Heart*, New York, Harper and Row.
9 See van Gunsteren's essay which outlines some of the problematic elements of theories of citizenship, especially from a European class awareness. Van Gunsteren, H. 'Notes on a Theory of Citizenship', in Birnbaum, P., Lively, J., and Parry, G. (1978) *Democracy, Consensus and Social Contract*, Beverly Hills, CA, Sage Publications.
10 See Lesko, N. (1988) *Symbolizing Society*, Lewes, Palmer Press.
11 See Gerald Holton, (1984) 'A Nation at Risk revisited', *Daedalus*, 113, pp. 1–27.
12 The Committee for Economic Development (1985) *Investing in our Children: Business and the Public Schools*, Washington, D.C.; Doyle, D. and Levine, M. (1985) 'Business and the public schools: Observations on the policy statement of the committee for economic development', *Phi Delta Kappan*, 67 (October), pp. 113–118.

13 Carnoy, M. (1987) 'High technology and education: An economist's view', in Benne, K. and Tozer, S. (Eds) *Society as Educator in an Age of Transition*, Chicago, University of Chicago Press, pp. 88–111.
14 Wirth, A. (1987) 'Contemporary work and the quality of life', in Benne, K. and Tozer, S. (Eds) *Society as Educator in an Age of Transition*, Chicago, University of Chicago Press, pp. 54–87.
15 See, among others, Keohane, N., Rosaldo, M., and Gelpi, B. (Eds) (1982) *Feminist Theory: A Critique of Ideology*, Chicago, University of Chicago Press; Clarke, M. and Lange, L. (Eds) (1979) *The Sexism of Social and Political Theory: Women and Reproduction from Plato to Nietzsche*, Toronto, University of Toronto Press; Thompson, P. (1986) 'Beyond gender: Equity issues for home economics education', *Theory Into Practice*, 24, 4, pp. 276–283; Weiler, K. (1988) *Women Teaching for Change: Gender, Class and Power*, Granby, MA, Bergin and Garvey.
16 See Bowles, S. and Gintis, H. (1976) *Schooling in Capitalist America*, New York, Basic Books; Bourdieu, P. and Passeron, J. (1977) *Reproduction: In Education, Society and Culture*, London, Sage.
17 Apple, M. (1982) *Education and Power*, London, Routledge and Kegan Paul; Aronowitz, S. and Giroux, H. (1985) *Education Under Siege*, South Hadley, MA, Bergin and Garvey; Wexler, P. (1987) *Social Analysis of Education*, London, Routledge and Kegan Paul.
18 Greene, M. (1989) 'Cherishing the World: Toward a Pedagogy of Peace', a paper presented at the Annual Meeting of the American Educational Research Association, San Francisco.

CHAPTER FOUR

The challenging world of educational leadership

Former views of educational administration

For the past 40 years or more, educational administration has been assumed to be one of several types of a generalized, uniform activity labeled *administration*. This label was thought to encompass relatively similar characteristics. That is, if a person were a good administrator in one setting, presumably he or she would be a good administrator in another setting. Sometimes a more idealized form of administration was considered to be found in a specific type of administration, such as military or business administration. Indeed, it has been suggested in the United States and other countries that school administrators should imitate business administrators or, further, that schools be run by people with training and experience in business administration.

This kind of thinking is often based on the assumption that there is a kind of science of administration that, through empirical research extending over decades, has established certain universal principles and management techniques that can be applied in diverse administrative and organizational settings. This belief was well expressed in an influential volume edited by Sergiovanni and Carver (1969):

> Research to date has revealed that human behavior, as a result of organizational life, manifests remarkable similarities as one moves from hospital, to school, to retail store, to welfare agency, and to military unit. Thus, while the school administrator is particularly concerned with one kind of formal organization, his vision may very well be improved by studying organizations in general. (p. ix)

Early in the 20th century, Taylor (1911) sought to create a science of management based on his time and motion studies of a manufacturing process. Cubberly (1916) was an early proponent of the application of scientific principles generated through empirical research in educational administration. Later, the work of Simon (1957) rekindled an interest in administrative theory based on scientific research on the behavior of managers in organizations. His work influenced the administrative theory movement in educational administration. Griffiths (1959) advocated the use of scientific research methods and theories from the social sciences to construct a theory and science of educational administration. He believed that only in this way would educational administration gain the legitimacy and respect accorded to true professionals. Consequently, he stressed the rationality and objectivity that administrators, having been exposed to these studies, would bring to their tasks. Such rationality and objectivity would ensure professional judgment in circumstances of organizational life in the pursuit of rational goals.

Not every scholar, however, endorsed the scientism and rationalism of the mainstream theorists of the 1950s and 1960s. Studies by Lindbloom (1959) and others (Cohen, March, & Olsen, 1972) questioned the assumed rationality and objectivity of administrators in all organizations. Cyert and March (1963) suggested that administrators exercise a bounded rationality: They may make decisions with goals in mind, but they cannot consider all the alternative choices available and then make the best choice among those alternatives according to an independently objective standard. Administrators' understanding of the alternatives is limited by their own experience, training, and imagination, and by the pressure to make timely decisions. Administrators tend to choose a course of action that resolves the immediate situation in some way or another. These decisions, however, may not necessarily be the best decisions for the long run. Lindbloom (1959) also found that administrators tend to make short-term decisions that are not necessarily consistent with earlier short-term decisions, nor with those they make the next day. Their decisions tend to be disjointed and incremental, rather than rationally consistent with long-term, prioritized goals.

Other scholars such as Apple (1982), Bates (1987), and Giroux (1991) reported that, beyond the disjointed and bounded nature of the rationality found in the actions of educational administrators, one finds ideological assumptions and beliefs. These assumptions and beliefs are not subject to empirical proof. More important, they are rarely articulated and indeed consciously attended to, and hence are all the more influential. These criticisms of the *administration as science* perspective are highlighted to caution the well-intentioned administrator to recognize that the job entails more than making decisions based on a rational assessment of the facts. Interpretation, bias, distortion, subjective feelings, beliefs, and assumptions are all at work in determining what one considers as facts, and indeed influence how one goes about gathering facts. Furthermore, administration as science tends to ignore or marginalize the complex moral issues involved in administrative activity.

Administrators need not surrender to the seeming impossibility of acting rationally and simply follow their own private hunches and beliefs. Educational administration requires a constant effort to introduce rationality into decisions. That rationality does not come exclusively from the individual administrator, but comes more from the individuals involved in the decision discussing the merits of alternative choices. Even then, decisions rarely if ever are purely rational; to seek for that kind of rational purity is to chase an unattainable ideal. Rather, what administrators should seek are the most reasonable decisions under the circumstances—decisions for which others can take responsibility because they have been involved in making them.

Besides the assumption of an ever-present rationality, there has been another harmful side effect from the effort to think of educational administration as one form of a general science or theory of administration. That harmful effect has been encouraging school principals to think of themselves primarily as managers rather than educators. Such thinking has led administrators to concentrate on structures, procedures, and the smooth running of the school organization. It has encouraged an emphasis on mechanical control and maintenance through reliance on administrative technique (good public relations, open communications, well-organized meetings, delegation of responsibilities with attendant accountability and reporting structures, etc.).

More recently, that view has come under fire. As Purpel and Shapiro (1985) put it: "Schools are not shops that require clever and ingenious bits of engineering to increase productivity and morale, but major social institutions where wisdom and courage are required to infuse practice with our highest hopes" (p. xvii). Educational administration is coming to be seen by practitioners, policymakers, and scholars as unique among forms of administration and management; it should be shaped and directed by the essential work of learning.

New views of educational administration

As school renewal policies are legislated and refined in state after state and country after country, we find a much greater emphasis on teachers and principals being held accountable for improved student performances on national and international tests. Under earlier accountability policies, school officials were held responsible for providing multiple opportunities for students to achieve success in school. Now they are held responsible for student outcomes—for actual student success with more rigorous curriculum demands than ever before. Previously, teachers and administrators could claim that they provided the opportunities for students to learn, shifting the blame for poor student performance on lack of student effort and motivation, unsupportive home environments, inadequate educational provisions in earlier grades, and so forth. Now principals can be removed when their students do not show sufficient improvement in test scores over a specified number of years. This kind of pressure has shifted the attention of administrators from general management concerns to more focused educational concerns. Their job is seen more clearly as involving continuous work with teachers to improve the quality of instruction, and to map classroom curriculum to state curriculum standards, the mastery of which state exams are supposed to assess.

Gradually this stress on improved student learning has drawn negative attention to administrators in underperforming school and led to threats of and actual removal from their positions. This attention to ineffective administrators has led to criticisms of the way administrators are selected and prepared for their job. State licensing criteria began to change to reflect this focus on administrative accountability for promoting improved student performance on high-stakes tests. In turn, university preparation programs in educational administration have come under increasing scrutiny by university accrediting associations. Those associations have begun to change their accreditation requirements for graduate departments of school administration, insisting more and more that the graduates of these programs demonstrate in the field that they are acting as instructional leaders involved with improving student success on high-stakes tests. Where these accountability schemes will end is uncertain at present, but professors of educational administration and their deans are feeling the pressure to guarantee the performance of their graduates by pointing to their success at improving student performance. That has already led to a redesign of field/practicum requirements, more performance-based assessments of graduate students, and greater attention to program requirements in curriculum and learning theory.

Two national groups in the late 1980s attempted to draw attention to the unfocused nature of university degree programs in educational administration. The University Council for Educational Administration (UCEA) published a report by the National Commission on Excellence in Educational Administration (1987) calling for more rigorous and selective university programs in educational administration. This led to an effort by the University Council on Educational Administration (1992) to identify the crucial knowledge base for the preparation of school administrators. In turn, this generated intense debate among scholars in educational administration who resisted the epistemology and the theory perspectives behind the UCEA proposal (Donmoyer, Imber, & Scheurich, 1995). This ferment of scholarly discussion was fueled by the report of the National Policy Board for Educational Administration (1989). This group, representing the major national associations of educational administrators, urged the reform of university-based educational administrator certification programs in the strongest of terms, urging more rigorous admission requirements, greater depth of academic courses, and more careful attention to field or practicum experiences under the guidance of proved educational leaders in the field. The National Policy Board for Educational Administration recently teamed up with the National Council for the Accreditation of Teacher Education (NCATE) to produce a comprehensive curriculum required of all university programs in educational administration, at least those that seek NCATE accreditation.

During this period of intense discussions about the future of educational administration within the UCEA and the National Policy Board, the Danforth Foundation also decided to get involved. That foundation funded specific efforts to revitalize educational administration programs (Milstein, 1993). Those efforts included a 5-year cycle of conversations among universities seeking to improve their educational administration programs. This national exchange of ideas led to further publications (Mulkeen, Cambron-McCabe, & Anderson, 1994; Murphy, 1992) and many improvements in university programs (Milstein, 1993).

At the end of the 1990s, three influential scholars of educational administration —Kenneth Leithwood, Richard Elmore, and Joseph Murphy—called for a major reorientation of the theory and practice of educational administration. Their work decidedly influenced the positioning of this book in the ongoing dialogue about transforming educational administration.

Kenneth Leithwood

With his customary scholarly thoroughness, Kenneth Leithwood and two colleagues, Doris Jentzi and Rosanne Steinbach, explicitly embraced the ambitious theme of *transformational leadership* as the necessary (not simply an ideal) framework for the future work of educational administration (Leithwood, Jentzi, & Steinbach, 1999). Based on the earlier work of Burns (1978) and adapted for empirical studies by Bass (1985), this notion of transformational leadership includes components such as charisma, idealized influence, inspirational motivation, intellectual stimulation, and individualized consideration. Leithwood and his colleagues reviewed 20 empirical studies in educational administration that tested the effects of transformational leaders on students, teachers' perceptions, behavior and psychological states of followers, and aspects of organizational life. They went on to identify features of transformational leadership in specific schools. These features are summarized as (a) setting directions, (b) developing people, and (c) redesigning the organization. Leithwood and his colleagues examined the cognitive processes that transformational leaders employ in solving problems, and they explored transformational leadership among teachers.

Although Leithwood, Jentzi, and Steinbach advanced thinking about educational leadership to include the theme of transformation, they focused attention exclusively on the organizational work of the adults in schools. From my perspective, they did not ground their exploration of educational leadership on a close analysis of *what* schools teach and *what* students learn, but more on how adults engage in organizational change. I endorse their claiming the theme of transformation as necessary for educational leadership, as an earlier work of mine witnessed (Starratt, 1993a). I find their analysis of how transformational educational leaders behave illuminating. I believe, however, that their work needs to be complemented by a closer look at the potential of transforming the learning agenda of schools.

Richard Elmore

Richard Elmore, a scholar at the forefront of thinking about school renewal, has also called for a new structure for school leadership (Elmore, 2000). Elmore proposed that the widespread national and international efforts at standards-based, large-scale instructional change carries with it a wholly different set of demands for school administrators at the system and school levels. Through state-administered exams, the state now has the means to hold individual schools accountable for student achievement in mastering a standards-based curriculum. Hence, local administrators can no longer hide their schools' record of long-term student failure and underachievement. Administrators can no longer function as managers of organizational procedures. They must be knowledgeable about the complexities of teaching and learning. They must work on instructional improvement as their top priority, making all other administrative activity serve that priority.

Elmore's call to the field of educational administration is this: Turn your schools into learning organizations, for only by being involved with the teachers in learning how to bring *all* students up to acceptable achievement of the standards-based curriculum will you and your schools survive. The future of public schools is in the balance. Elmore provided, I believe, a framework for transforming the work of educational administration. Again, I am concerned that his reach does not extend beyond standards-based curriculum and the testing process that drives them. I believe that the transformative work of educational leadership needs to fully explore the *what* of curriculum and *how* it is learned in order to unlock the human side of the learning agenda.

Joseph Murphy

During these same years, Joseph Murphy composed a challenging analysis of the current state of educational administration programs published by the University

Council for Educational Administration (1999). Murphy provided a comprehensive overview of the considerable efforts of the field of educational administration to reform its practice and theory over the past 20 years. Despite these efforts, Murphy asserted, the field remains diffuse and disunited, representing a hodge-podge of interests, functions, and scholarship, not a profession moving forward with a clear purpose. Murphy contended that currently the practice of educational administration as well as the academic field of educational administration has no integrating principle, no "center"—no central focus that integrates the many disparate functions, concerns, activities, or concepts about educational administration. That lack of a center has allowed the profession to drift during the past 20 years despite the efforts of its leading scholars, leaving the profession more or less ineffective in responding to the numerous criticisms leveled against schools, administrators, and educational administration programs.

Murphy (1999) identified three large concerns that seem to surface with increasing repetition within both the scholarship about and the practice of administration—"three powerful synthesizing paradigms" (p. 54) that could provide this center for educational administration. The three themes are: democratic community, social justice, and school improvement.

Murphy argued for accepting the theme of school improvement as the centerpiece for the revitalization and centering of educational administration. He argued that school improvement has a broad appeal for both the academic and practitioner branches of the field of educational administration—two groups that have all too often appeared to be working from different cognitive and value perspectives. Attention to this core focus by both academics and practitioners could lead to an ongoing collaboration where practitioners' efforts to improve student performance would be supported by research on the effectiveness of these efforts and by university preparation programs that now prepare new administrators more clearly focused and enabled to take on these educational leadership roles.

Murphy went on to encourage a complementary role for the other two themes—democratic community and concern for social justice—as integral components of the effort at school renewal. Work on democratic community and social justice would be seen as part of the core work of teaching and learning. Despite Murphy's inclusive posture toward the other two themes, his choice of the school improvement theme as the dominant theme (for both professional, political, and pragmatic reasons) has drawn criticism from those who prefer to see one of the other themes at the center.

It would be an unfortunate mistake for advocates of each of these three positions to compete for dominance of the field because these positions are necessarily and organically related to one another. They should imply each other. The focus on student achievement is a social justice issue; the emphasis here is on success for *all* children, not just for the bright or economically advantaged. Academic achievement in isolation from a societal context is chimerical; learning involves relationships with teachers and other students in some kind of functional community; learning has to be related to responsible participation in various social institutions. Democratic community implies a learning community that engages in discussion and debate about social policy and the common good. Social progress requires reasoned discourse and a continuous assessment of social policy. The critique of structural and cultural injustice in society on behalf of social justice has to be constructed from factual evidence as well as moral argument. All three themes require one another if we wish to create a robust educational program; neither one in isolation from the others can bring about the desired results.

Murphy is correct, I believe, in insisting that educators have to focus on the core work of students—namely, their learning. Educators have to continue to explore with one another and with their students how the learning in the school can become meaningful, deep, lasting, and reflective—whether that learning concerns the elements of rocket technology, computer graphics, group dynamics, poetic expression, conflict resolution, or the difficult balancing of loyalty and justice. By retaining the necessary interpenetration of all three themes, educators will be able to resist the current overemphasis on narrowly academic tests as the sole measure of a school's mission. Because students' mastery of the academic curriculum appears weak—in some communities, more than half of the student body is performing at an unsatisfactory level—this clearly requires vigorous and prolonged attention, but not necessarily the draconian and punitive measures some school systems have adopted. States have imposed stringent demands on schools while offering little or no additional support to achieve those demands—not in professional development funding, not in smaller class sizes, not in better science or library resources, not in more responsive and imaginative remediation programs, to mention a few obvious examples. Instead, the victims of an inadequate system—students, teachers, and administrators—get blamed for all the system's shortcomings.

Another perspective

In this book, I offer a perspective on this *center* for educational administration that is somewhat similar to Murphy's position, but takes it deeper. It is similar in that it argues for an interpenetration of three themes as the center while focusing on a common emphasis on learning in all three themes. It is similar in that I too am concerned about school improvement, but a school improvement that includes assessment and accountability issues in a larger perspective. I also want to employ the theme of transformational leadership emphasized by Leithwood, Jantzi, and Steinbach, but I want to emphasize that what needs transforming is the large agenda of student learning and the curriculum and teaching that support that learning. Like Elmore, I believe that the core work of school leaders must be involved with teachers in seeking to promote quality learning for all children, and that all management tasks serve that core work. Unlike Elmore, I want that core work to extend beyond state mandated curriculum standards to a broader curriculum that cultivates meaning, community and responsibility at the same time the school is responding to state standards and testing.

This book's perspective differs from the work of these three scholars, moreover, by looking beyond the present positioning of the argument about a center or focus for educational leadership. This book positions the argument in the larger historical transition from an early, *naive* era of modernity to a later, *reflexive* era of modernity. This enables me to highlight the cognitive and cultural landscape behind the present school reform agenda and thereby reach beyond the glaring shortcomings of that agenda to a deeper and more inclusive vision of what school reform *might* or *should* look like. I also want to recast the vocabulary of the present argument into terminology that I consider more inclusive and interactive—that is, fresher than the more abstract terminology of *higher achievement for all students, school renewal, democratic community,* and *social justice*. I use the phrases *cultivating meaning, cultivating community,* and *cultivating responsibility*.

The agricultural metaphor of *cultivation* suggests the work of the gardener: planting, fertilizing, weeding, watering, pruning (Louis, Toole, & Hargreaves, 1999). That is the work of someone who works with nature, with what nature provides. It involves educators understanding the qualities of soil and terrain, the chemistry of acids and alkaloids, the virtues of sun and shade, and the peculiar energies of winter and spring as metaphors of schooling realities. It is an aesthetic work, as well, appreciating the different colors and hues, variations in blossoming, and harmonies of size, color, and texture in the life one is cultivating. The cultivating work of educators is the work of understanding the native talents and interests of students, their cultural backgrounds, learning styles, and developmental readiness. It is a work of understanding both cognitive and affective development and the psychological logic of certain teaching protocols. It is dialogical work with fellow teachers and students to find out what blocks learning and what facilitates and enables learning to blossom.

Using the phrase *cultivating meaning* in place of Murphy's focus on the core work of teaching and learning enables me to focus on the outcome of teaching and learning, which is the construction of meaning. Within that theme, I can distinguish between *personal* meanings and *public* meanings, between *applied* meanings and *academic* meanings. Each of these differentiations requires different pedagogies, leaning processes, and assessment protocols. The phrase *cultivating community* rather than *democratic community* enables me to bypass what I consider to be a heatedly ideological argument about the meaning of democracy while exploring an education in pluralistic sociality, collaborative civility, and participatory self-governance. The phrase "cultivating responsibility" enables me to speak both to the neglected issues of social justice in the education of poor and minority children, as well as to the education of the young in moral values of justice, care and critique. The rhetoric of responsibility is both more inclusive of conflicting viewpoints and less inflammatory to the ears of a politically complacent public.

By incorporating the three themes into the center of administrators' work, both in theory and in practice, this book advances the basic thrust of Murphy's position. Through the elaboration of the themes we enrich Murphy's initial articulation of the three potential centers. This elaboration, in turn, enables us to develop the implications of these themes in specific curricula—what I have named the curriculum of meaning, the curriculum of community and the curriculum of responsibility. By drawing out the learning implications of these curricula, I can further specify the leadership focus of administrative work with teachers.

The consciousness of an educational administrator

Educational administration, however intense its focus on teaching and learning, is nevertheless different from classroom teaching. Whereas teachers focus on specific students and specific areas of subject matter, administrators must think of the education of the whole community of youngsters in the school. This requires them to think of the scope and sequence of all the learning activities occurring in the school, not simply as a collection of activities, but as activities that comprise a unity.

These activities make up a fitting education for human beings living in this moment of history, in this society, who are preparing for a challenging and demanding future in an increasingly globalized world. A rich grounding in the three foundational themes of cultivating meaning, community, and responsibility provides a focus for a broad consciousness of the desired purposes being served throughout the school.

An educational administrator today, working with the school board and the school district officers, is expected to have a larger sense of what constitutes an educated person and to bring this perspective to the task of coordinating and harmonizing the various separate areas of learning. Although teachers are expected to have a detailed understanding of specific learnings in their curriculum areas, administrators are supposed to bring the work of individual teachers into balance and unity by coordinating the varied activities of the youngsters during the years they spend in school. For example, one might expect that an educated person in 21st-century America would have an understanding of the natural environment and the importance of national and international policies enacted to protect this environment from excessive exploitation and deterioration. Hence, an educational administrator would be concerned that, in various science and social studies courses offered in the school curriculum, such understandings would be nurtured, although he or she might not know at what specific moment in any given course such considerations should be raised.

Similarly, one might expect that educated persons in 21st-century America would have developed an appreciation of the cultural diversity of the region in which they were raised and would have some understanding of the history and culture of communities that are culturally different from their own. That understanding must include a critical awareness of the historical oppression of various racial and ethnic groups by the White community. Thus, an educational administrator would be concerned that, in a variety of classes and extracurricular activities, a proactive multicultural sensitivity would be developed, although the administrator might not know how to bring about such sensitivity in every particular instance.

From the teacher's perspective, we could say that the teacher has a large sense of what youngsters in a particular course are supposed to be learning and a wide variety of learning activities by which the youngsters can arrive at those learnings. One might say that each teacher, after a few years of teaching, carries the course in his or her head. Educational administrators, however, must carry around in their heads the whole school's learning agenda as an integrated unity. One might say that a concert violinist carries the violin score of the symphony in his or her head, but that the conductor must carry the whole symphony in his or her head so that the playing of the various instruments can be integrated. Such an analogy helps explain the difference between the consciousness of the administrator and that of the teacher. The analogy appears to illuminate the difficulty of the administrator's task when we think of the individual musicians not as the teachers, but as the students who are just beginning to learn to play the various instruments. The administrator has to have some sense of how learning musical scales is an appropriate step in learning to play a symphony and, indeed, that both teachers and students need to keep the playing of the symphony in mind as they learn the mechanics of the instrument or the first simple melodies. The administrator also has to recognize that the symphony includes African, Asian, Latin and other motifs and instrumentation, and to allow for both cacophony and invention in the score.

It is the vision of what all individual learning activities, linked together and intertwined over the course of several years, are intended to produce that educators must remember. This vision includes the gradual emergence of autonomous, intelligent, caring, and socially responsible human beings who will comprise a community struggling with the wounds of the past, yet full of promise for the future. This is the vision that truly activates transformational leaders of schools.

While keeping in mind the ideal of the *educated person* who understands the tragedies and triumphs of the community and is prepared to participate fully in its public life, the administrator should realize that few youngsters ever achieve the full and harmonious balance of understandings and skills contained in the ideal. Youngsters bring individual talents and liabilities with them to school. They have different interests, abilities, and learning styles. Teachers struggle to bring children to a minimal level of mastery in many areas, yet they find that individual youngsters perform better on some tasks than on others, and their readiness for some tasks differs from their readiness for other tasks. Some youngsters come from homes where English is not spoken, and hence their learning activities may have to be structured to take into account the strengths and diversity of the cultures in which the children were raised. Some youngsters may come from dysfunctional home environments, and thus their educational program may have to be supplemented with other support services.

Educators' ideal of an educated person may reflect class, gender, and racial bias. The ideal of an educated person should always be contextualized by the youngsters being served. In other words, educators have to look at the total condition of the children and respond to it. The symphony may not be Mozart's; for now it might be a symphony in fingerpaint, the symphony of a child learning for the first time how to play with other children, or a symphony of linguistic expression with Latin inflections. In every instance, the educator must work with whatever the youngster brings to the learning situation, but the educator must never stop believing that each child is capable of something wonderful and heroic and that he or she will never exhaust his or her possibilities.

The vision behind administrative leadership

The prior considerations lead us to consider an all-important quality of administrative leadership—*vision*. I use that term here in two senses. The first refers to a firm commitment to an ideal—the educated person and an ideal educational process for cultivating that person. Educational leaders know full well the difference between the ideal and the realities in schools. Senge (1990) suggested that a tension necessarily exists in corporations between a shared vision and perceived organizational limitations. Senge asserted that this tension can be generative when leaders mobilize the members to use that tension creatively. It is the awareness of the unnecessarily large gap between the ideal and the real that fuels the commitment of educational leaders to close that gap.

Included in the ideal of the educated person is the autonomy of the educated person to choose the direction of his or her life. Hence, that ideal implies a dialogical relationship between the educator and student in which the process of cultivating meaning, community, and responsibility involves both invitation and response—a necessary mutuality in the learning process.

The second sense of vision is the sense of sight: the seeing things clearly, seeing both the foreground and background and being able to situate the foreground within the background. This sense of the educational leader's vision suggests that leaders look into the full reality of what stands before them, see it in its complexity, in its human, existential, and moral dimensions, as well as in its educational and organizational dimensions. This sense of insight refers to *in-sight*—to the grasp of both the deeper and pragmatic dimensions of situations. This sense of vision enables leaders to respond on several levels to the multidimensional quality of situations, to offer short-term responses and accommodate long-term needs. These two senses of vision—the ideal and the talent of insight—are mutually reinforcing. The ideal provides an interpretive lens for seeing into the deeper dimensions of present situations. The talent of insight enables the leader to connect the immediate realities to a larger framework of meaning and value.

This approach to educational leadership enables us to create a model of leadership that illustrates how the leader's vision eventually becomes embodied in the institutional structures and frameworks and policies of the school.[1] There are five basic elements to this leadership:

1. It is grounded in basic meanings about human persons, society, knowledge, human development, the natural world, and schooling.
2. It is energized by a dramatic vision of what education might and should be.
3. It involves the articulation of that vision and the invitation to others to articulate a communal vision of schooling.
4. It seeks to embody the vision in the institutional mission, goals, policies, programs, and organizational structures.
5. It celebrates the vision in ordinary and special activities and seeks a continuous renewal of both the vision and its embodiment.

In succeeding chapters, I lay out a vision of schooling that is grounded in basic meanings about human persons, society, the nature of knowledge, human development, and the natural word. Those chapters challenge the reader to engage those elements of the vision and modify or create their own vision statement. The chapters also suggest ways to engage members of the school staff in discussions about their vision for the school.

The articulation of the vision is crucial. Unless the school community gets its personal visions out on the table for public dialogue, it is difficult for that community to move beyond the customary daily routines into any sense of re-new-ing themselves and their work. Without a communal vision of who they are and where they want to go, the school functions as a shopping mall, with each classroom reflecting the idiosyncratic preferences of each teacher. Inevitably, a vision is imposed from outside. Indeed, state departments of education, pressured by political and corporate leaders whose views of schooling are one dimensional and simplistic, seem quite willing to step in and impose their view of schooling. A local vision of schooling endorsed by the staff can serve as an interpretive framework for discussing state curriculum mandates.

Often the leader has to take the initiative and put forth a vision statement. That provides the rest of the staff something to consider, but not necessarily to endorse. Individually and in teams, the staff should be encouraged to come up with their own vision—not of where they are now, of how they understand what their work currently consists of, but a vision of who they might become—a vision of new understandings of their work, a vision of where they want to go with the students. Because it is not an exercise most staff are comfortable with, some time and space, structure and coaching should be provided. Most university preparation programs do not require its prospective administrators to come up with a vision statement that they are required to defend in some kind of public forum. But that is precisely one of the leadership skills needed by educational administrators (Hargreaves & Fullan, 1998). Neither are these candidates required to work with a group to generate a group vision—again, a key leadership skill needed in the field.

Beyond creating one's own vision statement and collaborating with others on a communal vision statement, administrators need to assess the gap between the communal vision and the institutional processes, structures, policies, and programs that get in the way of the vision ever becoming operationalized. The following diagrams may help visualize this process.

Using what I refer to as the Onion Model of Schools we can visualize a school being made up of layers of intelligible activity (see Figure 4.1). The outer layer represents the operational level of the school. This is what one sees on walking around the school building on a given day: teachers in front of their classrooms explaining something on the blackboard; students struggling to enact the curriculum; students moving from one classroom to another, banging locker doors, calling out to one another; assistant principals standing in the corridors scowling at the students as they pass by; bulletin boards displaying students' work; bells ringing; announcements coming over the PA system reminding students and teachers about the days events; teachers discussing new textbooks; and so forth. Underneath that layer, one would find a pattern of organization: a class schedule for each day of the week, distribution of subject matter across the class schedule, allocation of 25 students or so to each classroom, marking of time by bells, allocation of support staff doing their respective jobs, weekly, monthly, and yearly calendar, schedule of meals and busses, and arrivals and departure arrangements.

Beneath that layer is the deeper layer of schoolwide programs—the various academic disciplines with their scope and sequence for each year, the guidance program, the discipline program, the health program, the athletic program, and school–parent programs. These programs provide the substance of the teachers' and students' work.

Under the program layer is the policy layer. This layer guides the execution of the programs and operations and includes grading and promotion policies, personnel policies for teachers and staff, pupil personnel policies, home–school communication policies, crisis management procedures, and so forth. These are the general rules that govern many of the day-to-day decisions made by everyone in the school community. Beneath the policy layer is the layer of goals and purposes. This includes the mission statement, perhaps a statement on the core values the school espouses, and goals referring to students' intellectual, social, and personal development.

Beneath those layers, one finds the level of beliefs and assumptions. Often these are not articulated clearly. Although tacit, they nevertheless exercise an enormous influence over the behavior and routines of people in the school. When these beliefs

50 *The challenging world of educational leadership*

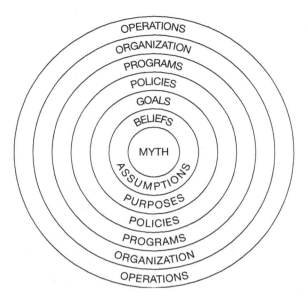

Figure 4.1 Dimensions of school life.

and assumptions are made explicit, they comprise the foundation for a vision statement. Sometimes the unarticulated beliefs and assumptions can be limiting. They might imply an attitude toward students as problems, focused on their limits rather than on their potential, containing subtle forms of bias toward some children and their communities. The unarticulated beliefs and assumptions may imply a vision of teaching and learning that focuses on passive learning, rote memorization of textbook materials, and an assessment system designed to reproduce the normal curve of intelligence. By contrast, these beliefs and assumptions might focus on the enormous potential of the children, on the role of teaching as the highly creative design of exciting learning activities that motivate students to high-quality learning, as well as focus on the importance of fostering community as the stimulus for individual growth. When those latter beliefs and assumptions are made public and become coalesced into a communal vision, they have enormous potential to energize a school.

At the core of the onion, often flowing into the unarticulated beliefs and assumptions, are the myths and meanings by which people make sense out of their lives. By labeling them *myths*, I do not imply that they are fairy-tale phantasies fed by infantile fears, desires, and superstitions. Rather, these myths are stories whose symbolism enable us to define value, judge human striving, and place ourselves in an identifiable order of things. This core is almost beyond articulation. It includes the myth of heroism, human destiny, and the sacred nature of all life; myths about society's relationships to nature, about values underlying the nation's identity, about those values considered to comprise the essence of humanity. Those myths—often embodied in story, poetry, highly symbolic literature, sacred texts—shape people's convictions, beliefs, and attitudes about most things. It is in that core of myth, meaning, and belief that leaders find the foundation for their vision of what the school can and should become: the greenhouse for cultivating the educated person.

The leader's work is not completed when the school community has articulated its communal vision. The vision must become embodied in the other layers of the school organization. The onion must be energized by its core. The difficulty experienced by many educators is that they function in schools that, for all intents and purposes, have no center, no articulated vision, mission, or sense of purpose, other than the daily delivery of programs governed by schedules and operating procedures (see Figure 4.2). In contrast, Figure 4.3 suggests a school in which the outer layers reflect those core beliefs, values, and meanings. The articulation of a vision enables those school communities to intentionally pursue the vision by means of the programs and structural organization of the school, rather than pursuing the vision by *fighting against* the routines of those outer layers.

A vision statement is not a full-blown philosophy or long-range plan. Much of its power comes from capturing three or four central meanings that are open to multiple applications and representations within the school. The vision statement does not have an impact on student learning unless it is institutionalized in the various layers of school life. Schools that fail to confront their organizational structures' resistance to the vision remain dysfunctional.

Figure 4.4 helps identify and distinguish more clearly the leadership side of administrative work and the managerial side of administrative work. Much of the leader's work lies at the left side of the figure, whereas much of the manager's work lies at the right side of the figure, involved in the organization and daily operation of the school. The important work of institutionalizing the vision calls on the complementary skills of both leadership and management, the former to insist on bringing the

Figure 4.2 A school with no vision.

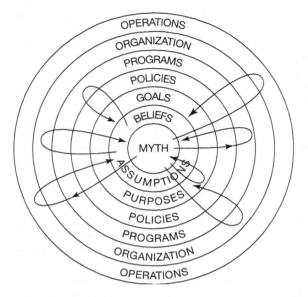

Figure 4.3 A school with an integrated vision.

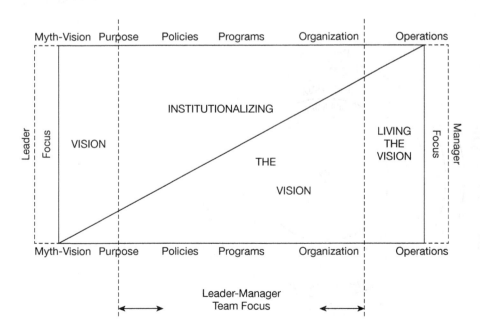

Figure 4.4 Bringing separated focus to a team focus.

vision forward into the practical functioning of the school and the latter insisting on bringing some kind of structure, predictability, and form to the vision. The figure brings the leader and the manager work into dialogue at the center of the figure. In a different context, Hill and Guthrie (1999) emphasized the integrative function of leadership, the work of bringing powerful perspectives and resources together so that their mutual interaction can produce the necessary effect. Here we see the integration of leadership and managerial work necessary for the re-creation of the school as a viable social institution, with the strengths of both approaches to administrative work coming together to effect what neither one of them singly could achieve. Obviously, we are talking not only of the integrative work of one person here, but a teamwork of all those in the school community who have talents in both areas.

Finally, Figure 4.5 lays out in a more logical-sequential diagram the work of administrative leadership, moving from the visioning and purposing work through the restructuring work toward coordinating the daily operations of the school. Thus, we see the work of school renewal that Murphy (1999) urged as the core work of administrative leadership represented in a model of administrative leadership that elaborates that work in its reach and depth. The model strongly suggests that the work of school renewal cannot progress in more than a superficial rearrangement at the program and organizational level unless it is energized by a communal vision of who teachers and students are, what authentic learning involves, and what the social and academic purposes of schools are. The remaining chapters in Part One attempt to explore dimensions of the vision, employing the three themes of cultivating meaning, cultivating community, and cultivating responsibility. In the process of suggesting consideration of these themes as providing a fuller vision of what schools and therefore administrators should be seeking, I hope to include the other two concerns that Murphy (1999) identified as needing to be included with school renewal—namely, democratic community and social justice. In Part Two, I touch on the integrative work of administrative leadership—namely, the embodiment of the vision into the core structures that shape and sustain the daily operation of the school. In Part Two, it becomes more obvious that the transformational leadership called for by Leithwood, Jantzi, and Steinbach, as well as (implicitly, at least) Elmore and Murphy, requires a healthy blending with transactional leadership (Bass, 1988) as the details of the vision get worked out in practical detail.

Recapitulation

The ingredients for reform are known at least in general outline. The political mandate is there. Public opinion seems rather firmly behind school reform. Anyone familiar with large-scale organizational change, however, knows that the transformation of schools—one of the more conservative institutions in society—requires leadership on a broad and continuous scale for at least a generation. Persons at the forefront of these changes may find themselves embroiled in controversy with teachers' unions, special interest groups in the community, and fiscal conservatives who oppose increased spending for schools (Cusick, 1992). The task requires facility in building coalitions, arbitration and conflict resolution, and communicating an appealing vision of the human benefits to be derived from changes in the form and substance of schooling.

54 The challenging world of educational leadership

ROOTS OF THE VISION	ARTICULATION OF THE VISION	INSTITUTIONALISATION OF THE VISION	OPERATIONALIZATION OF THE VISION
Meaning associated with: Human destiny The nature of the individual The nature of human society View of the past and of the future Frequency embedded in imagery, metaphor, myth, and story	Beliefs about: – the human mind and how one knows – how children develop as full human beings – how children should be socialized – varieties of learning – moral values – political values – religious values – what kind of future the young will face	Formal Statement of the Mission of the School Cultural purposes Political purposes Academic purposes Moral purposes Economic purposes Social purposes Religious purposes Process of Communicating the Vision – Thematic purposing – Rituals – Celebrations – Championing – Heroes – Rewards	Formal Organization Policies Programs Procedures – Graduation requirements – Curriculum – Course selection and assignment – Grading criteria – Discipline – Student activities – Staffing – Budget Informal Organization Community spirit Style of communications Tone of relationships Informal groups Informal curriculum	Woodrow Wilson School A school that opens its doors and looks like: People coming and going to – classes – activities – interactions making up a fabric of experience – meanings – patterns – rituals – symbolic action – celebration
MYTH	ASSUMPTIONS, BELIEFS	GOALS, OBJECTIVES	POLICIES, PROGRAMS, STRUCTURES	OPERATIONS

Figure 4.5 The communal institutionalization of vision.

To exercise leadership in this climate of change requires deep convictions, strong commitments, and clear ideas about directions for change in the form and content of schooling. There should be no illusions about this. The people leading the way in school transformation must have thought and read their way through the complex issues at stake in school reform. They must be people who see a clear connection between the public program of schooling and the kind of society that will carry the human adventure into the future; that is, they will understand the human and technical challenges that the community faces and will bring the understanding of these challenges to bear on the design of the form and content of the schools they are redesigning.

Aware of the dangers and dysfunction of imposing policy from the top down, future administrators should also realize that their ideas about the shape and content of schooling must be tested in the forum of public debate. Such public debate is often a raucous, contentious, self-interested power struggle. One's bright ideas can be misunderstood, misinterpreted, distorted, ridiculed, and contested. One is subjected to personal accusations, verbal abuse, betrayals, threats to one's job, and various forms of raw hatred. Through all this, one must attempt to keep people talking about the issues, appealing to people's better sides, finding common ground, bargaining for more resources, bringing disparate interests together, and keeping one's dreams and hopes alive month after month, year after year.

Such a prospect is not for the faint-hearted or weekend enthusiast. Rather, it is for people who see the possibility for a better life for children and youth, who dream of a better tomorrow for all members of their society, and who have the inner strength of their convictions and ideals, as well as the humility to know that they need to join themselves to the ideas, talents, and energies of countless others if their hopes and dreams are to be realized. The school administrator of the future needs a different mindset and skills than the status quo administrator of the past; the dramatic challenges facing schools call for a different kind of vision and commitment. Schools are not served well by people who go into school administration primarily for the increased salary, the greater prestige and power in the community, or a heightened sense of self-importance, all the while assuming that schools are more or less fine the way they are. Those contemplating a career in educational administration need to make a sober assessment of their own talents, motivations, and dispositions for meeting the challenges in educational administration in the 21st century. Such an assessment is necessary before rather than after a decision has been taken to become an educational administrator. For those who do choose to pursue such a career, the foundational orientations provided in these chapters can expose them to exciting possibilities.

Activities

1. Write out your understanding of educational administration prior to reading this chapter. Compare your prior understanding with that of your classmates. Does that shared understanding of administration represent what you perceive as standard practice in the workplace?
2. Assess your motivation for choosing to move into administrative work. What personal and professional values energize your motivations?

3. Assume that the view of educational administration present in this chapter is to be used as the basis for standards of hiring and evaluating administrators in the near future. Assess your strengths and shortcomings for success in this kind of educational administration. What does this assessment suggest to you?

Note

1 This material is adapted from my earlier works such as *Leaders with vision: The quest for school renewal*. Thousand Oaks, CA: Corwin Press, 1995, pp. 14–18 and 50–58; and *Supervision: A redefinition* (5th ed.). New York: McGraw-Hill, 1993, pp. 188–198, co-authored with Thomas J. Sergiovanni.

References

Apple, M. W. (1982). *Education and power*. Boston: Routledge & Kegan Paul.
Bass, B. M. (1985). *Leadership and performance beyond expectations*. New York: Free Press.
Bass, B. M. (1998). The ethics of transformational leadership. In J. B. Ciulla (Ed.), *Ethics, the heart of leadership* (pp. 169–192). Westport, CT: Quorum.
Bates, R. (1987). Corporate culture, schooling, and educational administration. *Educational Administration Quarterly, 23*(4), 79–115.
Burns, J. M. (1978). *Leadership*. New York: Harper & Row.
Cohen, M. D., March, J. G., & Olsen, J.P. (1972). A garbage can model of organizational choice. *Administrative Science Quarterly, 17*(1), 1–25.
Cubberly, E. (1916). *Public school administration*. Boston: Houghton Mifflin.
Cusick, P. (1992). *The educational system: Its nature and logic*. New York: McGraw-Hill.
Cyert, R. M., & March, J. G. (1963). *A behavioral theory of the firm*. Englewood Cliffs, NJ: Prentice-Hall.
Donmoyer, R., Imber, M., & Scheurich, J. J. (1995). *The knowledge base in educational administration: Multiple perspectives*. Albany, NY: State University of New York Press.
Elmore, R. (2000). *Building a new structure for school leadership*. Washington, DC: The Albert Shanker Institute.
Giroux, H. A. (1991). Curriculum planning, public schooling, and democratic struggle. *NASSP Bulletin, 75*(532), 12–25.
Griffiths, D. E. (1959). *Administrative theory*. New York: Appleton-Century-Crofts.
Hargreaves, A., & Fullan, M. (1998). *What's worth fighting for out there?* New York: Teachers College Press.
Hill, P. T., & Guthrie, J. W. (1999). A new research paradigm for understanding (and improving) twenty-first century schooling. In J. Murphy & K. S. Louis (Eds.), *Handbook of research on educational administration* (2nd ed., pp. 511–523). San Francisco: Jossey-Bass.
Leithwood, K., Jantzi, D., & Steinbach, R. (1999). *Changing leadership for changing times*. Philadelphia: Open University Press.
Lindbloom, C. E. (1959). The science of muddling through. *Public Administration Review, 19*(1), 79–88.
Louis, K. S., Toole, J., & Hargreaves, A. (1999). Rethinking school improvement. In J. Murphy & K. S. Louis (Eds.), *Handbook of research on educational administration* (2nd ed., pp. 251–276). San Francisco: Jossey-Bass.
Milstein, M. M., & Associates. (1993). *Changing the way we prepare educational leaders: The Danforth experience*. Newbury Park, CA: Corwin.
Mulkeen, T. A., Cambron-McCabe, N. H., & Anderson, B. J. (1994). *Democratic leadership: The changing context of administrative preparation*. Norwood, NJ: Ablex.
Murphy, J. (1992). *The landscape of leadership preparation: Reframing the education of school administrators*. Newbury Park, CA: Corwin.

Murphy, J. (1999). *The quest for a center: Notes on the state of the profession of educational leadership*. Columbia, MO: University Council for Educational Administration.
National Commission on Excellence in Educational Administration. (1987). *Leaders for America's schools*. Tempe, AZ: University Council for Educational Administration.
National Policy Board for Educational Administration. (1989). *Improving the preparation of school administrators: An agenda for reform*. Charlottesville, VA: Author.
Purpel, D. E. (1985). Introduction. In D. E. Purpel & H. Z. Shapiro (Eds.), *Schools and Meaning: Essays on the moral nature of schooling* (p. XVII). Lanham, MD: University Press of America.
Senge, P. M. (1990). *The fifth discipline: The art and practice of the learning organization*. New York: Doubleday.
Sergiovanni, T. J., & Carver, F. D. (1969). *Organizations and human behavior: Focus on schools*. New York: McGraw-Hill.
Simon, H. A. (1957). *Administrative behavior: A study of decision-making processes in administrative organization*. New York: Macmillan.
Starratt, R. J. (1993a). *The drama of leadership*. London: Falmer.
Starratt, R. J. (1993b). *Supervision: A redefinition* (5th ed.). New York: McGraw-Hill.
Starratt, R. J. (1995). *Leaders with vision*. Thousand Oaks, CA: Corwin.
Taylor, F. (1911). *The principles of scientific management*. New York: Harper & Row.
University Council on Educational Administration. (1992). *Essential knowledge for school leaders: A proposal to map the knowledge base of educational administration*. Unpublished proposal.

CHAPTER FIVE

Cultivating a perspective on learning

In the first part of the book, we developed the foundational themes of cultivating meaning, community, and responsibility as the primary focus for educational leadership. In the second part of the book, we draw out some of the implications of these foundational themes for the way schools conduct themselves, and for the work of administrators in leading schools committed to cultivating meaning, community, and responsibility. In this chapter, we focus on applying those themes to the fundamental work of the school—namely, student learning. By gaining a clearer idea of what constitutes the student's work, we gain a clearer perspective on the teacher's work, and thereby a clearer idea of how administrator's work supports the teachers' and students' work. Many administrators have forgotten how complex the process of learning can be and how carefully teachers have to plan and design a variety of learning activities that stimulate and guide this process. By and large, books on educational administration do not review the complex processes of learning and teaching, assuming that their readers are already familiar with those understandings or that that material is treated somewhere else in the university preparation of administrators. Curriculum courses, teaching methods courses, and learning theory courses, however, are usually conducted for teachers, not administrators. This chapter provides a model of learning and teaching that administrators might employ in their all-important work with teachers on improving the depth and quality of learning for all students. The model does not cover all the microaspects of teaching. Rather, it provides a large conceptual map that administrators can use in their conversations with teachers for cultivating meaning, community, and responsibility.

The student as worker

Schools are currently organized under the assumption that teachers are the primary workers. Through their instructional strategies—their work—it is assumed that they produce learning in the students—learning that can be replicated by the student on standardized tests. Behind this view of teachers' work in schools lies the assumption that knowledge is *out there* somewhere waiting to be packaged by a curriculum designer and textbook writer and then explained, treated, and passed along by the teacher. The techniques of teaching—the teacher's *bag of tricks*—consist in the shaping of the lesson material so that students will *get it*—be able to repeat the definition, use the words of the vocabulary lesson in a proper sentence, apply the mathematical formula to a series of simple problems that resemble the model problem, memorize the textbook explanation of the mercantile system, describe the eating and hunting customs of native peoples of the Arctic, and so forth. In this arrangement, the student is thought of as a passive recipient of nuggets of information being delivered by the teacher.

To be sure, there has to be some activity on the part of students, just as there has to be some activity on the part of anyone being fed (chewing, swallowing, etc.). Yet the teacher is the one who selects what is to be learned, how it is to be learned, how the learning is to be evaluated, and according to what measurable standards of mastery it will be judged. Even where the teacher is urged to help students relate the present learnings to prior learning or personal experiences, the focus is on a motivational strategy, not an epistemological value. The point is not for students to construct or produce something that is personally and singularly their own, but to see their own experience as simply an example of the abstract textbook learning defined in the curriculum. Testing and grading convey this message: The personal life of the student does not count; the replication of a predetermined piece of material is what counts. It is as though students are expected to leave their own lives at the schoolhouse door; they—or at least their minds—belong to the school during the school day. It is what the school determines is to be learned that matters, nothing else.

If we make the student the worker, then this form of schooling has to change. The student now enters more actively into the learning process. Learning is the active engagement of the student, including all the sensitivities, points of view, talents, and imagination that he or she possesses, with the material under study, whether it is a short story, an algebraic operation, a question in biology, a comparison of the technique of Matisse with that of Pissarro, or his or her own poem about the season of spring. In the process of learning, and as a result of their active engagement with the material, students are asked to produce something that expresses their learning.

It may be helpful to highlight what has already been developed about the nature of learning. Learning is not exclusively or primarily a matter of passive intake of information. Arguments continue in the field of cognitive science about the relative importance in the activity of knowing attached to the built-in neural wiring of the learner's mind as opposed to the active construction of knowledge and meaning by the learner (Frawley, 1997). It seems clear that the claims of both groups of cognitive psychologists need to be taken into account. Learning involves a conditioned processing of intake data acted on by different parts of the brain, but it also involves an active effort of the individual who chooses to pursue inquires further to explore various relationships within multiple frameworks of intelligibility. The educational policy community seems committed to the view that students can and must make their brains work harder, can and must enter much more actively and intentionally into the construction of knowledge. School renewal policy is based on this premise. The spirit of the arguments of the first part of the book also endorses this perspective. In summary, we have proposed that:

- learning involves an active construction of knowledge and understanding in a sociocultural context;

- learning is a reflexive shaping of the self;
- learning is intrinsically social;
- learning involves a striving for and development of personal and social excellence;
- learning is an intrinsically moral activity; and
- personal learning has to become public learning and applied learning on the way to generating academic understanding.

Personal, public, applied, and academic meanings: A model of learning

In the work of learning, students need to generate four kinds of meaning: personal, public, applied, and academic. For learning to be anchored in the life world of the student, it has to be personal. The student should always be able to say in a variety of ways,

> This is what my work in school today or this week means to me; it talks to me about this aspect of nature or of human nature, which I find in myself or in my circumstances; I can see examples of this in my own family, circle of friends, in my neighborhood or larger civic and natural community. What I learned helps me to understand myself better, to reposition myself in relation to nature, to social practices, to the cultural or political world I inhabit. What I learned teaches me a moral lesson about what I should do in similar circumstances, or what I need to watch out for, or avoid, or try out.

Obviously, younger students cannot present their personal appropriation of the material under study in such abstract terms; in their concrete narratives, however, their teachers can discern how the material is affecting them. The personal meanings each student derives from the learning activities are diverse, representing the cultural background, interests, motivations, self-image, and socialization of each youngster. Nevertheless, it is important for students to voice them—to weigh their importance and value in the construction of themselves as the person they want to be and to become.

The student then has to bring those personal meanings to the table of public discourse to see how those personal meanings relate to the personal meanings that other learners bring to the table. As students share the personal meanings they derived from the material under study, they can enter conversations about the similarities and differences among their personal meanings and explore common knowledge and understandings from their joint learning. They can construct provisional definitions of things on which they agree. They also need to relate their common understandings to the wider public. How are these matters talked about and understood in the wider public? Here the teacher can act as a Socratic facilitator, asking questions that stretch their understanding of the public views of the topics under discussion. This also can be a stimulus for the students to converse with their parents and members of their extended family about how they understand the material they have been studying. Although time constraints limit the extent of these explorations of public understandings, as they become a habitual part of the ongoing learning process, students gain an appreciation of the connections that their work of learning has to the larger public world. They become increasingly facile in placing their classroom understandings within larger public contexts.

As an extension of students' discussions of the public meanings of what they are learning, they should be required to generate at least two potential or actual applications of what they have learned to life in the home or larger community. They should pose questions such as the following: "What would this knowledge be useful for?" "What problem or issue in our home or community could be addressed by this knowledge or understanding?" "How would this be used in two or three occupations?" "Suppose a team of us from the class were called in by the Mayor to help the community solve this particular problem. How would what we just learned help us address the problem?" As students work to apply their knowledge to a new situation, the new situation requires understanding it from different perspectives, seeing the knowledge put to use, now in one context, now in another. Often the context requires them to modify their understanding or create analogies with more familiar contexts. As more than a few scholars have noted, our knowledge in the abstract may remain rather simplistic or one dimensional; when we have to do something with it, we understand it differently and can call on that understanding for use in other contexts (Newman, Secada, & Wehlage, 1995).

When the learning has generated personal, public, and applied meanings, we are in a better position to appreciate the academic meanings behind or within the learning activities. Academic meanings refer to those abstract principles, definitions, constant relationships, logical arguments, methodological principles, or large cognitive patterns or frameworks that lend an underlying intelligibility to the academic discipline, whether we are talking about the discipline of chemistry, history, geography, or poetry. The Harvard project, *Teaching for Understanding* (Wiske, 1998), has mapped the terrain of academic meaning quite clearly and provided rubrics for assessing various levels of academic mastery. Teachers, however, need to recognize that students are often unprepared to absorb the alphabet soup of academic meanings. Teachers who jump right into the academic meanings of the topic under study presume that students have the same readiness and interest as the academic scholar. All too often, students are required to grapple with new words, definitions, and formulas without any context in which to place them. Unless the learner has had an opportunity to muddle around with the material, look at its connection to his or her own life or the life of the public community, or test it out in various experiments and applications, the academic meanings become simply things to be memorized for tests and exams, but easily forgotten after classes are dismissed.

The model of learning presented here insists that for every significant unit of the curriculum, students should be required as part of the assessment process to articulate the personal, public, applied, and academic meanings they generated during that unit. If students are to enter into the learning process as a way of actively constructing themselves, if they are to develop a sensitivity to a plurality of points of view as well as work within that plurality for some pragmatic agreements on what will constitute some necessary public activity needed by the community, if they are to develop a sense of the usefulness of their learning in their present and future lives, then the weekly requirement that they generate personal, public, applied, *and* academic meanings from their learning activities will develop the kind of necessary foundation for these habits of mind and heart. As students complete the product or performance of their understanding of the curricular material, they should engage in a reflective assessment exercise. This reflective assessment exercise is different from and precedes the summative assessment exercises that involve using agreed-on rubrics to assess the quality of the performance or product (cf. Figures 5.1 and 5.2). This latter exercise involves not only the student assessing his or her own work in the light of the rubrics, but also peer assessment of the various products and performances of the class in the light of the rubrics, the teacher's assessment of each student's product or performance in the light of the rubrics, and, from time to time, the public (parents and/or community experts) assessment of students' products and performances.

Figures 5.1 and 5.2 attempt to visually represent the desired components involved in student learning. They comprise a model of student learning that can inform discussions administrators have with teachers about the way they design the antecedents and feedback elements of students' work. Both diagrams involve a form of backward mapping. More and more scholars of learning are tending to stress that the design of student work has to begin at the end (Newman et al., 1995; Perkins, 1998; Wiggins & McTighe, 1998). A performance view of understanding

Creating Readiness For the Work	Purpose/rationale for this unit
	Expected Outcomes for this Unit: • Science Project Demonstration • Musical Performance • Historical Research Report • Policy Debate • Composition of a Story in Writing or Film
	Rubrics for Assessment of Learning Outcomes

Doing the Work	Learning Activities: analyzing a political or economic issue, narrating a human drama, designing an experiment, comparing the work of two artists, debating two interpretations of a historical event, composing a letter in Spanish to a person in Argentina, explaining a chemical effect on brain cells, composing a response to drought in the sub-Sahara, testing water contamination in a nearby river, writing an op-ed piece on low-income housing, and so on.
	Learning Outcomes: Expressions of • Personal Meanings • Public Meanings • Applied Meanings • Academic Meanings

Assessing the Work	Review of Rubrics for Assessing Personal, Public, Applied, and Academic Learning
	Student Reflective Assessment of Personal, Public, Applied and Academic Learnings
	Teacher, Peer, and Public Assessment of Personal, Public, Applied and Academic Learnings
	Reflection on Feedback from Assessment for Future Learning (anticipatory scaffolding for new learning activities)

Figure 5.1 Framing student work.

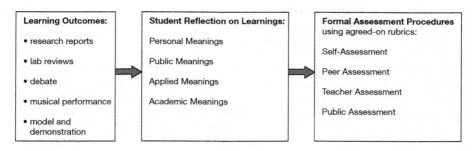

Figure 5.2 Reflection on and assessment of students' learning.

requires that teachers think about what kind of performances will reveal an understanding of the material under study and what qualities of the performance will reveal deeper understandings than others. That is why we began with the importance of having the student engage in reflective assessment on the personal, public, applied, and academic meanings generated by the learning activities. All too often, teachers begin their instructional planning by designing what appear to be interesting learning activities (coloring maps, making costumes, reading a story, doing mathematical word problems) before clarifying for themselves what it is they want the students to learn by engaging in these activities. What are the large ideas they want the students to grasp? What is the lesson they should all take away from the activity? What kinds of things should students be able to do at the end of these activities to authenticate that they have a rich understanding of the material? What products or performances would be legitimate expressions of the students' understandings of the material?

More recently, teachers are being asked to relate learning activities in the classroom to curriculum standards adopted by the district. Before designing the activity, they should look at the standards and think about the *many* activities that can be used to generate ideas and skills contained in the standards and then choose the activities that best and most richly respond to the standards. I would take the design and planning work back even farther. I would have the teachers ask themselves to provide a clear purpose or rationale for taking up the curriculum unit they are planning to engage. Without going off on an abstract or philosophical explanation, the teacher should be able to briefly explain why this curriculum unit they are about to take up is considered important within the academic area; what relationship this material has to real issues in the contemporary world; how this material could be useful to them. With this brief explanation of purpose, the teacher can then introduce the material and point to the kind of product or performance that is expected of the students as a result of their engaging the material. Depending on the material under consideration, the teacher may propose several exemplary types of products (a documentary film with accompanying commentary; the staging of a debate; a scholarly research report; an op-ed piece for the local newspaper; a series of illustrative drawings that sequence the procedures under study, a powerpoint presentation, a story using imaginary creatures to dramatize the understanding, etc.).

As indicated in Figure 5.1, these steps help create a readiness on the part of the student to take up the work. Presenting and explaining rubrics for assessing the quality of expected student products or performances comprise an additional part of the readiness stage. Teachers should provide examples of student performances that reflect the assessment rubrics (e.g., a research report on a topic in the science curriculum that provides abundant evidence for the conclusions of the report, clearly indicates how the research methods were employed, qualifies the findings by pointing out inherent limitations to the research, etc.; or a scrapbook biography of a grandparent, including photographs of three important times in the grandparent's life, illustrations of various technologies employed in the grandparent's home, stories about the grandparent's education, an account of two or three significant national or international events that the grandparent remembers from earlier years, and an account of the grandparent's major joys, struggles, and life lessons). Students would also see examples of student work that failed to meet one or more of the rubrics or met them only partway. Exposure to the rubrics at the start of the lesson allows them to see the criteria for how they will be graded on their own work.

As students are about to engage the material in a variety of learning activities, the teacher can provide one more important element in creating readiness for learning. This is referred to as *scaffolding*. The teacher asks the students to recall earlier learning activities and the skills and perspectives they engaged. The teacher asks them whether the present learning challenge reminds them of any they encountered in the past. When students volunteer that this lesson looks something like what they studied last month, the teacher can draw out of the students the ways they tackled that earlier learning, what worked and what did not work then, and how they might apply both the key concepts and inquiry skills from what they learned earlier to the study of the present material. By spending a little time at the beginning of a new learning unit, the teacher helps the students get focused, develop potential strategies to tackle the material, and see similarities to earlier inquiry procedures. In this way, the teacher brings prior learnings into active play in the new work.

At this point, the students should be quite ready to engage the material through a variety of learning activities. This may involve reading and note taking from two or three historical sources; conducting a science experiment employing careful measurement and mathematical computation; analyzing maps for significant geographical information; comparing and contrasting the editorial positions of two regional newspapers on political, economic, and ecological issues; reading a short story and writing a different ending that remains consistent with the initial characters' personalities; creating a still-life watercolor; writing a letter to the editor of the regional newspaper about a hotly contested issue in the community, after having carefully assessed the merits of the three major perspectives on the issue; researching the nature symbols in textiles used for Japanese kimonos for the comparative cultures course; researching the mathematics used in navigation on the high seas; or analyzing, comparing, and contrasting the design of cities with a view toward writing a recommendation to the local urban planning commission for improvements in the transportation system.

These examples illustrate how the learning activities are closely tied to producing or performing a product of some kind. Although the product requires considerable antecedent exploration and analysis of the material at hand, and strategizing how to construct or perform the product, a significant part of the learning is involved in the creation of the product itself. Students do not understand what they know until they have actively created something with that knowledge. Thus, in Figure 5.2, the learning activities and learning outcomes overlap, indicating that one is still learning while producing the outcome, and that producing the outcome is a learning activity in its own right. In their coaching role, teachers encourage students to refer back to the assessment rubrics before composing the final version of their product or performance. This additional review of the assessment rubrics enters into the learning process as well, and can cement a clearer understanding of the methodological requirements or inquiry skills the lesson intends to reinforce.

A major mistake educators make is to disassociate learning from assessment. An enormous amount of learning can take place by careful attention to assessment. That is why in Figs. 5.1 and 5.2 so much appears to be made of assessment. The reflective assessment already referred to should follow the performance of the learning. This enables students to further clarify what the learning meant to them personally, discuss with peers the common public meanings to be derived from the learning activity, imagine the various applications the new learning might have to several different situations, and place the new learning within frameworks of intelligibility that are reflective of the academic disciplines (e.g., "That's how gasses are supposed to react"; "That is what we should have expected from a colonial power in the 19th century"; "That is just another example of the slope-intercept formula"; "That conforms to the methodology of a controlled laboratory experiment"; "That is simply a variant in Elizabethan rhyming"; "That nature symbolism in Japanese textiles is another example of the Japanese borrowing from the earlier Chinese culture and creating their own local variations"). The value of this kind of reflective assessment seems so obvious, yet it is so often neglected.

The recent emphasis on teaching to state curriculum standards and preparing youngsters for high-stakes tests has reinforced the use of assessment rubrics by more and more teachers. Again, the opportunity for important learning is present in the summative assessment exercises. These summative exercises should involve personal assessment, peer assessment, teacher assessment, and, on occasion, public assessment. In this step of the learning process, students should be asked to judge their own work according to the criteria contained in the rubrics provided at the beginning of the unit. Their assigning a grade to their work should require justification by clear references to the performance criteria of the rubrics. This kind of self-assessment indicates whether the student has grasped the understandings of the unit implied in the rubrics. It also helps students see where they can improve in future learning assignments.

The whole class should be shown the products of two students—one superior and one average, according to the rubrics—(without identifying to whom they belong) so they might practice evaluating performances according to the criteria contained in the rubrics for that unit. In the interests of time, each student might then be asked to evaluate two or three peer products according to the rubrics. This exercise provides students with further experience with the rubrics and helps them see the reasoning behind them. It also provides the student whose work is anonymously being assessed by some of his or her peers additional feedback. From them, he may learn that assessments may vary depending on how one interprets the criteria in the rubrics and how one analyzes the performance or product. When this feedback is joined to the feedback of the teacher, the student should get a clear understanding of the quality of learning expected from the unit. If on occasion someone from the community (usually fairly knowledgeable in the matter) is asked to comment on the quality of the student's product or performance, it helps the student recognize the further significance of the learnings achieved in that unit. One final learning exercise should bring the student work in this unit full circle. The student should be asked to reflect on what he or she learned through the assessment exercises that will be useful in responding to future learning opportunities. These reflections (e.g., "I need to review how that slope-intercept formula really works"; "I need to be more aware of how one culture borrows from another, but how in the translation, those cultural borrowings are always changed"; "I need to cite more examples when making generalizations"; "I have to be more careful about incomplete sentences") provide some anticipatory scaffolding for future learning activities. They also develop a habit of reflection on ways to improve one's work.

The Model of Student Learning (Figure 5.3) attempts to place this student's work in a larger context. The work of learning is strongly influenced by what the student brings to the work at hand. That includes the various qualities in the student's make-up: the emerging self-image; what particular interests capture the student's attention (athletics, politics, music, science fiction); what level of initiative the student tends to bring to school work; what motivates the student to work hard, to persevere; what learning skills the student brings to the work; how well the student works with others; and how creative a student is in brainstorming various strategies for tackling a learning challenge.

Besides the student's make-up, there is the student's personal life world that exercises a continuing influence on the quality of learning. If a student experiences confusion, ambiguity, unpredictability, humiliation, and rejection in his or her life world, that will negatively influence the student's ability and motivation to engage the learning activities. A student coming from a working-class family situated in a working-class neighborhood brings different experiences, perspectives, and attitudes to school than those of his or her peers who come from affluent families in affluent neighborhoods. Youngsters who have frequently changed residences bring a different set of life-world experiences than those who continue to live in the same home where they were born. The life world of the youngsters is strongly influenced by the family's race, religion, culture, and class; that life world nurtures various interpretations of cultivating meaning, community, and responsibility, some of which conflict with the interpretations within the school or classroom. Therefore, the learning of the student is continuously influenced, for better or worse, by all those influences in the life world. Insofar as the learning can be connected directly or indirectly to that life world, it engages the student at a deeper level.

Another major influence on the student's learning are the existing conditions, challenges, and issues in society at large. Included here, of course, would be issues within the youth culture of that society—issues that get reflected in music, dress, lifestyle, language, and popular heroes. Insofar as the work of learning can have some direct or indirect relationship to the larger youth culture, it engages the student more deeply. Many teachers are decidedly uncomfortable, however, with what they perceive to be the values portrayed in the youth culture. Nevertheless, school learning occasionally has to engage that culture, look beneath the sometimes silly

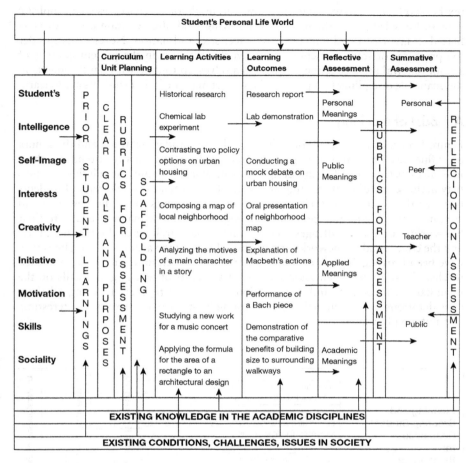

Figure 5.3 A model of student learning.

surface expressions of that culture to the deeper yearnings, dreams, and human struggles seeking a voice, and build bridges between what is being learned in school and what is being explored in the youth culture.

Beyond the youth culture, the larger society is struggling with multiple issues and challenges to which the school learning should be connected. Not only should students be taken seriously enough to be invited to study these issues and challenges, but they must be convinced that these struggles and challenges are theirs—the stuff that will affect their adult lives as well.

A third major influence on student learning is the existing knowledge, understandings, and challenges in the various academic disciplines. These academic disciplines exert a huge influence through their dominance of university studies that in turn strongly influence the curricula of K–12 school systems. Furthermore, the academic disciplines strongly determine the subject matter and materials in textbooks. As advances in the academic disciplines progress, the subject matter in

68 *Cultivating a perspective on learning*

textbooks changes. As we have seen, however, textbooks tend to present a simplistic view of knowledge and the process of knowing, and often contain points of view biased in favor of the dominant class, race, sex, and nation. Nevertheless, under the pressures of state curriculum frameworks, teachers in the present context of school renewal are struggling to keep themselves up to date with developments in the academic disciplines that provide the subject matter of what students are to learn.

A model of teaching

Figure 5.3 presents in visual form the logic driving student learning and the syntax of influences on that learning. Teachers need to continually attend to these influences as they plan for and design student work, bringing these influences into play in the scaffolding of the students' work. Thus, teachers should remind students of what they learned in their previous curriculum units, how the new material continues building on that previous learning, how the new material relates to their life world, interests, challenges facing society, the searching of the youth culture, and the conceptual frameworks and methodologies of the academic disciplines they have been learning. This scaffolding is different for each unit, each class, and each teacher. It is, however, an essential part of the craft of teaching and calls on the imagination, invention, and organizational talents of teachers to bring all these considerations to bear on making the learning in this new unit exciting, interesting, and potentially useful.

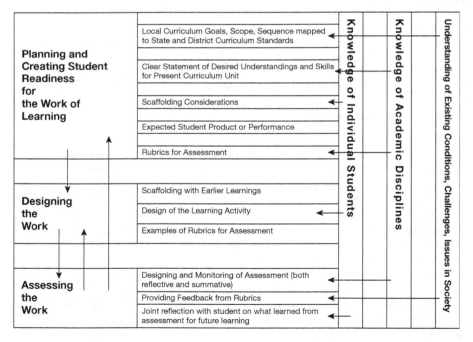

Figure 5.4 Mapping teachers' work.

Figure 5.4 attempts to diagram the teacher's backward mapping of the work of teaching. Keeping in mind the curriculum standards that are to guide student achievement, the teacher prepares a clear statement of the purpose and rationale behind this new learning unit. That purpose and rationale is related both to the academic discipline as it is embedded in the year's curriculum as well as to the existing conditions, challenges, and issues in present society. The teacher explains what are the large, desired, and expected understandings that result from their engaging the material in this unit and indicates the one or several ways that understanding can be represented in a product or performance. The teacher then explains the rubrics for assessment of that product or performance, indicating the criteria to be met for a high grade and, when ignored, for a low or failing grade. The teacher then engages in scaffolding the new material to be studied, drawing attention to similarities in earlier learnings that assist them in engaging the new material. As the students engage in the learning activity and prepare to translate their learning into authentic performances or products, the teacher engages in coaching, Socratic questioning, encouraging, suggesting a second look at the evidence, and so forth, all the while recognizing that the student has to produce the learning rather than repeat information delivered by the teacher. Another crucial aspect of the teacher's work is to monitor the assessment exercises carefully, recognizing that they contribute mightily to the student's deep understanding of the material of the unit.

A lesson from rocks

Some illustrations might clarify the teacher's monitoring of the assessment process. As students are completing their product or performance, teachers might ask them how their learning affected their understandings of themselves. They may have just finished an interdisciplinary unit on rocks. That unit began with a story about the rabbit's encounter with the lonely rock. In discussing the story, they were encouraged to reflect on what it feels like to be lonely, on the importance of friends to play with, on the need to be sensitive listeners when someone confides how they feel to us. They also reflected on how they take rocks for granted, how each rock has a history much longer than their own, that each rock has a unique composition of minerals. They were encouraged to look more closely at various rocks in their neighborhood environment and note the unique features of each rock. They were asked to choose a pet rock, give it a name, and talk to it about stuff going on in their lives. These encounters with rocks were enriched by the work they did in science class where they analyzed the minerals in their rock, classifying them and measuring them at least in rough proportions, and learning about how and when the rock was formed geologically. In art class, they drew several sketches of their rock seen from different sides and different lighting. Further nuancing of those learnings occurred in their social studies classes where they studied the rock and sand gardens in Japanese culture, and how, within that culture, such gardens are considered an art form. Additionally, the father of one of the students, a stone mason, showed a slide lecture to the class on various types and shapes of rocks used in various types of construction, from garden walls to fireplaces to foundations for homes and to exteriors of whole buildings. Besides the practical properties of various rocks, the stonemason also spoke about the aesthetics of color, shapes, position, and balance in working with rocks, and how different types of rocks have different personalities.

In this example, students are developing a set of personal meanings about rocks, as well as gaining scientific, aesthetic, and craft understandings about rocks. They are also learning to look more closely at nature to understand more about evolutionary and cosmic time, and to consider the many human uses natural objects can be put to, both functionally and aesthetically. Students might perform their knowledge about rocks in a variety of media and a variety of presentations. These presentations contain both personal and public meanings. When their fellow students present their performance of their knowledge, then students hear their peers express their personal appropriation of the unit on rocks and thereby learn how various interpretations of the material help to enrich and complement their own understanding. The teacher also asks the students to converse about the public meanings about rocks. This would include the obvious scientific facts about rocks, especially to be found in the science of geology, but it would also include public knowledge about the aesthetic properties of rocks (marble, sandstone, gemstones, slate, granite, etc.), the various crafts associated with rocks, famous rocks around the world (Uluru, Gibraltar, Shiprock, etc.), famous sculptors of rock, and so forth. The teacher can also structure several exercises that require students to apply their knowledge to solving a problem (e.g., in designing a sea wall out of rocks, creating a poem about rocks, or creating a company that sold a variety of rock [not rock 'n roll] products). Finally, the teacher can coach students into generating academic meaning from all these exercises (scientific categories and temporal frameworks in geology and paleontology, aesthetic principles in rock gardens and sculptures, principles of measurement involved in classifying rocks, the physics of mass and gravity to be found in handling rocks).

After students have completed the reflective assessment in their journals, they should engage in exercises of summative assessment. In these exercises, students should be asked to evaluate how well their own work and that of other students has measured up to the assessment rubrics for the assignment. The first summative assessment exercise, the personal assessment, is crucial because the student has to engage the intelligibility of the rubrics and his or her own work according to standards of performance. Beyond the students' personal assessment of their own work (as produced individually or by a team), students should also be required to do a summative assessment of other students' or one team of students' work. Again, this requires the students to attend to the intelligibility of the assessment rubrics now applied to another project. The exercise should further reinforce their understandings of the substance, methodology, and applicability of the materials under study, and lead to a more articulate grasp of the standards embedded in the various academic disciplines. Peer assessments should not be entered into the final grades of the students being assessed. Grading is the sole prerogative of the teacher.

When those assessments are completed, the teacher provides his or her own summative assessment of all this work. Although the assessment is summative—that is, it leads to a judgment of whether this block of work measures up to the performance rubrics for that work—the teacher may engage in formative assessment as well, pointing out to students aspects of their work that need further refinement as they approach the next learning unit. In subsequent classes dealing with that next learning unit, the teacher can repeat those points from the prior summative assessment, urging the students to avoid making the same mistakes this time, helping them to see, in the presentation of the assessment rubrics for that next learning unit, how to carry on their work more effectively.

Finally, these summative assessment exercises should, at least occasionally, be complemented by parental commentary and by having appropriate people from the community offer feedback on students' work in some kind of open forum, either at the school or in a community agency. In this way, students can gain an appreciation of how their work in school is seen as related to the life of the larger community.

Administrators' work

At this point, we have a clearer idea of the work of administrators in the cultivation of meaning, community, and responsibility. This work consists of conversations with external and internal constituencies and, in the light of these conversations, follow-up work on the restructuring of various institutional components of the school. It should be noted, however, that prior to these conversations, the preliminary work of exploring and clarifying the central focus of the school on cultivating meaning, community, and responsibility has to occur. In the light of these clarifications, a new look at the teaching–learning process is also necessary. I am not implying that administrators should have a blueprint etched in stone that they can then impose on all internal and external constituencies. Rather, administrators should develop clear ideas about a blueprint that provide a starting point for conversations. That blueprint is adapted by additional local concerns, filled out by the pregnant ideas of others, and constrained (at least for the present) by political, fiscal, and other entrenched positions in the community. Even where the local environment is weakly disposed to look beyond anything other than the familiar (however dysfunctional) routine, the preliminary work of clarifying a well thought-out and defensible educational blueprint provides administrators a starting point for changing the system over time. It also provides administrators a well-articulated platform for influence within the educational policy community, as well as within the larger civic leadership community, both of which have tended to view the educational agenda both superficially and simplistically.

In Figure 5.5, we can see the work of administrators sketched on a large canvas. Obviously, the conversations on that canvas do not include the many microdetails of administrative work. Those microdetails, however, should be enacted in the service of the central conversations with those constituencies.

Conversations with external constituencies

Administrators' work involves conversations with parents, civic leaders, and various cultural communities and organizations within the larger civic community. In other words, administrators should use their position within a visible public institution as a kind of bully pulpit—a dialogical bully pulpit to be sure—to state their position about the central focus of the school on cultivating meaning, community, and responsibility. Presentations and conversations vary in complexity depending on the audience. Administrators need to craft multiple versions of their message for a variety of audiences. For not a few administrators, it may mean sharpening their

72 Cultivating a perspective on learning

command of rhetorical argument and, initially, even going through several rehearsals with critical friends to ensure both clarity and brevity. Even the best preachers can put the most sympathetic congregations to sleep after 5 minutes. Besides oral presentations to various audiences, newsletters, and op-ed pieces in the regional newspapers, position papers and other forms of the written media can also carry the conversation forward. Conversations with various parent groups are essential so that the focus of the school curriculum can be echoed in a variety of ways in the home. These conversations should also seek to involve parents as volunteers in communicating with other parents so that the message gets communicated in vocabularies and examples that parents can identify with.

An important part of the dialogue is to relate the cultivation of meaning, community, and responsibility to the agenda of school renewal. Illustrating how the emphasis on authentic student performance of their understandings relates to

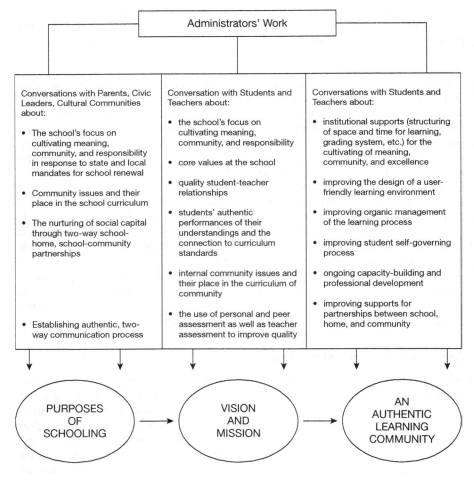

Figure 5.5 The core work of administrative leadership.

various curriculum standards helps the external constituencies grasp the needed connection with the mandates of local and state educational authorities. These conversations should also involve discussions about various forms of testing and the sometimes simplistic and inflammatory judgments expressed in the media about test scores. Questions about the types of knowledge and understanding tests are looking for, issues about opportunities to learn, funding of professional development for teachers to develop appropriate instructional materials for newly imposed curriculum standards, issues around the testing of recently arrived immigrant children with limited proficiency in English, assumptions about the significance of testing children with severe disabilities, discussions about within-school and within-class variance in students' readiness for the curriculum, and the resulting statistical distortions that occur in grouping student test scores—all of these complexities should be raised and aired so that the public better understands how to interpret reports of aggregate student scores on state and national tests.

Administrators need to dialogue with their external constituencies to stay familiar with long-standing and emerging community issues. Various community groups may want the school to teach (or demand that the school *not* teach) perspectives on a host of topics, from AIDS education and its corresponding relationship to sex education and health education, driver safety, drug and alcohol education, religious education, character education, gay and lesbian studies, ecology education, civil rights and active antiracism, multicultural education, global issues, vocational education, cooking, and a variety of other issues. Administrators can all too often adopt a cynical or patronizing attitude toward some or all of these groups, failing to recognize that these groups have constitutionally guaranteed rights to voice their opinions, and that as public servants they have a responsibility to listen attentively and sympathetically. As public servants, they also have a role to play in calling to the attention of these groups the conflicting demands and perspectives of other groups, and to legal decisions already made in the adjudication of these conflicting demands (e.g., legislation concerning children with special needs or bilingual/bicultural children, local school board rulings on program cuts or reductions). As educators, they should also have worked out reasoned *educational* positions in response to these various demands so that the dialogue can remain focused on the educational implications of various demands, as well as on various institutional constraints on schools.

Another valuable outcome of these conversations with external constituencies concerns the inclusion of specific local issues in classroom applications of the curriculum. For example, state investigators may have recently required the community to monitor more closely the pollution of a river flowing through its area to determine whether three local industries were observing industrial waste disposal requirements. That issue could be included in one or more science and social studies classes where students were required to apply scientific, political, and economic understandings learned in class to respond to this issue. They might work with one or more representatives of the local agencies responsible for monitoring water quality in the river, as well as representatives from the companies involved. In another example, the community might be facing a debate on whether to build mixed-income housing with a small adjoining park on an open parcel of land or turn it over to a developer to build a golf course surrounded by expensive homes. Students might be asked to apply what they knew about the principles of urban planning to this debate and offer a reasoned argument for one or the other position. In another example, the local library may have received a generous grant from a local millionaire who was interested in documenting the history of the community. His grant would enable the library to compose and publish the biographies of 100 of their most senior citizens. This might provide a wonderful opportunity for a significant number of high school students whose participation would thereby enable them to apply their understandings of historical research and connect the writing of the biography with a major writing project. Each student might work in collaboration with one or more adults in the community who were assigned to interview a particular senior citizen in the community. In another example, students might be asked to report on all the computer applications used in the work setting of one of their parents. Such a project might involve students meeting with the person responsible for computer technology in that parent's work environment, as well as having the parent explain the company's computer technology from the parent's perspective.

These examples point to a few of the many ways schools may engage in learning partnerships with the community. These learning partnerships develop the social and cultural capital of the school. By that I mean that students come to see that their learning in school is supported by their parents and by groups in the community. These partnerships enable the students to appreciate that their school learnings can be connected to important issues in the community, can open them to new cultural learnings, and can enable them to explore possible career opportunities. Administrators who remain in an ongoing series of conversations with various groups in the community can initially explore potential learning opportunities with these groups and bring those ideas back to the school for consideration by the teachers.

Conversations with internal constituencies

Administrators can bring the focus on cultivating meaning, community, and responsibility to conversations with teachers, students, and support staff. Initially, administrators need to propose these ideas within the framework of state and locally mandated school renewal. As seen in Part I of this book, the focus on cultivating meaning, community, and responsibility provides multiple avenues for approaching school renewal and connecting school learnings to the state and local curriculum standards while providing a larger, more fully developed learning environment within which attention to curriculum standards constitute one essential focus. Each local school setting should be unique, with its own history, internal chemistry, and relationship to the larger community. This means that administrators should craft their presentation of the cultivation of meaning, community, and responsibility to fit the local school. The school may already enjoy a tradition of a rich and highly professional learning environment, a supportive and participative parent community and school board, and a well-integrated student body. The initial conversations with that teaching faculty and student body about cultivating meaning, community, and responsibility would be quite different from the initial conversations with the internal constituencies of a school with a history of poor relations with the teachers' union, a culture of teacher isolation and autonomy, a curriculum with no schoolwide sense of scope and sequence, and a student body polarized by race, athletics, and college-bound versus job-bound students. Different schools require not only different conversations, but also different strategies for approaching various groups within the school. What is common to all schools, however, is the necessity of continuing to focus on school renewal. That provides the initial opening for administrators to address the importance of quality learning for all students. From those initial conversations, administrators gather clues about directions to take to enlarge the conversation to the larger focus on cultivating meaning, community, and responsibility.

However those conversations develop, they must include discussions about the students' authentic performance of their understandings and the connections of those products and performances to the state and local curriculum standards. As an integral part of these conversations, administrators bring teachers to ongoing discussions about assessment rubrics for those products and performances. The continuing dialogue among teachers about assessment rubrics constitutes one of the most crucial influences on a school's progress toward authentic learning.

As those conversations develop, administrators can introduce considerations about the place of internal community issues among the student body as well as issues in the larger community within the formal curriculum. In other words, the learning of being and becoming a community is presented as something of equal importance to the learning of the academic curriculum. Indeed, the learning of one curriculum is seen as implying a great deal of learning of the other curriculum. Furthermore, the enriching of the academic learning depends on the variety of applications the students are encouraged to make to real problems and issues within the home, neighborhood, and larger civic community. Administrators can encourage teacher groups to brainstorm a variety of applications of classroom learnings to real issues in the larger community. From their conversations with parents and various groups within the larger community, administrators can offer additional potential applications of classroom learning to issues and problems within the community.

Other conversations with the teaching faculty should take up the connection between various forms of assessment and the enrichment of student learning. Sometimes these conversations should come first as a lead in to the larger considerations about school renewal and cultivating meaning, community, and responsibility depending on the readiness of the teachers to take one perspective or the other. In either case, administrators need to raise issues around assessment to review how the teachers engage and monitor a variety of assessment procedures and activities.

Conversations about institutional arrangements

As those two sets of conversations with the external and internal constituencies unfold, administrators also need to look at the present institutional arrangements at the school in the light of the focus on cultivating meaning, community, and responsibility. These arrangements include the daily, weekly and semester schedules; allocation of instructional spaces; time available for teachers to work together in planning and strategizing new classroom protocols and for visiting each other's classes; decision-making procedures; relationships with central office authorities; budget preparation and budget administration procedures; student assessment systems and grade reporting systems; presence and functioning of any kind of student government; parental partnership arrangements; student discipline policies; any co-curricular organizations and how they function to create or divide the community; the school's reward and award systems; student counseling and health arrangements; institutional communication patterns and media employed; student and faculty committees; and so forth. Along with the administrators' assessment of how well these institutional arrangements support a focus on cultivating meaning, community, and responsibility, students and teachers should be invited to engage in similar assessments and offer suggestions on how those institutional arrangements can be improved in a system design of a user-friendly learning environment. Parents should be invited to converse with teachers on ways to enhance the school–home partnerships that nurture enriched student learning.

What is sought is the development of an organic management of the learning process in the pursuit of meaning, community, and responsibility. By that is meant the creation of a learning community in which all decisions are related to the support and encouragement of quality learning for each and every student, in which decisions are made by those closest to the activity of learning, or by those most directly affected by the decision. Attention to these institutional arrangements is taken up in subsequent chapters.

Recapitulation

In this chapter, we have seen the development of a model of student learning that points to a model of teaching. Elaboration of these two models, at least in a summary fashion, points to the essential work of administrators. As this work becomes clarified, it becomes evident how much a redirection of administrative work is called for in this era of school renewal. This clarification of the essential work of administrators does not eradicate their concern about the *administration* of the daily life of the school, nor about the necessary administrative coordination with the central office of the local school district or authority. Rather, it places that administrative work within a larger framework, *in the service* of that work of the school community, rather than in the service of some kind of abstract organizational efficiency. In one sense, it partakes of some characteristics of mass administration, in the sense that it belongs to a local, state, and federal system of school administration. Nevertheless, educational administrative work has as its essential purpose the fostering of a learning community engaged in cultivating meaning, community, and responsibility. That essential purpose overrides and integrates all other administrative work.

Activities

1. Talk with three outstanding teachers at your school. Ask them whether they have students reflect on personal meanings they might derive from the learning activity. Do these teachers prepare students for this kind of personal reflection when they introduce the curriculum unit to the class by suggesting possible connections to their lived experience? Discuss Figs. 5.1 through 5.4 with them.
2. Ask the same teachers whether and how they use explicit rubrics for assessing student learning.

3. Do any teachers in your school require students to keep a portfolio of their work? If so, how are portfolios used?
4. Name all the examples that indicate your school's commitment to the principle of student active performance of their learning. Share your list with three other teachers in the school to see whether they can add to it.
5. Are teachers required, in the teacher supervision/evaluation process at the school, to present examples of student work?
6. What ideas from this chapter might you easily put in practice in your own work? What ideas for schoolwide practice?

References

Frawley, W. (1997). *Vygotsky and cognitive science: Language and the unification of the social and computational mind.* Cambridge, MA: Harvard University Press.

Newman, F., Secada, W. G., & Wehlage, G. G. (1995). *A guide to authentic instruction and assessment: Vision, standards and scoring.* Madison, WI: Wisconsin Center for Educational Research.

Perkins, D. (1998). What is understanding? In M. S. Wiske (Ed.), *Teaching for understanding* (pp. 39–57). San Francisco: Jossey-Bass.

Wiggins, G., & McTighe, J. (1998). *Understanding by design.* Alexandria, VA: Association for Supervision and Curriculum Development.

Wiske, M. S. (Ed.). (1998). *Teaching for understanding.* San Francisco: Jossey-Bass.

CHAPTER SIX

Building an ethical school
A theory for practice in educational leadership

The social sciences are undergoing a major shift away from a dogmatic positivism that relegates ethics and morality to a stereotyped realm of personal preferences, prejudices, and tastes unsupportable by scientific argument, toward an acknowledgment of organizational and public life as a legitimate arena of moral striving and human fulfillment (Bellah, Madsen, Sullivan, Swidler, & Tipton, 1985; Jennings, 1983; Sullivan, 1986; Walzer, 1985). In the field of education, talk about ethics and morality tends to divide between public rhetoric and academic theory. In the public arena, some call for a return to a hypothetical time when people agreed on moral values, when teachers were not ashamed to preach morality in the classroom. Others worry that these proposals are simplistic attempts to impose "fundamentalist" definitions of right and wrong (supposedly with Biblical grounding) on everyone, to impose repressive attitudes about sex, spontaneity, and material enjoyments. The public rhetoric tends to frame the debate over morality in education in extreme and sometimes inflammatory imagery, but a more restrained shift has slowly been taking place among researchers and theorists.

Whether this shift is labeled as ushering in a "Post-Positivism" (Jennings, 1983), "Post-Structuralism" (Cherryholmes, 1988), or "Post-Liberal" (Bowers, 1987) era or as a reconceptualization of traditional categories of virtue and character and justice (MacIntyre, 1984; Purpel, 1989; Walzer, 1985; Wynne, 1982), there is clearly a movement away from an overly rationalistic approach, despite some rear guard action in defense of positivism (Lakomski, 1987). This shift in educational policy formation and implementation, in organizational analysis, in program evaluation, and in curriculum theory, is toward an inclusion of human factors, expressly moral in nature, previously neglected.

The literature in educational administration similarly reflects growing concerns about moral and ethical issues (Foster, 1986; Greenfield, 1987; Kimbrough, 1985; Raywid, 1986; Sergiovanni & Starratt, 1988; Strike, Haller, & Soltis, 1988; Vandenberg, 1990). However, the literature may be yet a step away from speaking concretely enough to practitioners. The abstractions of moral philosophers and social theorists are difficult to translate into practical guidelines that influence everyday actions. Theory needs to approach close enough to practice so that it becomes a theory for practice, something the reflective practitioner can use in everyday encounters while walking about the school or the district (Schon, 1983; Sergiovanni, 1985; Starratt, 1990). A theory for practice does not imply a collection of generic recipes for moral choices, but rather a theory that helps practitioners frame moral situations encountered in practice so that their moral content becomes more intelligible and more available to the practical intuitive sense of the practitioner.

What follows is an attempt to bring ethical inquiry much closer to the workplace of educational administrators. It will not attempt to build an ethical theory, but rather to bring ethical themes developed by other theorists into a multidimensional construct that offers practicing administrators a way to think about their work and their workplace from ethical perspectives. The attempt will probably offend ethical purists because it borrows from ethical theories that seem incompatible with one another. On the other hand, the construct accepts the substantial conceptual tensions between the themes and highlights those tensions to illuminate the very ethical issues at stake. If the construct appears to offer useful, or even interesting, clarifications for the practitioner, then perhaps ethical theorists can follow up this attempt with a more foundational synthesis of their own.

What is suggested, in brief, is the joining of three ethics: the ethic of critique, the ethic of justice, and the ethic of caring. None of these ethics by itself offers an educational administrator a fully adequate framework for making ethical judgments; together, however, each ethic complements the others in a developmental context of practice. Each fills out an ethical perspective on policy choices. Because none of these ethics compels choice in every instance, one perfect choice does not exist; the three perspectives, however, enable one to make choices with the consequences more clearly delineated, to move toward the "best" choice under the circumstances, or to a choice that, although it favors one ethical demand, will probably be balanced later on by other choices.

The ethics of educational administration: Building and administering an ethical school

The ethics of educational administration being advanced here is different from that offered by other scholars on the topic, such as Kimbrough (1985) or Strike et al. (1988). They tend to focus on individual ethical choices of administrators regarding how to deal with individual persons or with individual situations. In other words, the ethics of educational administration from their perspectives is about the ethics of choices that administrators make in given circumstances. The position taken here is that the much larger ethical task of educational administrators is to establish an ethical school environment in which education can take place ethically. Individual choices regarding individual circumstances are seen as taking place in this larger ethical context. Hence the administrator who assumes that the educational environment, the organization, the system, the institutional arrangements (the curriculum, the daily and weekly schedule, the assessment and discipline and placement and promotion policies) enjoy a value neutrality, or worse, already embody the desirable ethical standards, is ethically naive, if not culpable.

Educational administrators are supposed to manage, not simply any old organization, but an educational organization. The educational program housed in that organization is supposed to serve moral purposes (the nurturing of the human, social, and intellectual growth of the youngsters). Hence, although educational administrators do many generic things common to all administrators (coordinate the scheduling of multiple activities simultaneously under one system, monitor budgetary expenditures, monitor health hazards, delegate responsibilities, and so forth), these activities are aimed at promoting the educational goals of the institution. The qualitative elements essential to educating give those administrative choices a different finality than choices made, for example, by hospital administrators, military officers, or corporate managers. Hence the ethical position taken here is that educational administrators have a moral responsibility to be proactive about creating an ethical environment for the conduct of education. They will no doubt be faced with individual ethical choices about whether to suspend a custodian for certain actions or whether to accept a gratuity from the parent who wants her son to make the basketball team. Those individual choices, however, do not constitute the ethical agenda of the educational administrator; they are a small part of the large agenda of building an ethical school.

Presently, the political climate is encouraging educators to restructure schools, which provides a certain opportunity for the building of ethical schools. Assuming that this means, among other things, a move toward school-based management, teacher empowerment, and participatory decision making, then schools will be freed from systemic, bureaucratic controls and enabled to exercise greater autonomy in their attempts to create a more humanly responsive environment. This implies that the school community will be engaged in an ongoing effort to govern itself, and that, in turn, implies pursing a moral purpose. From this vantage point, then, the educational administrator faces a difficult task. How is he or she to conceptualize the ethical task? This is where the ethical inquiry of this article begins.

Each theme will be developed consecutively. Although attempting to remain faithful to the theory, or body of theory, from which the theme was selected, the exposition will be guided in equal part by the ethical demands of the educating context. Hence, if a distortion, bending, or thinning out of the force of the original theory seems to some readers to be taking place, they may be right; however, such interpretation is grounded in the effort to offer a larger synthesis in the service of practice. Underneath this synthesis, of course, are the irreducible assumptions and myths about what is valuable in human life in which every theory is grounded. A discussion of the ontology and epistemology behind this construct, however, would paralyze, I fear, the very attempt to develop the construct in this article. If the construct offers possibilities for ethical clarification and development, then subsequent debate and criticism can lead either to its further elaboration or to its rejection. In either case, the conversation over the meaning of ethics in educational administration may be enriched.

The ethic of critique

Because the historical moment appears to be one of transition and transformation, this article begins with the ethic of critique. Whether one begins from the less radical perspective of the recent proponents of school reform, such as Boyer (1983), Goodlad (1984), or Sizer (1984), or from the deeper critique of Freire (1970), Apple (1982), Bates (1984), or Giroux (1988), it has become increasingly evident that schools and school systems are structurally ineffective. Moreover, the awareness of the structural obstacles to renewal and change is taking on a historical dimension. The bureaucracy of school systems is coming to be seen as an enduring problem, not simply a contemporary phenomenon. Hence an ethic of educational administration appropriately begins with the theme of critique, a critique aimed at its own bureaucratic context, its own bureaucratic mind-set. As the school community, under the leadership of educational administrators and teachers, faces the possibility of creating an ethical school, it will also face the necessity of critiquing both the adversarial, contractual mind-set of the unions, as well as the hierarchically structured, impersonality of the administration of the school. Beyond that critique awaits the critique of the overly (if not exclusively) technicist approach to teaching and learning tied to narrowly conceived learning outcomes and simplistic, quantifiable measures of learning.

Because it goes well beyond the functional critique of contemporary reformers such as Goodlad and Boyer, the ethic of critique employed in this article draws its force from "critical theory," that body of thought deriving from the Frankfurt School of philosophers and others sympathetic to their perspectives (Adorno, 1973; Habermas, 1973; Horkheimer, 1974; Young, 1990). These thinkers explore social life as intrinsically problematic because it exhibits the struggle between competing interests and wants among various groups and individuals in society. Whether considering social relationships, social customs, laws, social institutions grounded in structured power relationships, or language itself, these thinkers ask questions such as the following: "Who benefits by these arrangements?" "Which group dominates this social arrangement?" "Who defines the way things are structured here?" "Who defines what is valued and disvalued in this situation?" The point of this critical stance is to uncover which group has the advantage over the others, how things got to be the way they are, and to expose how situations are structured and language used so as to maintain the legitimacy of social arrangements. By uncovering inherent injustice or dehumanization imbedded in the language and structures of society, critical analysts invite others to act to redress such injustice. Hence their basic stance is ethical for they are dealing with questions of social justice and human dignity, although not with individual choices.

Examples of issues confronted by critical ethics include (a) sexist language and structured bias in the workplace and in legal structures; (b) racial bias in educational arrangements and in the very language used to define social life; (c) the preservation of powerful groups' hegemony over the media and the political process; (d) the rationalization and legitimation of institutions such as prisons, orphanages, armies, nuclear industries, and the state itself. The point the critical ethician stresses is that no social arrangement is neutral. It is usually structured to benefit some segments of society at the expense of others. The ethical challenge is to make these social arrangements more responsive to the human and social rights of all the citizens, to enable those affected by social arrangements to have a voice in evaluating their results and in altering them in the interests of the common good and of fuller participation and justice for individuals.

This ethical perspective provides a framework for enabling educational administrators to move from a kind of naivete about "the way things are" to an awareness that the social and political arena reflect arrangements of power and privilege, interest and influence, often legitimized by an assumed rationality and by law and custom. The theme of critique forces administrators to confront the moral issues involved when schools disproportionately benefit some groups in society and fail others. Furthermore, as a bureaucratic organization, the school exhibits structural properties that may promote a misuse of power and authority among its members. From a critical perspective, no organizational arrangements in schools "have to be" that way; they are all open to rearrangement in the interest of greater fairness to their members. Where unjust arrangements reflect school board or state policy, they can be appealed and restructured.

When an educational administrator confronts the structural issues involved in the management of education, such as the process of teacher evaluation, homogeneous tracking systems, the process of grading on a curve, the process of calculating class rank, the absence of important topics in textbooks, the lack of adequate due process for students, the labeling criteria for naming some children gifted and others handicapped, the daily interruptions of the instructional process by uniform time allotments for class periods, he or she discovers ethical burdens to all of them because they contain unjustifiable assumptions and impose a disproportionate advantage to some at the expense of others.

The ethic of critique poses the fundamental ethical challenge to the educational administrator: how to construct an environment in which education can take place ethically. The ethic of critique reveals that the organization in its present forms is a source of unethical consequences in the educational process.

Some would say that all organizations, of their very nature, precipitate unethical consequences. All organizations tend to make the rules and standard operating procedures the dominant force in organizational life, smothering initiative, instilling fear of not being promoted or approved by one's superiors, severely limiting freedom of choice, reinforcing "groupthink" and the official rationalizations for the way things are. On the other hand, organizations, paradoxically, are the only places in the modern world where freedom and creativity can be exercised in any significant way (Eisenstadt, 1968). In the restructuring of human institutions to meet the human purposes for which they were originally designed one finds significant moral fulfillment (Starratt, 1990).

Thus educational administrators will face the continuing paradox of their institutional position in the school. On the one hand, they must acknowledge the tendency built into management processes to inhibit freedom, creativity, and autonomy, and to structure unequal power relationships to insure institutional uniformity, predictability, and order. On the other hand, they must acknowledge their responsibility to continually overcome that tendency to promote that kind of freedom, creativity, and autonomy *without which* the school simply cannot fulfill its mission.

Hence the ethic of critique, based as it is on assumptions about the social nature of human beings and on the human purposes to be served by social organization, calls the educational administrator to a social responsibility, not simply to the individuals in the school or school system, not simply to the education profession, but to the society of whom, and for whom, he or she is an agent. In other words, schools were established to serve a high moral purpose, to prepare the young to take their responsible place in and for the community. Besides the legal and professional obligations of the educational administrator, the moral obligation is to see that the institution of the school serves society the way it was intended. Hence the challenge to restructure schools is a moral as well as a technical and professional challenge.

The ethic of justice

One of the shortcomings of the ethic of critique is that it rarely offers a blueprint for reconstructing the social order it is criticizing. The problem for the educational administrator is one of governance. How do we govern ourselves while carrying out educating activities? The ethic of critique illuminates unethical practices in governing and managing organizations and implies in its critique some ethical values such as equality, the common good, human and civil rights, democratic participation, and the like. An ethic of justice provides a more explicit response to the question, even though that response may itself be flawed.

We govern ourselves by observing justice. That is to say, we treat each other according to some standard of justice that is uniformly applied to all our relationships. To understand the theory of justice that we employ requires an understanding of anthropology and epistemology. Socrates explored the basis of justice in *The Republic*; his search was to be pursued by a long line of philosophers up to the present day.

Currently, there are two general schools of thought concerning the ethic of justice. One school traces its roots to Thomas Hobbes and John Locke in the 17th century and finds its contemporary expression in the work of John Rawls (1971). In this school, the primary human reality is the individual, independent of social relationships; the individual is conceived as logically prior to society. Individuals are driven by their passions and interests, especially by fear of harm and desire for comfort. Individuals enter into social relations to advance their own advantage. Individual will and preference are the only sources of value. Therefore, social relationships are essentially artificial and governed by self-interest. The issue of social governance assumes a social contract in which individuals agree to surrender some of their freedom in return for the state's protection from the otherwise unbridled self-seeking of others. In this school, human reason is the instrument that individuals use to analyze in a more or less scientific fashion what is to their advantage, and to calculate the obligations to social justice called for by the social contract. As Sullivan commented, in its more benign application, this theory conceives of social justice as "a social engineering to harmonize needs and wants" of self-serving individuals in society (Sullivan, 1986, p. 19).

Kant, however, wanted to ground morality in something more than the passions. Hence his philosophical search led him to postulate moral categories of obligation inherent in the practical reasoning of humans. However, the individual was still the source of moral activity. The obligation to act ethically came from the individual, not from society. Rawls (1971) attempted to explain this Kantian moral intuition as a reconstruction of the intuition of justice as fairness. He constructed a coherent context of general rules by which a moral community can reach agreement in much the same way that a community judges linguistically correct expression according to the rules to which all users of the language subscribe (Rawls, 1971). His development of fairness and fair play avoids some of the minimalist rationalizing of the utilitarians, although he continues to hold on to a kind of practical reason to work out individual instances of the universal fairness principle.

Kohlberg (1971) carried on this tradition, only he claimed to go beyond the traditional standoff between "is" and "ought" found in Hume and Kant. That is to say, Kohlberg claimed to have documented in his research an isomorphism between psychological development of moral reasoning and normative ethical theory (Schindler, 1986). His research indicated that as humans moved from one moral stage to a higher moral stage, they moved toward formal moral criteria of prescriptiveness and universality. (Kohlberg, 1971, pp. 224–225). Their higher moral reasoning conformed to what moral theorists from Kant to Rawls had postulated as universal principles to guide ethical behavior. Once again, note that Kohlberg postulates the individual as the source of ethical judgment, and reason as the instrument of morality, although reason is now seen more in a developmental perspective.

The second school of thought on the ethic of justice finds its roots in Aristotle, Rousseau, Hegel, Marx, and Dewey. A contemporary scholar in this school, William Sullivan (1986), placed society as the prior reality within which individuality develops. Furthermore, through experience, through living in society one learns the lessons of morality. Participation in the life of the community teaches individuals how to think about their own behavior in terms of the larger common good of the community. In this school, freedom "is ultimately the ability to realize a responsible selfhood, which is necessarily a cooperative project" (Sullivan, 1986, p. 21). Ethics is grounded in practice within the community. The protection of human dignity depends on the moral quality of social relationships and this is finally a public and political concern. Citizenship is a shared initiative and responsibility among persons committed to mutual care (Sullivan, 1986, p. 22). From this perspective, a communal understanding of the requirements of justice and governance flows from both tradition and the present effort of the community to manage its affairs in the midst of competing claims of the common good and individual rights. That understanding is never complete; it will always be limited by the inadequacy of tradition to respond to changing circumstances and by the impossibility of settling conflicting claims conclusively and completely. The choices, however, will always be made with sensitivity to the bonds that tie individuals to their communities.

Kohlberg himself (1980) believed that moral reasoning and choices were best made in a communitarian setting (Blatt, 1970; Higgins, Power, & Kohlberg, 1984). He played an active role in the formation of "just community" schools. Hence it can be argued that an ethic of justice, especially when focused on issues of governance in a school setting, can encompass *in practice* the two understandings of justice, namely, justice understood as individual choices to act justly and justice understood as the community's choice to direct or govern its actions justly. In a school setting, both are required. In practice, individual choices are made with some awareness of what the community's choices are (school policies), and school community choices are made with some awareness of the kinds of individual choices that are being made every day in the school.

An educational administrator encouraging an ethic of justice will see to it that specific ethical learning activities are structured within curricular and extra curricular programs to encourage discussion of individual choices as well as discussions of school community choices. This may mean extensive faculty *and* student workshops on active listening, group dynamics, conflict resolution, values clarification, problem naming, and the like. Teachers familiar with Kohlberg's stages of moral reasoning (Kohlberg, 1969, 1981), can more easily understand the general frame of reference students are using (e.g., instrumental hedonism, negotiation of the social contract, and so forth).

In a school that takes site-based management seriously, issues of the day-to-day governance of life in the school are inescapable. The ethic of justice demands that the claims of the institution serve both the common good and the rights of the individuals in the school. Ongoing discussions of student discipline policies, of faculty and student due-process procedures, of agreements about faculty time commitments, and so on are absolutely necessary. Furthermore, discussions about the curriculum, about appropriate textbooks, about a visiting speakers' program, and the like will need to be carried on, not simply for their appropriateness for standardized tests, but for the moral questions they raise about public life in the community. Approaches to multicultural education should include not only the standard attempts to create better understanding of cultural differences, but also, and most important, discussions of historical and present social conditions that breed unjust relationships between people of different cultures and explorations of ways to alter those social conditions. Issues of grading and testing could be examined from the perspective of justice, with such discussions leading to the development of alternatives to present practices that benefit some to the disadvantage of others.

No doubt such freewheeling discussion of so many taken-for-granted elements of schooling will get messy and unmanageable. Most administrators dread such initial lack of definition. On the other hand, the debate is in itself educative. The only way to promote ethical attitudes and understandings about self governance is to engage in debate. Someone might object that there will be little time left for the business of teaching and learning if schools spend so much time restructuring the institution. Although that criticism betrays too narrow a view of teaching and learning, let us take it seriously. Then the question for the community to decide is precisely how to manage its time in such a way as to attend to the more traditional academic agenda while still carrying out its activities of self-governance.

Even this brief dusting off of the school's involvement in promoting an ethic of justice points to the close relationship of the ethic of critique and the ethic of justice. To promote a just social order in the school, the school community must carry out an outgoing critique of those structural features of the school that work against human beings. Often the naming of the problem (critique) will suggest new directions or alternatives for restructuring the practice or process in a fairer manner. For example, the administration of a policy that provides a disproportionate share of resources to students in the upper decile of the student body results in inequities that affect large numbers of "average" students unfairly (Cusick & Wheeler, 1988). It raises questions about the responsibility of brighter students to share their gifts for the larger good of the community, perhaps in some peer tutoring activities.

Ethics of caring

One of the limitations of an ethics of justice is the inability of the theory to determine claims in conflict (Hollenbach, 1979). What is just for one person might not be considered just by another person. Hence discussions of what is just in any given situation, can tend to become mired down in minimalist considerations (What minimal conditions must be met to fulfill the claims of justice?). For an ethic of justice to serve its more generous purpose, it must be complemented or fulfilled in an ethic of love. Although earlier discussions of the incompleteness of the ethic of justice took place in a theological context (Niebuhr, 1935), more recent discussions have tended to ground the ethic of love and caring in a philosophy of the person (Buber, 1970; MacMurray, 1961). Scholars such as Gilligan (1977) and Noddings (1984, 1988) promoted these ethical directions from a vantage point of psychology, especially women's moral development, in the current literature on the ethic of caring.

Such an ethic focuses on the demands of relationships, not from a contractual or legalistic standpoint, but from a standpoint of absolute regard. This ethic places the human persons-in-relationship as occupying a position for each other of absolute value; neither one can be used as a means to an end; each enjoys an intrinsic dignity and worth, and given the chance, will reveal genuinely loveable qualities. An ethics of caring requires fidelity to persons, a willingness to acknowledge their right to be who they are, an openness to encountering them in their authentic individuality, a loyalty to the relationship. Such an ethic does not demand relationships of intimacy; rather, it postulates a level of caring that honors the dignity of each person and desires to see that person enjoy a fully human life. Furthermore, it recognizes that it is in the relationship that the specifically human is grounded; isolated individuals functioning only for themselves are but half persons. One becomes whole when one is in relationship with another and with many others.

Educational administrators committed to an ethic of caring will be grounded in the belief that the integrity of human relationships should be held sacred and that the school as an organization should hold the good of human beings within it as sacred. This ethic reaches beyond concerns with efficiency, which can easily lead to using human beings as merely the means to some larger purpose of productivity, such as an increase in the district's average scores on standardized tests or the lowering of per-pupil costs.

Administration based on an ethic of caring will attend to the "underside" of administration (Starratt, 1984), that is, to those motives that sometimes intrude, even slightly, on an exchange with a teacher, student, or parent. Sometimes those motives involve the desire to dominate, to intimidate, to control. Sometimes those motives involve racial, sexual, ethnic, and age stereotypes that block the possibility of honest communication. Sometimes the administrator feels insecure in the face of a strong and assertive teacher and feels the need to put that teacher in his or her place. Sometimes the administrator is not even aware of the power he or she has in the eyes of teachers and recklessly toys with the teacher's insecurity by some light-hearted ridicule of a classroom activity.

When these underside issues dominate an administrative exchange, they block any possibility of open, trusting, professional communication. Mistrust, manipulation, aggressive and controlling actions or language on the part of the administrator or the teacher or both can lead to a relationship that is hypocritical, dishonest, disloyal, vicious, and dehumanizing.

An administrative exchange can move beyond a superficial ritual to a contractual obligation to a relationship of caring when there is a deep attention to the unique human beings involved in the exchange and to issues of self-esteem, personal confidence, and ego anxieties. People who are fairly secure in their sense of themselves and in their professional role are not overly affected by these underside motives; few, however, are entirely free from them in every circumstance. If these motives are understood and acknowledged initially, they will not distort the exchange in excessively manipulative or negative ways.

The administrator who is concerned with nurturing the growth of teachers will have to ensure that teachers experience the relationship with the administrator as one of regard, mutual respect, and honest contact between two persons. Even though their traditional organizational roles have conditioned administrators and teachers to an antagonistic relationship (Blumberg, 1974; Starratt, 1990), in a school intentionally restructuring itself and concerned about issues of empowerment, it is possible to move toward a relationship based on caring. For relationships of caring to develop, administrators will initially explore with their teachers those conditions necessary to initiate and maintain trust, honesty, and open communication (Hoy & Kupwersmith, 1984).

Besides developing sensitivity to the dignity and uniqueness of each person in the school, the administrator can promote an ethic of caring by attending to the cultural tone of the school. Often the use of language in official communiques will tell the story. Formal, abstract language is the language of bureaucracy, of distance; humor, familiar imagery and metaphor, and personalized messages are the language of caring. Through reward procedures and ceremonies as well as through school emblems, school mottos, school songs, and other symbols, the school communicates what it cares about. When the school rewards academic competition in ways that pit students against each other, when the awards are few and go only to the top students in the formal academic disciplines, then the school makes a clear statement of what it values. Other ceremonies and awards that stress caring, cooperation, service, teamwork, and the like send different messages. Some schools clearly promote a feeling of family and celebrate friendship, loyalty, and service. Laughter in the halls, frequent greetings of each other by name, symbols of congratulations for successful projects, frequent displays of student work, hallways containing pictures of groups of youngsters engaged in school activities, cartoons poking fun at teachers and administrators—these are all signs of a school environment that values people for who they are. When youngsters engage every day in such a school community, they learn the lessons of caring, respect, and service to each other. With some help from peers and teachers, they also learn how to forgive, mend a bruised relationship, accept criticism, and debate different points of view.

For most educational administrators, a brief reflection on their own ethical caring will occasion some embarrassment. By confronting their own flawed performance, administrators can discover, with a moment's reflection, the subtle but constant intrusion of self-interest. Without excusing it, they learn to acknowledge it as a part of them. Recognizing their own failures will help them avoid the tendency to self-righteous judgment of others' ethical mistakes.

The ethics of caring brings us full circle at this point. Knowing our own failures to care for others, our own immature ways of rationalizing moral choices, knowing our own reluctance to challenge questionable school arrangements, we are able to confront the general weakness in the human community. That weakness is part of being human. Despite our heroic ideals, we often act in distinctly unheroic ways. A sense of compassion is needed for one who would act ethically, compassion for himself and compassion for others. We have to extend our caring to forgiving. The forgiveness extended, we then go on with the business of making things right.

Summary

Two questions remain, the response to which may close out this inquiry into an ethical perspective for practitioners. The first question involves the legitimacy of combining themes derived from three different ethical theories, despite what some might claim are irreconcilable differences among the theories (Pateman, 1980). The second question deals with the practicality of the construct for the practitioner. Namely, does it offer the administrator a perspective that allows him or her to frame the most important ethical issues encountered in schools and to shape an environment that encourages ethical choice?

The answer to the first question deserves a lengthy development that space does not allow. For now, this author argues that the three theories are not irreconcilable. They can be grounded on both the essential nature of human beings and on the essential nature of human society. That is to say, one can argue for the necessary interpenetration of each theme by the others if one is to argue for a fully developed moral person and a fully developed human society. Even a superficial familiarity with the themes, which this article attempts to communicate, suggests that each theme implies something of the other theme. The ethic of critique assumes a point of view about social justice and human rights and about the way communities ought to govern themselves. The ethic of justice assumes an ability to perceive injustice in the social order as well as some minimal level of caring about relationships in that social order. The ethic of caring does not ignore the demands of community governance issues, but claims that caring is the ideal fulfillment of all social relationships, even though most relationships among members of a community function according to a more remote form of caring.

Moreover, each ethic needs the very strong convictions embedded in the other. The ethic of justice needs the profound commitment to the dignity of the individual person found in the ethic of caring. The ethic of caring needs the larger attention to social order and fairness of the ethic of justice if it is to avoid an entirely idiosyncratic involvement in social policy. The ethic of critique requires an ethic of caring if it is to avoid the cynical and depressing ravings of the habitual malcontent, and the ethic of justice requires the profound social analysis of the ethic of critique, to move beyond the naive fine tuning of social arrangements in a social system with inequities built into the very structures by which justice is supposed to be measured. The response to the first question, then, is that the themes are not incompatible but, on the contrary, complement and enrich each other in a more complete ethic. Uniting themes from different theoretical foundations attempts to use the genuine strengths and the genius of each theoretical position in the interests of building a rich and pluriform ethical environment.

The response to the second question is likewise affirmative. An educational administrator's day is filled with ethical situations and challenges. Sometimes those situations clearly call for a critique of unfair school procedures; sometimes they involve debate over school policy in an effort to balance the common good with individual rights; and sometimes they involve the demands of an individual person to be recognized and cherished for who he or she is. At other times, more complex problems require that the administrator examine the problem from each framework and perhaps balance the demands of all three ethics in his or response to the problem. Given the proactive position of an ethics of educational administration

Building an ethical school 89

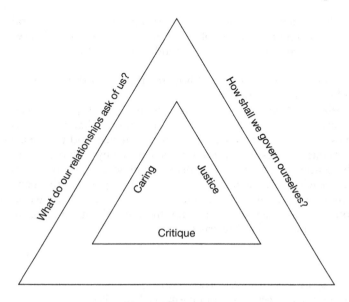

Figure 6.1 The multidimensional ethic

Figure 6.2 The multidimensional ethic at work in a school setting—an ethical school environment

advocated in this article, namely the building of an ethical school as an integral part of a national effort to restructure schools, the larger construct of all three ethical themes offers a more comprehensive and multidimensional foundation for such a reconstruction.

Figures 6.1 and 6.2 offer a visual diagram of how the themes work together to provide such a multidimensional perspective.

This article has attempted to develop a tapestry of ethical perspectives, specifically for those involved with educational administration. That tapestry is woven of three themes: the theme of caring, the theme of justice, and the theme of criticism. An ethical consciousness that is not interpenetrated by each theme can be captured either by sentimentality, by rationalistic simplification, or by social naivete. The blending of each theme encourages a rich human response to the many uncertain ethical situations administrators face every day in their work. Furthermore, they offer complementary frames for thinking about building an ethical school during this time of school restructuring.

References

Adorno, T. W. (1973). *Negative dialectics*. New York: Seabury.
Apple, M. (1982). *Education and power*. Boston: Routledge & Kegan Paul.
Bates, R. J. (1984). Toward a critical practice of educational administration. In T. J. Sergiovanni & J. E. Corbally (Eds.), *Leadership and organizational culture* (pp. 260–274). Urbana, IL: University of Illinois Press.
Bellah, R., Madsen, R., Sullivan, W. M., Swidler, A., & Tipton, S. M. (1985). *Habits of the heart: Individualism and commitment in American life*. New York: Harper & Row.
Blatt, N. (1970). *Studies on the effects of classroom discussion upon children's moral development*. Unpublished doctoral dissertation, University of Chicago.
Blumberg, A. (1974). *Supervisors and teachers, a private cold war*. Berkeley, CA: McCutchan.
Bowers, C. A. (1987). *Elements of a post-liberal theory of education*. New York: Teachers College Press.
Boyer, E. (1983). *High school: A report on secondary education in America*. New York: Harper & Row.
Buber, M. (1970). *I and thou* (W. Kaufmann, Trans.). New York: Scribner.
Cherryholmes, C. H. (1988). *Power and criticism: Poststructural investigations in education*. New York: Teachers College Press.
Cusick, P. A., & Wheeler, C. W. (1988). Educational morality and organizational reform. *American Journal of Education, 96*, 231–255.
Eisenstadt, S. N. (1968). *Max Weber: On charisma and institution building*. Chicago: University of Chicago Press.
Foster, W. (1986). *Paradigms and promises: New approaches to educational administration*. Buffalo, NY: Prometheus.
Freire, P. (1970). *Pedagogy of the oppressed* (M. B. Ramos, Trans.). New York: Herder & Herder.
Gilligan, C. (1977). *In a different voice: Women's conception of self and morality*. Cambridge, MA: Harvard University Press.
Giroux, H. A. (1988). *Schooling and the struggle for public life*. Minneapolis: University of Minnesota Press.
Goodlad, J. I. (1984). *A place called school*. New York: McGraw-Hill.
Greenfield, W. (1987, April). *Moral imagination and value leadership in schools*. Paper presented at the annual meeting of the American Educational Research Association, Washington, DC.

Habermas, J. (1973). *Legitimation crisis*. Boston: Beacon.
Higgins, A., Power, C., & Kohlberg, L. (1984). The relationship of moral atmosphere to judgements of responsibility. In W. Kurtines & J. Gerwirtz (Eds.), *Morality, moral behavior and development*. New York: Wiley Interscience.
Hollenbach, D. (1979). *Claims in conflict*. New York: Paulist.
Horkheimer, M. (1974). *Eclipse of reason*. New York: Seabury.
Hoy, W. K., & Kupwersmith, W. (1984). Principal authenticity and faculty trust. *Planning and Changing, 15,* 80–88.
Jennings, B. (1983). Interpretive social sciences and policy analysis. In D. Callahan & B. Jennings (Eds.), *Ethics, the social sciences and policy analysis* (pp. 3–35). New York: Plenum.
Kimbrough, R. B. (1985). *Ethics: A current study for educational leaders*. Arlington, VA: American Association of School Administrators.
Kohlberg, L. (1969). Stage and sequence: The cognitive-developmental approach to socialization. In D. Goslin (Ed.), *Handbook on socialization theory and research* (pp. 347–480). Chicago: Rand McNally.
Kohlberg, L. (1971). From is to ought: How to commit the naturalistic fallacy and get away with it in the study of moral development. In T. Mischel (Ed.), *Cognitive development and epistemolgy* (pp. 151–235). New York: Academic Press.
Kohlberg, L. (1980). High school democracy and educating for a just society. In R. L. Mosher (Ed.), *Moral education: A first generation of research and development* (pp. 20–57). New York: Praeger.
Kohlberg, L. (1981). *The meaning and measurement of moral development*. Worchester, MA: Clark University Press.
Lakomski, G. (1987). Values and decision making in educational administration. *Educational Administration Quarterly, 23(3),* 71–82.
MacIntyre, A. (1984). *After virtue* (2nd ed.). Notre Dame, IN: University of Notre Dame Press.
MacMurray, J. (1961). *Persons in relation*. London: Faber and Faber.
Niebuhr, R. (1935). *An interpretation of Christian ethics*. New York: Harper & Brothers.
Noddings, N. (1984). *Caring: A feminine approach to ethics and moral education*. Berkeley, CA: University of California Press.
Noddings, N. (1988). An ethic of caring and its implications for instructional arrangements. *American Journal of Education, 96,* 215–230.
Pateman, C. (1980). "The disorder of women": Women, love and the sense of justice. *Ethics, 91(1),* 20–34.
Purpel, D. (1989). *The moral & spiritual crisis in education*. Granby, MA: Bergin & Garvey.
Rawls, J. A. (1971). *A theory of justice*. Cambridge, MA: Harvard University Press.
Raywid, M. A. (1986, April). *Some moral dimensions of administrative theory and practice*. Paper presented at the annual meeting of the American Educational Research Association, San Francisco.
Schindler, D. L. (1986). On the foundations of moral judgment. In G. F. McLean, F. E. Ellrod, D. L. Schindler, & J. L. Mann (Eds.), *Act and agent: Philosophical foundations for moral education and character development* (pp. 271–305). Lanham, MD: University Press of America.
Schon, D. A. (1983). *The reflective practitioner: How professionals think and act*. New York: Basic Books.
Sergiovanni, T. J. (1985). Landscapes, mindscapes and reflective practice in supervision. *Journal of Curriculum and Supervision, 1,* 5–17.
Sergiovanni, T. J., & Starratt, R. J. (1988). *Supervision: Human perspectives* (4th ed.). New York: McGraw-Hill.
Sizer, T. R. (1984). *Horace's compromise: The dilemma of the American high school*. Boston: Houghton Mifflin.
Starratt, R. J. (1984). The underside of supervision. *Impact, 19,* 5–16.

Starratt, R. J. (1990). *The drama of schooling/the schooling of drama*. London: Falmer.
Strike, K., Haller, M., & Soltis, J. (1988). *Ethics of school administration*. New York: Teachers College Press.
Sullivan, W. M. (1986). *Reconstructing public philosophy*. Berkeley, CA: University of California Press.
Vandenberg, D. (1990). *Education as a human right*. New York: Teachers College Press.
Walzer, M. (1985). *Exodus and revolution*. New York: Basic Books.
Wynne, E. A. (Ed.). (1982). *Character policy: An emerging issue*. Washington, DC: University Press of America.
Young, R. (1990). *A critical theory of education*. New York: Teachers College Press.

CHAPTER SEVEN

Working within the geography of human development

Introduction

One approach to the study of leadership is to ask, leadership of what, for what? Educational leaders should be leading a community and an institution that is committed to the growth of human beings *as* human beings, as they engage in the work of the school. Granted that the policy agenda speaks of all children meeting high standards of academic achievement; granted that states and the profession are calling teachers to meet high standards of content knowledge and sophisticated pedagogy—nonetheless, that academic achievement and those professional standards will be met by human beings serving human purposes. High standards are not ends in themselves. Rather, they are policy goals intended to ensure the development of those human competencies that will enrich and further the growth of communities of free, creative, and responsible humans who participate in their raising of coming generations, in their work, in their neighborhoods and community involvements in furthering the multiple varieties of human fulfillment within a social and political context.

Human resource leadership can be and often is interpreted as primarily or exclusively an exercise of managing organizational and bureaucratic functions such as recruiting, hiring, and evaluating employees and coordinating their ongoing training and skill development. Often these functions are administered by one person or one unit within the central administration of a school district. The perspective this book embraces, however, is that every educator, whether an administrator, teacher, counselor, coach, or school nurse should be both a human resource manager and a leader of human resource development, a person who works with and through human resources in their charge to transform the work of the school or school system into a humanly fulfilling experience.

How can this system of human resource development move beyond the "feel good" impressions of these lofty goals to operationalizing the means to realize them? As a starting point, this chapter sets out to map out the terrain to guide the effort and commitment of educational leaders. To repeat, this book is attempting to compose a *system* of human resource development in which all organizational units and structures and processes of the school system will focus organically around clearly articulated human purposes in enacting the core work of the school system, namely the work of learning. Learning and all the structured and collective effort that goes into it will be seen as a continuous human activity that engages the individual and communal humanity of the learners in the pursuit of human purposes. Leading the learning, no matter at what level—in classrooms, in counseling offices, in the cafeteria and on the playground, in school clusters and departments, whole school projects, or school system initiatives—is understood as part of an organic process of human resource development that begins and ends with the young learners in the school.

This effort to map the terrain of human resource leadership must rest on some well-grounded understandings of human development seen from a whole human lifetime. In other words, if the work of human resource development includes the human resources of the young learners in the school, as well as the young adults beginning their careers in education, as well as the more veteran and senior members of the learning community, then it would help to start with a large view of how humans develop from infancy through adulthood.

Such a view enables educators to comprehend what young learners are going through in their life experiences, their challenges, their capabilities, their developmental readiness for more demanding learning adventures. Furthermore, this life-span view encompasses young adulthood, enabling human resource leaders to more readily perceive and attend to the developmental needs and challenges facing neophyte teachers, and to promote the integration of the learnings of their craft as educators into their development as adult human beings. Furthermore, as these young educators master the basics of their craft and continue to open up to larger adult concerns, their humanity seeks deeper satisfactions in their work beyond the routines they have grown comfortable with. Human resource leaders' work is not completed with the successful induction of young adults into the profession. It requires working with the increasingly mature professional on finding new ways to reach underperforming or unmotivated or struggling students and to reach a deeper understanding of the curriculum content they are teaching so as to more effectively invite learners to encounter the curriculum as something that holds real meaning for them (Brophy, 2001; Freire, 1998; Nixon, Martin, McKeown, & Ransom, 1996, Perkins, 1992).

The theory of human development of Erik Erikson

The landscape of human development that can provide a grounding for the work of human resource administration has been admirably mapped by the psychologist Erik Erikson. While his interpretation of human development is one of several scholarly perspectives, it is a particularly dynamic heuristic tool for understanding the repetitive cycle of challenges that humans face as they grow toward a mature adult humanity.

First, a mention of Erikson's scholarly credentials. Erikson as a young man moved to Vienna where he studied under Sigmund and Anna Freud. Though initially enthusiastic with psychoanalysis, he grew increasingly disillusioned with what he perceived to be a narrow dogmatism of the Vienna Institute. He moved with his wife and two young children to the United States, settling initially in Boston. His scholarly career included teaching and research at Harvard and Yale universities, as well as the University of California at Berkeley, and at the Austin Riggs Center in Stockbridge, Massachusetts, before returning again to Harvard in 1960. Though he retired from Harvard in 1970, he continued to lecture and write into the mid-1980s. Erikson's thinking about human development holds particular importance for educators because he is basically concerned about *healthy* human development. The primary question driving his work is: How do human beings develop toward a healthy, rich adulthood? In this he differed from his early teacher. Freud's primary question was: How did this maladapted human lose control over her or his life? What trauma and suffering caused this illness? Ironically, many followers of Freud have criticized Erikson for being naively optimistic, as though psychological health were a hopeless ideal or existential aberration. Erikson's theory of human development, however, has enjoyed great appeal to many in the helping professions. Furthermore, recent scholarly commentaries on the broad expanse of Erikson's work of almost fifty years point out the complexity and insightfulness of his thinking on human development (Arnett, 2004; Conn, 1977; Coté & Levine, 2002; Freidman, 1999; Hoare, 2002; Hoover, 2004; Knowles, 1986; Stevens, 2008; Wallerstein & Goldberger, 1998; Welchman, 2000).

Erikson's work broadened Freud's theory of human development to a larger biosocial psychological perspective. Erikson understood the tensions between the ego and the superego as crucial to human development, those tensions resulting more from the cultural context than the biological. For Erikson, the ego, rather than the id, is much more the source of agency in its synthetic processes of *making meaning*, and its executive process of *expression and action* (Coté & Levine, 2002). Depending on the severity and narrowness of adult controls through childhood—which initially translate into the superego—the ego will enjoy more or fewer opportunities to act autonomously. Those opportunities provide interactive experiences in shaping one's relationship with one's cultural and social environment.

Erikson saw human development as a developmental series of learnings about how one could manage one's own growth as a human being, in the process becoming more and more in charge of oneself, enlarging the sphere of one's agency, both physically and linguistically, imaginatively and willfully. Those learnings initially happened in a somewhat age-appropriate sequence, beginning in infancy and stretching forward through young adulthood into mature adulthood, parenthood, career, middle and old age. As we will see, however, this sequence gets repeated in a transformed and dynamic way as one progresses through the life cycle.

Erikson spoke of these learnings as being occasioned by a crisis, and here he continued with the vocabulary of his Freudian training (the oedipal crisis, etc.). Humans experience challenges or crises which must be met in order to grow into more mature human beings, challenges which are met in various degrees of success over the course of a specific range of years in a person's development. The relative success in meeting these challenges provides a platform for engaging the next developmental challenge. The severity of these challenges or crises depends on the flexibility or rigidity of the familial and cultural environment as well as the physical and psychic endowments of the person, and how well the person has met the earlier challenges in her or his human development. Furthermore, as we will see shortly, these challenges recur in more mature forms in later years, with different tonalities and coloration, as persons move into new life-circumstances.

As Table 7.1 indicates, each stage or life-challenge has a healthy or an unhealthy outcome, or, in most cases, a *relatively* satisfactory or unsatisfactory outcome. These outcomes, as we will see, are not necessarily definitive in fixing a person's development irrevocably. One can repair the damage, so to speak, through more positive experiences in later stages of one's life, through experiences that enable one to revisit the challenge perhaps now more intentionally, either through therapy, or through other positive experiences in one's life. Likewise, success at one stage does not guarantee continued success in meeting future challenges. Table 7.1 indicates when these crises or challenges originally occur though they may be implied in earlier challenges, and will reoccur throughout one's life's journey.

These challenges begin during infancy with the *challenge to trust* the mother's constancy of care and attention to the infant's basic needs. That trust in the mother lays the foundation for trusting other human beings in one's life, and for trusting the basic beneficence of one's world. It also establishes a foundational understanding that one's life *is inescapably relational*, that independence from relationships is not an option for a healthy and satisfying human life. Insecurity in one's relationships, however, is never decisively overcome, due both to the ego's drive for omnipotence, and due to the vicissitudes of life and fluctuating disappointments in one's relationships.

Many parents are familiar with the "terrible two's" when children begin to assert their autonomy, often in frustrating and unpredictable ways. The child's most frequent response is,

"No." That translates as "I won't do what *you* want. *I'll* do the choosing."

As their physical mobility and language mastery develops, the relatively autonomous child will then begin to explore the limits and boundaries of her or his environment, physical and imaginary, cultural, and sexual. Again, the child takes the initiative in exploring the various *relationships* within the environment, relationships that continue to communicate information about her or his identity and the social expectations of the immediate family and community that provide for a satisfying mutuality of relationships.

As the child experiences primary and middle school during the latency years, the youngster tries out a variety of tools, and tool-using processes, whether those involve sophisticated technology (computer games, play-station, Internet searches), craft or artistic skills (playing the piano or learning step-dancing), athletic skills (dribbling a soccer ball or basketball, playing hop-scotch or skipping rope), or a range of hobbies (chess, boy/girl scouts, co-curriculars at school). During these

Table 7.1 Life-cycle challenges and strengths to be developed

Erikson's Eight Stages of Human Development

Stage	EGO Development Outcomes	Resulting Strengths
Infancy	Trust vs. Mistrust	Drive & Hope
Early Childhood	Autonomy vs. Shame	Self-control, courage, will
Play Age	Initiative vs. Guilt	Purpose, Imagination
School Age	Industry vs. Inferiority	Method + Competence
Adolescence	Identity vs. Role Confusion	Consistency + Fidelity
Young Adult	Intimacy + Solidarity vs. Isolation	Affiliation + Love
Middle Adulthood	Generativity vs. Self-absorption or stagnation	Production + Care
Late Adulthood	Integrity vs. Despair	Wisdom

years, the youngster is finding out what she or he can do well, what natural talents or interests can be mastered. These learnings will further enlarge the child's sense of self and of the various ways she or he can *participate in the life of the community*. During elementary and middle school years, young learners begin to develop an academic self-image. Through their classroom activities and out of class assignments, they discover what they are good at and what they aren't. If the school work is not particularly meaningful, engaging, and somewhat satisfying, these young learners will turn their attention to mastering out of school skills and interests like sports, computer games, chess, surfing, or other hobbies, doing just enough to pass in order to keep the teachers and their parents "off their backs."

During the teen-age years, youngsters now begin to explore a variety of life-long choices about who they want to be as adults. Career explorations help to expose them to a variety of adult roles. Strong attachments to role models emerge. Sexual identity becomes solidified as rapid physical maturity makes them acutely aware of their sexuality and their sexual attractions. As they look forward to increasingly adult roles in their later teens, school work may begin to recede in importance, especially when school work appears quite disconnected to adult concerns in the "real world." Connecting school work to explicit applications to adult concerns such as careers, civic participation, and self-expression is especially crucial during these years when the force of adult authority is increasingly evanescing.

As the adolescent moves into young adulthood, the exploration of identity matures into a more intentional choice of an identity-trajectory of her or his life. This development in young adulthood completes, in one sense, the whole struggle of a young person's first third of her or his life, namely a struggle to construct and be true to a self, a self that is consistent and reasonably predictable. While the young adolescent is capable of grasping some meaning of altruistic generosity, and indeed, of imagining a somewhat romanticized picture of her or himself enacting a heroic life, the focus would tend to remain on the self and how admirable that heroic self would look in other people's eyes. The embracing of an altruistic cause would be more the embrace of an ideology, a set of high principles that would redound to the adolescents' self-image. The struggle to be a somebody is necessarily self-centered or self-focused, even among the healthiest of young humans.

This struggle, however, eventually leads the young adult to the point in his or her life when self-transcendence is possible, both in and through a career and in and through a relationship. Having a reasonably clear grasp of him or herself, it is now possible to let go of the *exclusive* concentration on becoming a somebody. Now it is more possible to be a self whose identity is more clearly fed by increasingly deeper relationships, leading to the gradual ability to give the self away, to give *from* the self, to give *of* the self—in short, to transcend the self in *reaching out* to bond with another, or with a cause that is much greater than self-development.

As Giddens (1991) argues, however, conditions of late modernity such as widespread divorce; multiple family moves from one locale to another; interracial, interethnic, and interreligious marriages; multiple changes within careers and to other careers in adulthood; multiple globalizing influences—all contribute to a weakening of traditional markers of self-identity. Humans have to participate more actively in the intentional invention of themselves. Understandably, therefore, the deeper establishment of a self-identity that remains consistent around a more permanent set of values takes a longer period of time to put together within a horizon of rapid change.

The self-identity challenge which Erikson saw in mid-twentieth century in the United States as being worked through in adolescence, appears now to be taking longer. Arnett's recent research (2004) indicates that many young adults are postponing marriage and a permanent career until reaching their late twenties and early thirties. The twenties seem much more a time for trying out various identities, various life partners, and various career commitments. Nevertheless, the life challenges as mapped by Erikson appear to maintain the same sequence, even though the move into the intimacy of marriage and a lifetime career seems to be taking longer now, at least in technologically developed countries around the world.

Conn (1977) points out that Erikson's mapping of human development enables a clear delineation between the "moral" (following adult-imposed rules) or pre-ethical stages that precede young adulthood, and the ethical stage, involving self-transcending-choices involved in mature intimacy and generativity and integration. In the earlier stages one is focused primarily on the self. Although there are obvious relationships of mutuality to be negotiated, the focus has been primarily on "what's in it for me?" As one enters into intimacy and generativity, one is clearly involved in a form of acting out of care and beneficence for others, which is so naturally identifiable as a virtuous or ethical form of human activity.

The next crisis or challenge emerges as an adult challenge, namely, the move towards intimacy. Here we see self-transcendence unfolding. Intimacy does not mean self-annihilation or self- abandonment. Rather, it means the meeting of two autonomous, humanly mature adults in a mutual invitation to share life together. As the metaphor of intimacy implies, the self is more able to dis-robe and dis-role in the presence of the other, to remove the cultural costumes one wears, to remove the social masks and disguises one uses to protect oneself from disclosing the insecurities and anxieties that gnaw beneath the surface of one's public life. In intimate relationships, the person is progressively able to be psychologically naked. That means being able to share one's fears and worries, one's silly routines, one's flights from reality—in short, to reveal both one's human poverty and one's inner beauty and humanity. In revealing that human insecurity to the intimate other, however, one finds a loving that accepts that fragility and returns the gift of trusting intimacy with disclosures of the other's own vulnerabilities. Those revelations of the partners' naked humanity actually endear them to each other more, call out for a tender loving that protects and pours life into the soul of the other.

In earlier years, the assumption was that in order to be able to love, one had to bring a fully developed, competent, and "put-together-self" that could be worthy of another's love. Now the opposite appears to be true, namely, that love confers on one's human limitations a fuller sense of life and dignity. Before, loving assumed *being* before loving, now loving confers being, and it sets one free to be oneself, not only in the intimate relationship, but also in other spheres of one's life. That dis-robing and dis-roleing is gradual, to be sure, as the mutual trust deepens, as the authenticity of the other is allowed fuller expression, as the exploration of each other's interior journey grows into a shared journey—not a fused journey, but a journey of partners whose identities remain intact within the union of their lives.

Neither does that intimacy preclude occasional retreats to self-concern, to defensiveness, to feeling wounded by the other, to having falling-outs over minor or major disagreements. Those painful experiences with the loved one, however, lead to moments of forgiving and forgiveness, when the loving heals the bruise, and bonds the union with a deeper, mutual compassion towards each other's humanity. Gradually the loving becomes *predisposed* to forgiving, knowing that the human way of relationships is always somewhat messy.

In marriage, that sharing involves (potentially, anyway) as much as is humanly possible. Having a clear sense of identity that one chooses and intends to be loyal to enables the *mature human, the adult* to emerge. The adult is now not only able to share the full nakedness of his or her person with another in intimacy, but can also intentionally choose to generate new life. In relationships of deep friendship and loyal companionship, that sharing may not involve such totality of daily living together, including the responsibilities of child rearing. In the generation of new life, mature humans embrace the responsibilities to nurture and care for that new life. The simple physical generation of new life, moreover, has to be carried forward to the protection and growth of that new life in its own journey towards full selfhood.

Furthermore, as one moves into the generativity stage of human life, there are other demands to transcend self-interests in order to contribute to new life within the civic and occupational communities one belongs to. At its most basic level, generativity involves the frequent sacrificing of self-interest and self-gratification in proffering care and nurturance to children in one's work of parenting.

As well, one's work in a career frequently entails going beyond the bare minimum to a larger effort to contribute something of genuine value in that work. Having experienced the lessons of intimacy, however, the generative career person recognizes that work gets done with others. One's human and technical limitations need the cooperation and collaboration of various others who make up, however briefly, a team whose collective talents and energies can far surpass the abilities of individual parts of the team. Generativity can involve generating inventions, new political policies, creating works of art, writing scholarly books, teaching young children in school, healing sickness through the healing professions, building a bridge, bringing criminals to justice, conducting research on new medicines, preaching inspiring sermons, and, indeed, being a nurturing foster parent. Generativity is an exercise of human virtue that extends over the last half or last two thirds of a person's life, even during retirement, and can be exercised in a multiplicity of ways by the same person enacting various social and cultural roles.

Finally, in the sunset years of life, there is the stage or life-challenge of bringing one's life into some kind of integrated whole. That challenge involves an acceptance of the totality of one's life, its joys as well as disappointments, its triumphs as well as its less than courageous moments, its mistakes as well as its satisfactions. All of one's experiences come to be seen somehow as necessary for one to have learned the many lessons life has to teach, to have arrived at the completion of one's journey, where the truth is that the journey, rather than the destination holds the truth about oneself. This life-challenge leads to a form of wisdom, a wisdom that can be passed along in a final form of generativity. A simple map of Erikson's life cycle is represented in Figure 7.1.

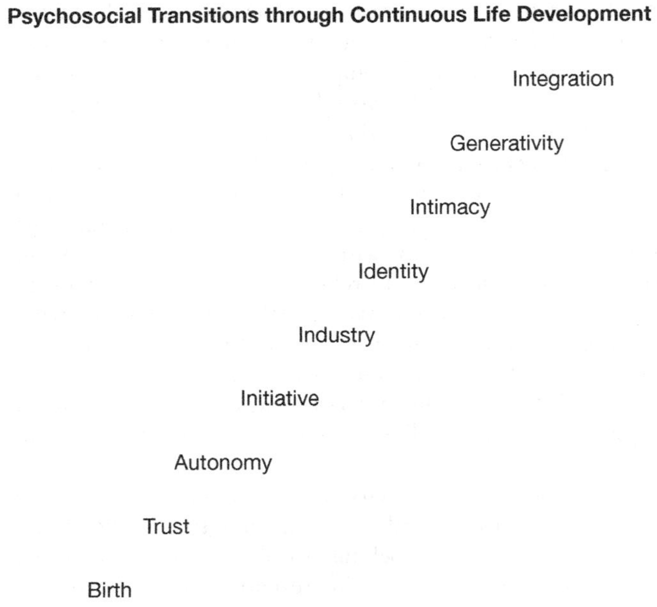

Psychosocial Transitions through Continuous Life Development

                                                     Integration

                                        Generativity

                                   Intimacy

                              Identity

                         Industry

                     Initiative

               Autonomy

           Trust

     Birth

Figure 7.1 Stages of life-cycle psychosocial transitions through continuous life development.

Cautions against simplifications

Erikson's understanding of the life cycle as shown in Figure 7.1 can induce several misinterpretations. One major misinterpretation is to see the map as expressing a static, once-and-for-all sequence of challenges resulting in either-or outcomes. First, the outcomes of engaging a life-challenge do not issue in a complete victory or complete defeat. Rather, the results will tend to be more-or-less success or more-or-less failure.

Depending on the quality of the maternal interactions, a child comes to trust either more completely in the adult world, or to recognize that sometimes one's trust is disappointed, even though, by and large, in most circumstances adults and the world in general can be trusted to be predictably responsive to one's expectations. That trust makes it more likely, though not inexorably guaranteed, that young persons will be able to bring that trust to support their instinctive drive for greater autonomy. That is to say that youngsters have an intuition that their struggle to be more independent will not turn their parents (whom they have grown to trust) against them in a punitive rejection. The struggle to gain autonomy, while frustrating for parents, is not a rejection by the child of the fundamental relationship of caring dependence. Rather, if the relationship is to grow into something more human, the child has to own itself in increasingly insistent agency in order to be in a *more genuine* relationship with the parent. This example also illustrates that the virtue of trust developed in infancy must itself be transformed into a more complex and deeper trust that will sustain the relationship even in the conflict of wills. Thus, it becomes apparent that in this developmental sequence of challenges, the prior learnings will become incorporated into the learnings called upon by the newer challenge; the earlier learnings are both *required* and further *deepened* in the new challenge.

Figure 7.2 attempts visually to indicate that, at every higher stage in the life cycle, resolutions of the earlier stage or stages continue to be folded into the working-through of the next challenge. The working-through of all the earlier stages continues to need attention but now in a more mature and complex working-through of the next stage. Thus, for example, the ability to take the initiative is different as one enters the stage of intimacy than taking the initiative in the earlier stage of identity formation.

The progression through life challenges, therefore, is not a once-and-for-all sequence. As one enters into every new experience, for example, moves into the first job as a teacher, it may very well be necessary to apply the sequence of earlier learnings all over again.

For example, the neophyte teacher may have to learn whether the new environment and new relationships are trustworthy, or at least to find out whom she or he can trust among teaching colleagues, how much to trust the principal, and how much of a trusting relationship is possible with students. With some positive results in that search, the teacher may then be able to explore how much autonomy is

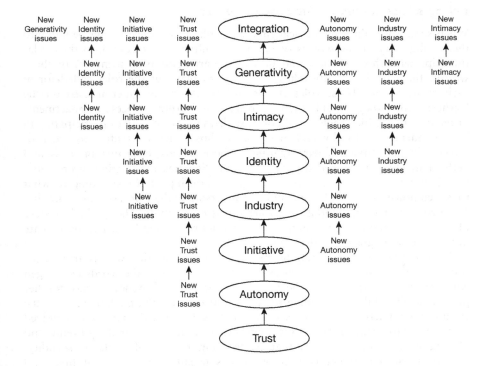

Figure 7.2 The gradual integration of earlier stage strengths into the work of more mature stages.

possible in the work of teaching. From there she may move on to explore the boundaries of her work and of her relationships with her colleagues and students, exploring where work should end and personal life begin. With those initiatives resolved, she may then be ready to tackle the work of gaining new skills and competencies in order to broaden her professional stature.

Another example of having to repeat the passage of earlier challenges would be in the initial stages of an intimate relationship. How much trust to invest in the potential life partner? How much of one's true self will be revealed; how much autonomy will the other tolerate? At the start, what boundaries will be set, what new interpersonal landscapes will be explored? And again, how to negotiate disagreements, how to develop skills of dancing and cooking? Thus, it becomes apparent (as in Figure 7.2) that each life-cycle challenge will be taken up again and again within the various higher stages of the life cycle. On the other hand, this point illustrates the intrinsic logic to the progression of stages or critical challenges.

With these cautions about simplified readings of Erikson's map of the life cycle, we can now turn to an analysis of the psychodynamics of the learning process that takes place every day as the person both fashions and engages his or her "true" self. At this point, we are better prepared to *link* this learning of how to meet the challenges of growing into an increasingly mature person *with* the learning process involved in engaging the academic curriculum of the school.

Linking school learnings to life-cycle challenges

When school learnings in the academic curriculum introduce young people into the intelligibility of the worlds of nature, of culture, of society; into their relationships with those worlds, and into their participation as members of those worlds, the school is tacitly rehearsing ways to play out the roles called for in such participation. Those roles should not be externally superimposed on the learner; rather, they should emerge through the learning process as enactments of relationships which each world contextualizes in the activity of participating in it. The learning and individual nuancing of those roles are tentatively worked-through in the activity of participating in those worlds, both imaginatively and performatively, over extended periods of time. Enacting the relationship to those worlds involves *both* understanding those relationships *and* responding to what those relationships imply. For example, membership in the world of culture implies a growing mastery of symbols and rules for using symbols. The gradual mastery of vocabulary and number manipulation enables the young learner to participate in the various languages of the culture.

Thus, the young child sitting in the cart which the mother wheels around the supermarket and brings to the check-out station, listens to the words exchanged with the clerk, and watches the mother count out her money to pay for her purchases. The child is beginning to acquire, at least tacitly, the languages of the culture of commerce. Under other circumstances, learning the mutuality involved in sibling relationships prepares the youngster for mutuality in making friends and playing neighborhood games, that is, learning the initial skills of sociality. Moreover, the enactment of relationships is usually exploratory at first, and becomes routinized as the feedback of "fit" with expectations of the world becomes, for that individual, the gradual and flexible adoption (usually quite tacit) of a role as a member of that world. Gradually the learner tacitly recognizes that those worlds are *in* him or her, and he or she lives *in* those worlds.

Sociologists and social psychologists, finding broad similarities among the enactments of large numbers of individuals, classify those similarities as roles.

"Role" is a metaphor derived from the theater, where actors perform the role of servant, jealous husband, arrogant bureaucrat, favor-currying sycophant, flirtatious female. Sociologists and social psychologists use the term in a more general sense, diluted of much of the theatrics, to describe behaviors one might observe in ordinary life—the role of mother, husband, consumer, conservative, feminist, fundamentalist, professor (Goffman, 1959). Roles can apply to gender, ideology, profession, economic activity, or class. They are ways the self is socialized into behaving. However, individuals give their own personal twist or nuance to how a role is enacted in a given circumstance. Improvisation of one's identity in a variety of role enactments is an essential ingredient of the learning process, and indeed lends to learning a weighty, dramatic quality as it implicates the learner in the construction of him or herself (McCarthy, 1996; Starratt, 1990).

In Figure 7.3, we have a visual image of how the ego is the core of the individual, making sense, at an unconscious level, of the information it receives from the I at the experiential level. The I functions at the surface of the individual, at the level of consciousness, of sensory experience, of behavior and social interaction. The I is organically and dynamically connected to the ego which is below consciousness. The ego is the collector of the residue of a lived history, of the hurts, the joys, the satisfactions and disappointments experienced and interpreted throughout that history. Those joys, hurts and disappointments have been interpreted through the filters of the body (its needs, drives, sensations, feelings), and through the filters of the superego (what parents want, encourage, forbid; what the culture approves, disapproves, sanctions, rewards; how religion represents one's relationship to God).

The I tells the ego what is happening in the immediate, experiential world. The message to the ego, however, has to pass through the filters of acquired social roles, cultural conditioning, the present bodily needs and learned emotional sensitivities of the person, and thus reaches the ego distorted, rescripted, and weighted by the tonalities added to the message by those filters. The ego tries to make sense of that initial gestalt of what is happening—sometimes successfully, sometimes incorrectly, sometimes bewildered or confused by the surface context, sometimes finding mixed value messages as the experiential world is filtered through the superego and the id. Through that interpretation, the ego scripts and clothes the general response of a self that corresponds to the situation. That response is a response to the initial intelligibility the ego makes of the situation (synthetic processing) and also an expression (the executive processing) of what the ego wants to do in the situation, what the ego wants out of the situation, what the ego senses is appropriate and consistent with the deepest intuition of who the person (the whole person—ego, body, cultural member, the social self, the I) *is*.

In order to grasp the deep connection of understanding (the cognitive aspect of learning) with responding (the affective, willful side of learning), we have to examine Erikson's understanding of the ego as *the source* of both understanding and agency. Note that the ego is the source *both* of understanding *and* of will and action. This point is often missed in the psychological literature that tends to locate

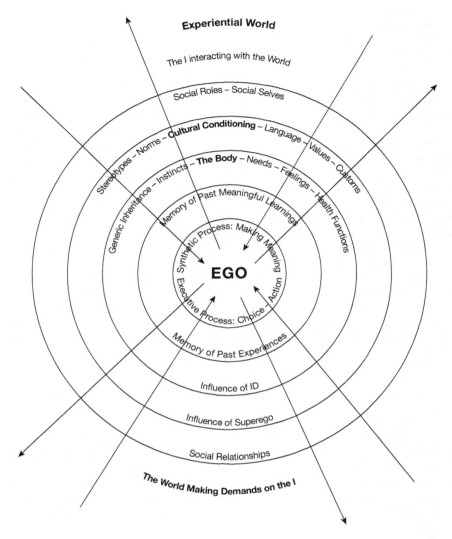

Figure 7.3 A psycho-social model of learning. The influence of the ego on meaning making, and action; the influence of present circumstances, external demands, and internal dispositions on meaning making and action.

understanding in "the mind" (Frawley, 1997). "Mind," however, is as much an abstraction as is "ego." Both are heuristic categories used to interpret and explain the functioning of human beings. The category of mind, however, often connotes an impersonal, information- processing mechanism, separate from emotion and affect, the latter interpreted as found in "the body" (as in mind-body dualisms, often found in the advice, "Think with your mind, not with your body."). By placing the activity of sense-making, of meaning-construction in the ego, Erikson is suggesting the immediacy of knowledge to the person, *within* a unity of knowledge, affect, and choice, each interpenetrating each other and influencing each other, even as they are filtered and expressed by social roles, bodily dispositions, and cultural values.

The heuristic model in Figure 7.3 (and one must remember that it is a visual theoretical model that uses interpretive categories to attempt to illustrate the way a person "works") indicates that the process of meaning making, which is the essential activity of learning, is affected by being filtered through successive layers that have come to constitute the rich structure of the human person. Those filtering layers include not only the immediacy of perception, but the limitations and possibilities of various social roles the person has been socialized to play, as well as the cross-hatching filter of cultural structuring by language, value and belief orientation, religious and parental teachings lodged in the superego, and the instinctual and genetic presuppositions of the body. While knowledge implies intelligibility, in this model it implies a very complex and continuous construction, probably synthesized over varying periods of time, built out of multiple external and internal influences.

Note that the ego is the source, not only of sense-making, but of action, of responding to the sense being made, of expressing how the ego sees itself in relationship to what is being made sense of. When the pedagogy that presents "the lesson" only asks for intelligibility, but not for an *active response* to the ego's perceived relationship to that intelligibility, the interaction with the world is truncated. The intelligibility of the lesson remains sterile because the pedagogy seems to imply that the lesson asks nothing of the learner except a repetition of its surface facticity. This kind of truncated learning leads to an identification of learning with memorized repetition of words and symbols. Higher order learning requires that the learner explain what the lesson means to the learner. In such explanation, the learner necessarily, though tacitly, connects the meaning to who the learner is and how the learner relates to that meaning. Again, it is the whole person, not the "mind" that makes meaning as that person engages the world in exploring how the person is in relationship to that world as it is revealing some of its intelligibility.

That may help to explain why some learners have difficulty understanding, let alone accepting curriculum knowledge, abstracted from the learner's cultural and psychodynamic biography. The learner should be asking, "How is this academic knowledge representing something that can become a part of me, something that I can relate to, become a part of, do something with, be in dialogue with?" The curriculum should entice the learner to ask, "How am I in a Shakespearean play, and how is it in me? How is the industrial revolution playing out in my life, and how is my life related to its history? How is gravity *in* me and how am I *in* gravity? How is DNA and RNA in me, and how am I in my DNA and RNA? How is language in me and how am I to be found in my language and in the language of others? How is cellular subdivision in me and how am I in cellular subdivision? How are equations in me and how am I in equations?" These questions are the unasked questions behind that earlier question: "Why do we have to study this stuff?"

Cultivating these kind of reflective learnings ties the life of the learner to curriculum in authentic ways, so different from a curriculum to be mastered so as to act out the charade of learning. That may also explain the initial impulse of the young learner to embed how he or she interprets curriculum knowledge in a story, rather than in an abstract definition or a formula. In its story form, knowledge is more personal and is constructed out of numerous personal experiences and associations.

Because of Piaget's bias toward science and mathematics, he ranked this narrative kind of cognitive processing, which he called "concrete operational thinking," as a less mature form of thinking than "formal operations"—the use of abstractions to think about other abstractions, following the rules of formal logic. Formal operations may be the more desirable level for scholars and professionals to employ, but is rarely found as the consistent mode of thinking even of 12th graders (Sprinthall & Theis-Sprinthall, 1983). Indeed, some research suggests that only about 30 percent of adults use some aspects of formal operations, and those adults belong to modern societies with complex technologies that require such levels of thought (Bart, 1977, referenced in Sprinthall & Theis-Sprinthall, 1983, p. 23).

This research does not argue against the desirability of attaining formal levels of thinking, nor, indeed, that the narrative way of making sense, though perhaps humanly richer than abstract, logical thinking, is always more appropriate. It leads, however, to the question of whether the attainment of formal logic is indeed developmentally possible (even though one can mimic the curriculum language of such logic in order to pass standards-based assessments), and, even if possible, whether it is humanly desirable as *the primary logic* for the vast majority of young people undergoing formal education in K–12 schools. It leads one to question the widespread insistence that schools should emphasize an intellectualized higher-order reasoning as the exclusive or primary criteria for quality learning, prior to more adult experiences of the need for such abstract levels of knowledge. In other words, one wonders whether the attempt to short-circuit the slower but more authentic process of learning results in a process of learning that is so truncated and speeded up as to eviscerate the rich and lasting quality of learning that is normal—that is, learning tied to the ego development of the learner.

Does enacting the role of "student" in K–12 schools, under the ever present pressure to produce "right answers"—the definition of school achievement—gradually lead the learner to reproduce in that role a form of make-believe learning that satisfies the role expectations of school authorities, but is completely disassociated from the agenda of the ego to define who one is or wants to become (Bonnet & Cuypers, 2003; Wiles, 1983). This disassociation, which is actually, if tacitly, encouraged by classroom routines, may explain the testimony of many students who characterize the learning process in schools as alienating, unreal, and meaningless (Pope, 2001; Shultz & Cook-Sather, 2001). In this regard, one can cite not only the critical reflections of John Dewey, but also of Ernest Becker (1971), Jerome Bruner (1987, 1990), Kieran Egan (1999, 1997, 1990), James Macdonald (1971), Reay and William (2001), Seymour Sarason (2004), and Patrick Shannon (1995), among other scholars.

In more adult stages of development, after resolving one's identity, after dealing with the demands of intimacy, and at the threshold of the generative stage, then the more habitual use of abstract formal logical thinking may indeed be the desirable and necessary way of thinking for engaging the demands of one's career. Even then, the slower, ego-satisfying type of personalized learning involved in cultural pursuits such as learning to play the piano, in relating to one's children, in coming to grips with painful or joyful family challenges, may be far more appropriate than the application of highly abstract analytical categories one uses in one's job, or when paying one's taxes, or planning to purchase a new house.

Connecting learning to the journey toward authenticity

Erikson placed great importance on ego identity, on the ego's sense of its own consistency throughout multiple and varied experiences, and on its ability to act appropriately—consistent with its past knowledge and understandings as well as its interests, wants and desires, and in response to the apparent demands of the present situation. In other words, the individual experiences both an insight into situations, often based on similar past situations, and a desire and a sense of obligation to act consistently, responsibly, and competently. Acting competently implies that one understands the demands of the situation and can exercise the skills and utilize the called-for affective and symbolic communication processes. Acting responsibly implies that one both *apprehends* and *responds* to the demands of the various relationships involved.

When this organic response of the whole person (ego and its memory, body, cultural guidelines and formats, role enactments of specific selves, and the agency of the I) is harmoniously and accurately responsive to the situation being experienced, the person derives a sense of *authenticity* in his or her activity. That is to say, the ego has a sense of competent expression of the *real* person one is. In that expression there is a sense that one's actions are consistent not only with how one understands who one is, but also with *who one wants to be*. It is as though the ego, in its synthetic and executive functions has more fully surfaced, has become conscious of itself in enacting its agency. What the person has said or done or chosen "feels right in my gut," even though the act may draw disapproval from the other players in the drama. The person has acted "responsibly"; that is, in the inner tribunal of ego reflectivity, the person has been true to him/herself and in the process has responded to the demands of the truth embedded in the situation. The truth embedded in the situation is often expressed as a value or ideal implied in the relationships embedded in the situation that cannot be violated except at the risk of violating oneself.

Here, however, the question arises whether the person in the situation, due to his or her socialization into the mainstream culture, might rather mindlessly go along with the social and cultural status quo implied in the situation. That indeed is a real possibility, and one reason why Erikson is sometimes accused of an underlying conservativism (Roazen, 1997). On the other hand, one may find a certain dissonance in a situation, where values embedded in the situation are contrary to those one holds closely and dearly, or where there is a clash of cultural expectations. In such instances, one's sense of authenticity might call for resistance to or questioning what the situation seems to call for. Often, in social situations involving bigotry or scapegoating, or caustic humor at the expense of some denigrated group, the authentic person has to resist the expected response. Likewise, this resistance and questioning is often required in the classroom, when the curriculum presents a distorted or one-sided view of reality.

Thus, one can begin to understand from a psychological standpoint (illuminated by the categories of Erikson's psychosocial model of the individual) the significance of Charles Taylor's ethic of authenticity. Taylor (1991) maintains that the construction and enactment of personal authenticity is the most fundamental and profound ethical responsibility all human beings face. Erikson and Taylor help us to understand the demands of authenticity. To own oneself, to sing one's song, to improvise one's place in the drama of life, to be real instead of phony, to be a somebody instead of a cardboard character mouthing a script someone else has provided, is to be responsible to the truth of who one is, has been, and is capable of becoming, and to the truth embedded in one's relationships. Being real, being authentic is the burden only the individual can bear, is the adventure only the individual can live, is the satisfaction and fulfillment only the individual can enjoy.

Make-believe learning in the pursuit of someone else's approval, when reinforced over twelve to eighteen years of schooling, can induce a habit of mindless inauthenticity. When young people are exposed to inauthentic learning for twelve or more years then it is little wonder that at the final bell of every day, and on the last day of school every year, so many young people depart with such feelings of emancipation. Freed from the constraints of school, they are free to be themselves. For many "successful" students enmeshed in a system of inauthentic learning, however, despite their grades and test scores, their relationships to the natural, social, or cultural world remain impoverished, and thus, they hardly know who they are.

The understanding of learning as involving the integration of ego development with cognitive development, and in turn, the challenge of teachers to advocate for that integration is, by and large, absent from the discourse around pedagogy and school renewal in teacher preparation programs, and indeed from the evaluation of the effectiveness of regular classroom teaching. It is the 600-pound gorilla sitting in the classroom that is consistently ignored by the policy community, until some sensational news story raises momentarily troubling questions about the sources of violence, drugs, homophobia, nervous breakdowns, bullying, weapons, bulimia, dropouts, suicide, and the persistence of the achievement gap in schools.

Hard questions

The burden of this chapter is to question whether teachers adequately integrate concerns for the psychosocial development of learners with their pedagogical approach to curriculum. Are teacher preparation programs even raising the question with teachers-to-be in their university classrooms about their own personal connection to the knowledge they are called upon to teach; raising the question about their own rights and responsibilities, as ethically responsible teachers, to lead students to a "something more" to be learned from the texts they are required to "master"; to allow students time—the opportunity to learn—for what, at their stage of cognitive and affective development, is possible for them to understand?

Should schools continue to promote the schizophrenic split between cognitive and psychosocial development among learners, a split to be found in the practice of relegating student "problems" in psychological development to the work of counselors and teachers of emotionally disturbed and behavior disorder children, as though psychosocial development becomes a school concern only in its pathological manifestations, as though for "normal children" teachers can continue to educate their minds, irrespective of that "other journey."

Summary

Undoubtedly Erikson's map of healthy human growth over the span of a human life will continue to be refined, corrected, expanded by other scholars of human psychology and anthropology. Women's studies have already amplified our understanding of women's distinctive life experiences, and scholarship in race and ethnic studies are similarly providing insights into the diverse patterns of human development contextualized by race and ethnic circumstances. For our purposes, however, Erikson's basic mapping of the life-cycle terrain offers a useful, however incomplete, perspective for human resource development within the context of formal education institutions.

The journey toward a full humanity, toward a fully mature and healthy adulthood can be understood as involving the meeting of initial *and repeated* challenges of trust, autonomy, initiative, industry, identity, intimacy, generativity and integration. For every person, however, there is the unique personal journey, influenced by one's biological and cultural inheritance, by the politics of family, neighborhood and tribe, by happenstance of accident, luck, warfare, poverty or privilege, talents and handicaps, dispositions and dreams, opportunities or dead-end experiments. Thus, the successful or unsuccessful meeting of those life-cycle challenges remains unique for every person at every stage of life.

The work of human resource leadership in education is therefore complex and multifaceted, involving professional, political, organizational, moral, and technical dimensions. Always, however, it remains work with humans by humans for human purposes. Because of this basic premise, an introduction to the work of leadership as human resource development begins with and continuously refers to the human journey and the need to help humans integrate elements of that journey into their work of educating and becoming educated. In succeeding chapters we will attempt to apply the lessons this overview provides to the various demands of the work of human resource development.

References

Arnett, J.J. (2004). *Emerging adulthood. The winding road from the late teens through the twenties.* New York: Oxford University Press.
Becker, E. (1971). *The birth and death of meaning* (second edition). New York: The Free Press.
Bonnet, M. & Cuypers, S. (2003). Autonomy and authenticity in education. In N. Blake, P. Smeyers, R. Smith, & P. Standish (Eds.), *The Blackwell guide to the philosophy of education* (pp. 326–340). Oxford, England: Blackwell.
Brophy, J. (Ed.) (2001). *Subject specific instructional methods and activities.* Amsterdam: Elsevier Science.
Bruner, J. (1987). The transactional self. In J. Bruner & H. Haste (Eds.), *Making sense: The child's construction of the world* (pp. 81–96). New York: Methuen.
Bruner, J. (1990). *Acts of meaning.* Cambridge, MA: Harvard University Press.

Conn, W. E. (1977). Erik Erikson: The ethical orientation, conscience, and the Golden Rule. *Journal of Religious Education, 5*(2), 249–266.
Coté J. & Levine, C. (2002). *Identity formation, agency, and culture: A social psychological synthesis.* Mahwah, NJ: Erlbaum.
Egan, K. (1990). *Romantic understanding: The development of rationality and imagination, ages 8–15.* New York: Routledge.
Egan, K. (1997). *The educated mind: How cognitive tools shape our understanding.* Chicago: University of Chicago Press.
Egan, K. (1999). *Children's minds, talking rabbits & clockwork oranges: Essays on education.* New York: Teachers College Press.
Frawley, W. (1997). *Vygotsky and cognitive science: Language and the unification of the social and computational mind.* Cambridge, MA: Harvard University Press.
Freidman, L.J. (1999). *Identity's architect: A biography of Erik H. Erikson.* New York: Scribner.
Freire, P. (1998). *Teachers as cultural workers: Letters to those who dare to teach.* Trans. by D. Macedo, D. Koike, & A. Oliveira. Denver, CO: Westview Press.
Freud, A. (1968). Psychoanalysis and education, 1954. In *Indications for child analysis and other papers, 1945–1956. The writings of Anna Freud* (Vol 4, pp. 317–326). New York: International Universities Press.
Giddens, A. (1991). *Modernity and self-identity: Self and society in the late modern age.* Stanford, CA: Stanford University Press.
Goffman, E. (1959). *The presentation of self in everyday life.* Garden City, NY: Doubleday Anchor Books.
Hoare, C.H. (2002). *Erikson on development in adulthood: New insights from unpublished papers.* New York: Oxford University Press.
Hoover, K.R. (Ed) (2004). *The future of identity: Centennial reflections on the legacy of Erik Erikson.* Lanham, MD: Lexington Books.
Knowles, R.T. (1986). *Human development and human possibility: Erikson in the light Heidegger.* Lanham, MD: University Press of America.
McCarthy, E.D. (1996). *Knowledge as culture: The new sociology of knowledge.* London: Routledge.
Macdonald, J.B. (1971). A vision of a humane school. In J.G. Saylor & J.L. Smith (Eds.), *Barriers to humanness in the high school* (pp. 2–20). Washington, DC: Association of Supervision and Curriculum Development.
Nixon, J., Martin, J., McKeown, P., & Ransom, S. (1996). *Encouraging learning: Towards a theory of the learning school.* Buckingham, England: Open University Press.
Perkins, D. (1992). *Smart schools.* New York: The Free Press.
Pope, D.C. (2001). *"Doing school": How we are creating a generation of stressed out, materialistic, and miseducated students.* New Haven, CT: Yale University Press.
Reay, D. & William, D. (2001). "I'll be a nothing": Structure, agency, and the construction of identity through assessment. In J. Collins & D. Cook (Eds.), *Understanding learning: Influences and outcomes* (pp. 149–161). London: Paul Chapman Publishers and Open University Press.
Roazen, P. (1997). *Erik Erikson: The power and limits of a vision.* Northvale, NJ: Jason Aronson.
Sarason, S.B. (2004). *And what do you mean by learning?* Portsmouth, NH: Heinemann.
Shannon, P. (1995). *Text, lies, and videotape. Stories about life, literacy and learning.* Portsmouth, NH: Heinemann.
Shultz, J.S. & Cook-Sather, A. (2001). *In our own words: Students' perspectives on school.* Lanham, MD: Rowman & Littlefield.
Sprinthall, N.A. & Theis-Sprinthall, L. (1983). The teacher as an adult learner. A cognitive-developmental view. In G. Griffin (Ed.), *Staff development.* Eighty Second Yearbook of the National Society for the Study of Education, Part II (pp. 13–35). Chicago: University of Chicago Press.

Starratt, R.J. (1990). *The drama of schooling/the schooling of drama*. London: Falmer Press.
Stevens, R. (2008). *Erik H. Erikson: Explorer of identity and the life cycle*. New York: Palgrave Macmillan.
Taylor, C. (1991). *The ethics of authenticity*. Cambridge, MA: Harvard University Press.
Wallerstein, R.S. & Goldberger, L. (1998). *Ideas and identities: The life and work of Erik Erikson*. Madison, CT: International Universities Press.
Welchman, K. (2000). *Eik Erikson: His life, work and significance*. Philadelphia: Open University Press.
Wiles, M. (1983). *Children into pupils*. London: Routledge and Kegan Paul.

CHAPTER EIGHT

Foundational qualities of an ethical person

Introduction

The assumption behind the last chapter is that schools should prepare young people for membership in a world confronting significant challenges and possibilities, challenges both new and perennial. As Dewey cautioned educators, however, schools should not be about preparing to live, but about living (Dewey, 1916). By that he meant learning by living and living by learning—engaging in age appropriate ways what it means to live in today's world in order to continue to live in tomorrow's world.

The title of this book, *Cultivating an Ethical School*, similarly intends the engagement of young people in living by learning and learning by living in age appropriate ways what it means to live ethically in today's world in order to live ethically in tomorrow's world as responsible members. Schools are about learning, about learning to be and become what we are not fully yet and learning how to get there through patient trial and error. That learning involves going through teacher-designed as well as unplanned learning experiences and reflecting on the lessons learned. That learning involves learning by failures, defeats, mistakes, as well as by successes, victories, and good luck. That learning involves relating to the world and its demands and challenges, learning how to become a human person in the adventures of everyday life with its rewards and disapprovals, learning how to do things, make things, share things. In age appropriate ways they are learning to be and to become the person who will someday graduate from school into a full, mature life.

At the outset of this chapter it is important to state how I conceive the convergence of ethical development with human development. That convergence has its foundation in the ontology of the human. Being ethical addresses the ontological relatedness of our being. We by nature are constituted by our relationality. We live by, with, and through other human beings. We do not constitute ourselves independent of our relationship to others. We are not stand-alone, stand apart, isolated and independent beings who come to birth, indeed, who come to exist at all by our own power. There was a time when we did not exist, and there will be a time when, at least in our embodied state, we will not exist. We did not come into being out of our own nothingness. We came into being as children begotten by parents who belonged to an existing community within an existing society and an existing culture, with physical attributes resulting from the genes of our parents, with a body grown inside another body. We did not make our own bodies and fly in with the stork to arrive at our parents' doorstep. We are constituted by our relationality to all that produced us, physically, socially, culturally, inside of a history that provides the possibilities and limitations of our common adventure into what we call our humanity. That adventure continues to involve struggles and dreams, beauty and terror, heroism and cowardice, triumphs and defeats, inventiveness and stubborn adherence to tradition.

Ethics is what our community and culture and society has come to recognize and name as what violates that relationality as well as honors that relationality. What choices and experiences grow us as fuller, more intentional human beings we call good and desirable; what choices and experiences frustrate or suppress us as fuller, more intentional human beings we call bad or evil, undesirable, dysfunctional, and unworthy of our humanity. Those good or bad choices and experiences either respect and honor our relationality, or disrespect and dishonor our relationality.

One way humans define their relationality is through the term, "membership." We are members of a family, a community, of a tribe or nation, of a cultural and a religious tradition, of an organization and a profession. Enacting one's membership in any one of these groups is the way we enact the relationality of our essential nature, our humanity. Membership confers many "goods" for our lives—friendships, security, work, recreation, language, imagery and rituals for self-expression, and for defending values tied to our relationality. Membership implies and invites participation in the life, values, struggles, and satisfactions of fellow members, by which participation we learn how to overcome an exclusive preoccupation with self, and discover the fulfillment of sharing our lives with others. Our membership also provides us with an identity, with possibilities for contributing something unique from ourselves.

Membership brings to the fore an awareness of rights as well as responsibilities of membership. Rights and responsibilities are two of the faces of relationality for humans. One of the basic responsibilities of membership is to see that the rights of all members are protected and sustained. Furthermore, the exercise of those rights and responsibilities by each individual contributes to the overall welfare of the community one belongs to.

What the preceding argument is getting at is the fundamental point that what societies and cultures consider ethical is very close to or synonymous with what it considers a minimal or virtuous exercise of the relationality that constitutes our lives as human beings. Learning to understand the specifics of our relationality within the worlds of culture, nature, and society, and learning to enact those basic responsibilities and rights of membership in those worlds is what schools promote, or are supposed to promote. Thus, if ethics implies the exercise of our relationality in ways that honor our humanity, the work of schools has to be an intrinsically ethical work in its efforts to promote such understanding and performance.

This chapter takes up what can be considered foundational human qualities of personhood that support living an ethical life. Those qualities will reflect the basic relationality of our humanity, and provide a compass for cultivating an ethical school. In any culture, one might be able to identify these qualities as belonging to persons whom their fellows would consider ethical persons. Persons lacking in these qualities would be less likely to be called ethical, except perhaps in rather superficial ways. A central task of an ethical school is to nurture those foundational human qualities of an ethical life in age appropriate ways. Schools might encourage their students to be law-abiding citizens, by a strict regimen of imposing rules and controlling external rewards and punishments. These efforts might or might not produce law-abiding citizens, but they will not cultivate ethical human beings. This chapter explores what these foundational human qualities are, and how the school might nurture them.

As one moves away from specific actions or choices that might be considered ethical in specific situations and circumstances toward more basic, predispositional ethical qualities, one moves away from ethical disputes about what is the ethical thing to do in this specific instance, toward greater agreement that these general qualities are indeed foundational dispositions for ethical living. These qualities inform all ethical living, although, in any specific instance, the predominance of one quality over the others or the mix of all of them together will differ according to circumstances and perceptions. These basic predispositions to ethical living can provide a broadly acceptable and well-focused foundation for cultivating an ethical education.

The truly ethical person acts as an autonomous agent, acts within the supports and constraints of relationships, and acts in ways that transcend immediate self-interest. In other words, the ethical person has developed relatively mature qualities of *autonomy, connectedness*, and *transcendence*. After exploring these foundational qualities or predispositions of an ethical person, we may draw some general implications for a school that would educate such a person.

In speaking about these qualities, we must first recognize that children and youngsters develop these qualities over time. At any given time in their development, youngsters will exhibit greater or lesser strength in these qualities. Likewise, adults will vary in the strength of these dispositions, depending on whether their development toward maturity has been arrested or supported by significant people and circumstances of their lives. At present, we will explore these qualities as we might find them in a more fully developed adult.

It is also important to acknowledge that the sexes will express these qualities differently. Males are socialized, for better or worse, differently toward autonomy than females. Nonetheless, females will learn to express their autonomy as they develop their human personhood. That expression will not be better than or inferior to the male expression. It will be and should be different in terms of their gendered lives, but as humans, it will be recognized in both as the quality of their autonomy. The same is true about the qualities of connectedness and transcendence. There are normal ways females learn and express their connectedness and transcendence that are different from males. As human beings, however, those qualities will be recognized in both males and females. Although these foundational human qualities will be critical for the ethical development of both boys and girls, the mutual interpenetration of these qualities in the different sexes will be reflected differently at different stages and with different intensities in their development. As teachers move through the various stages of building an ethical school, the men and the women on the faculty will have to discuss these differences and their implications for the design of specific learning activities.

Autonomy

Ethical persons are autonomous. That is, they are independent agents who act out of an intuition of what is right or appropriate in a given situation. Their autonomy is in contrast to those who act out of a mindless routine, or simply because others tell them to act that way, or who act out of a feeling of obligation to or fear of those in authority. Autonomy implies a sense of personal choice, of taking personal responsibility for one's actions, of claiming ownership of one's actions.

Assumed in the notion of autonomy is the sense that the autonomous person is an individual person who has a sense of him or herself as standing out from the crowd. It does not mean necessarily an opposition to all that the crowd stands for. Rather it means a willingness to oppose the crowd in certain circumstances, to walk in a direction different from the crowd if it seems called for. It conveys a certain independence, a definition of one's self that is self-chosen, not imposed by anyone else.

Obviously one does not exist in isolation from communities of meaning and memory. To a great extent, one's identity as a person is formed as a male or female member of a specific cultural community, with its traditions, myths and mores. Yet one becomes an individual by appropriating the community's meanings and mores in a personal and unique way. At times one breaks through the standardized, routinized habits of thinking and acting into new ways of thinking and acting. If one is to overcome the suffocation of the collective, one has to choose one's own meanings. One has, in a sense, continuously to create oneself; otherwise he or she becomes absorbed into the unreflective and undifferentiated ways of thinking and acting of the collective. For humans, it is the painful task of adolescence when one has to begin to separate from parents and from peers to forge one's own identity.

One forges one's own identity especially in creating a world of meaning. One's identity can be shaped by accepting the meanings that the culture conveys. There are customary ways to be feminine or masculine, to be successful, to be popular, to be good or to be bad. By simply doing what the culture (either the peer culture or the parental culture) dictates, one chooses an identity that is hardly differentiated from the generalized identities modeled by the culture. Others will seek to reject what the culture dictates in order to validate their individuality. In adolescence, that often takes the form of distinctive hairstyles, clothing, language and counter-cultural music, dances, and public heroes. The problem is that many others in one's peer group want to imitate the antiestablishment posture, and so one must go further and adopt an even more unique appearance within the antiestablishment group. Although viewed by adults as unhealthy or crazy, such behavior by adolescents is often a necessary interlude when youngsters can differentiate themselves. Unfortunately, because of involvement with drugs and alcohol, some attempts at self-definition often turn dangerously self-destructive.

However, the process of self-definition, begun early in childhood and a clear focus in adolescence, goes on through young adulthood. After the first extreme efforts at differentiation, the process settles into a less flamboyant, but usually deeper journey. Assuming that one chooses not to conform to socially defined prescriptions, at least in certain defined areas of one's life, how does one justify these choices? Often such choices carry waves of anxiety with them, for they imply that one is cutting oneself off from society's definitions. Staying with what society prescribes offers security and approval. Striking out into the unknown puts one's self at risk. To assume responsibility for one's life, to assert one's autonomy, to create one's meaning where none existed before, one needs to be strong to stand up to such anxiety.

From where does the strength to assume responsibility for one's life come? One source of strength comes from knowledge and understanding, although this knowledge is not necessarily scientific knowledge. Intuition and imagination also lead to knowledge and understanding. The strength comes from knowing that there are options, of knowing at least some of the options quite well. It also comes from knowing oneself well enough to know why one is afraid to define one's own meaning. Those who live amidst grinding poverty and little hope, however, cannot easily see options and believe that they are already defined by outside forces.

Becker, citing Adler and Fromm, asserts that "neurosis is a problem of the authority over one's life" (1968, p. 258). If one is afraid to move forward under one's own power, which is what it means to be autonomous, it is because that power has been turned over to someone or something else. In that case, one finds the source of power that sustains one's life externally to him or herself. The most common external source is the transference relationship in which one gets personal power from the father figure, from someone in authority. A second major source of power is from a supernatural, personal god, or some transcendent nature or world soul. A third source of power is in the cultural game itself, the everyday rituals and performances that are already in place and thoroughly scripted. Insofar as one turns over one's independence to any of these external sources of power, one loses autonomy.

The strength to be free comes not simply from knowledge, even the therapeutic knowledge of our former bondage to an external source of power. The strength to be oneself can only be fully gained in relationships to other human beings. In authentic relationships, others give us the courage to be ourselves. Here we have the paradox of autonomy. One cannot be autonomous in isolation. Striving to be totally oneself by oneself reveals one's incompleteness, one's poverty, one's existential loneliness. One makes contact with "reality," with the rich world of meaning, by reaching out beyond the isolated self. As Martin Buber put it:

> Human life touches on absoluteness in virtue of its dialogical character, for in spite of his uniqueness man can never find, when he plunges to the depth of his life, a being that is whole in itself and as such touches on the absolute. Man can become whole not in virtue of a relation to himself but only in virtue of a relation to another self. This other self may be just as limited and conditioned as he is; in being together the unlimited and the unconditioned is experienced. (Buber, 1955, pp. 167–168)

Our knowledge and our meanings and our uniqueness are validated in interpersonal relations. Our autonomous decisions reflect both our independent judgments and a choice to act in relation to others. Aggressive and adversarial competition, then, is not natural; when it leads to selfish isolationism, it is in fact destructive of both the individual and the community. Buber (1955) offers a way out of the either/or conundrum of narrow individualism or constricting collectivism by showing that the depth of reality is essentially relational. He offers us a vision of society working toward a transcending ideal, but an ideal rooted in autonomous individuals who find their fulfillment in living relationships.

Dewey (1927) also speaks of society working toward this transcending ideal, an ideal in which human beings, working together, each with a reservoir of talent and intelligence, continuously recreate their society in progressive transformations, and in the process find their own individual fulfillment. He called this the ideal of democracy. In reality, Dewey acknowledged, democracy always falls short of the ideal, but continues to work toward that ideal. The human condition is defined both by the failure and the successes of that effort.

The ethical person must be autonomous. Only in one's autonomy can one bring one's unique personal gifts to an ethical exchange. Only autonomous actors can claim responsibility for their choices. Only autonomous agents add a piece of their own lives, a quality of their unique selves to the ethical act. What constitutes the act as *ethical* is, as a matter of fact, that it is the intentional act of *this person*, not the act of an unreflecting, robot-like human who is following a routine prescribed by someone else, or is driven by irrational urges. Hence, we can see that one of the primary human tasks facing a young person is to become autonomous, to claim his or her own life. One can speak, then, of a deep moral obligation to become autonomous, for only then can one claim membership in a community of moral agents. It follows that the formation of autonomous persons is a primary ethical task of schooling.

Connectedness

The ethical person is connected (Scheler, 1957). As we saw above, the autonomous person cannot authentically express her or his autonomy except in relationships. Every relationship is distinct. It offers unique possibilities because of the qualities that each person brings to the relationship. It is also bounded by the limitations that each person brings to the exchange. What one might expect from one person might be unfair to expect from another. A woman brings certain qualities to a relationship; a man brings other qualities. An older person might be expected to be more flexible in a relationship than a younger person; relationships involving people from the same culture are often different than those involving people from different cultures (Hallowell, 1999).

Circumstances set limits as well as create opportunities in relationships. Work related relationships hold opportunities for creative teamwork in technical areas; neighborhood relationships offer opportunities for more family oriented or recreational activities. Customer or client relationships are different than employer–employee relationships.

Hence it is clear that ethical behavior, while always involving interpersonal relationships, is shaped by the circumstances and status of the persons involved. Acting ethically requires one to be sensitive and responsive to the other person *within* the circumstances and the context.

Within this theme of connectedness, we cannot avoid discussing relationships between the sexes. Here it is so important to be sensitive to the revolution going on in the redefinition of what constitutes masculinity and femininity. Since this revolution is still in its beginning stages, it would be premature to attempt to redefine an education that 'correctly' socializes young people into the possibilities and responsibilities involved in male–female relationships. Yet some attempt must be made, starting from the recognition that traditional definitions of male and female are distorting of the possibilities for both males and females, in their separate lives and for their lives in relationships with one another. No longer can education about the human be dominated by male categories and male frameworks.

The school agenda for both males and females requires the simultaneous attention to equity and to difference. Attention to equity requires that girls and boys have equal access to and encouragement in all programs in the schools. Attention to difference requires that girls and boys have opportunities for same-sex activities and for same-sex discussions of the social expectations of each sex role. It also requires appropriate cross-sex discussions of their differences and the issues and problems that flow from these differences. A variety of authors provide perspectives on either female or male developmental issues (Belenky, Clinchy, Goldberg, & Tarule, 1986; Gilligan, 1982; Hollway, 2006; Johnson, 1983, Jordan et al. 1991; Pearson, 1986; Sichtermann, 1986).

Attention to gender, circumstances, and context, however, calls our attention to the cultural scaffolding of all relationships. One does not act with another person according to a uniform, universal script. Rather, humans express themselves in relationships according to an infinite number of cultural artifacts and cultural signs (Chatwin 1987; Goffman, 1959; Green, 1985; Shils, 1981). The clothing one wears at various occasions, the language employed, the formality or informality one adopts—all these are culturally prescribed. Hence, acting ethically in any situation requires a knowledge of and respect for the culture one inhabits. Acting ethically means being sensitively connected to the values expressed by the sign and symbol system of that culture, for they make up the foreground and the background of relationships as they unfold. So it is not simply a question of one person in relation to another person; the relationship is supported as well as limited by the culture in which the two parties live their lives.

Every culture is a rich endowment, an enormous inheritance. It contains and expresses the history of a whole people over the course of many centuries: their struggles, their triumphs, their tragedies, their sense of heroism, their sense of failure, their ideals and their values. One acts ethically within that culture, within its possibilities and within its limits. No culture is perfect, no culture has finished its human journey. Hence the ethical person knows that the inheritance is also a burden. It has standards to be lived up to; it has standards to be surpassed; it has a bias against other cultures; it has a history of shameful behaviors as well as honorable behaviors; it has frontiers to be reached and perhaps expanded. Ethical persons, experiencing connectedness to their culture and to other persons, know that the culture sustains their lives, and that they have a responsibility to sustain the life of the culture. Sustaining that life happens in one's relationships and involves a kind of loyalty. Though the awareness is normally tacit, ethical persons approach one another as cultural beings, and yet because of the culture they share, they can approach each other in a discovery of uniqueness, where the humanity of the other person is discovered beyond, so to speak, cultural symbols, or as fresh embodiments of those symbols.

This adds, of course to the paradox of autonomy. One is autonomous, yet one's autonomy is as a cultural being. As one supported by that cultural life, one bears responsibilities to it, to uphold its honor, its ideals, and to pass on the best of that culture to the next generation. The autonomous cultural agent, however, is different from the unreflective cultural agent who is a slave to the culture, who cannot distinguish the shortcomings of the culture—for example, in the way it treats women, or peoples of certain other cultures. The autonomous cultural agent can be a critic of his or her culture and see that as an act of responsibility to the culture. For beyond culture, there is humanity, to which all cultures bear responsibility.

Ethical beings are also connected to their natural environment. That environment provides air to breathe, food to nourish, the raw materials for food and housing, transportation and industrial production. This connection to nature in the present has a long past as well. Every person contains in his or her genes, so to speak, the history of evolution and the effects of cosmic time. As beings embedded in nature, yet having enormous power to affect nature, we have responsibilities to preserve the natural world itself, not simply to ensure the survival of the human species (Macy, 1990). Unbounded human exploitation of nature seemed a human right not very long ago. Now we recognize that we have to be far more respectful of natural processes of a nature that is endangered. Our connectedness to the earth is now seen as bringing ethical obligations to preserve the earth (Augros & Stanciu, 1987; Bateson, 1979b; Macy, 1990; McKibben, 2010). Our connectedness to the race, in both evolutionary time and in the future, brings responsibilities both to our forebears and to our progeny.

We cannot leave this quality of connectedness without speaking of its political and social implications. In the United States, we happen to live in a democracy, which we are coming to realize is a fragile collage of many voices, many distinct communities. One view of democracy is that it is a society made up of separate individuals, each pursuing his or her own self-interest, joined together in a social contract which protects the rights of all individuals to pursue self-interest as long as it does not infringe on the rights of others. The problem with this view is that it ignores the real bonds that make life in the community morally compelling (Bellah et al., 1985).

Another view of democracy sees humans as inherently social, whose individual moral good is achieved and sustained only in community, through the bonds of blood to be sure, but also through the bonds of neighborliness, interdependence, and brotherly and sisterly affection. In this view, our humanity reaches its highest moral fulfillment in community. Without the relationships of community, which constitute not just necessary interdependencies, but also an intrinsic good, life would not be worth living. This is not to say that these relationships do not involve conflict, disloyalty, disagreement. But these relationships—even in conflict and struggle—define the context of human moral striving, the effort to agree on what constitutes our common good. Democratic political and social life does not guarantee a continuous experience of freedom, equality and brother/sisterhood; rather, those are the goals and purposes continually pursued in democratic give-and-take in public life. It is in being connected to that community with those very ideals, and the procedural rights and responsibilities that govern their pursuit, where we discover our truest moral selves (Sullivan, 1982).

In discussing 'conscience as membership', Green (1985) makes a point of fundamental educational importance to the formation of a sense of connectedness.

He speaks of the necessity of empathy. In any discussion of what the group or social collective should do, there will be differences of opinion. In order for a moral choice to emerge (not simply an arithmetical calculation of allowing the consequences of X's opinion and Y's opinion to be figured into the decision, nor a calculation of political favor-swapping) one has to engage seriously the perspective of others. This means entering into an empathetic appreciation of the value and legitimacy of those perspectives, a kind of taking those perspectives as if they were one's own in order to understand the reasoning and to feel the affective colorations embedded within them. For our purposes, this insight into the psychological and existential dynamic of empathy enables us to see how one gains a sense of connectedness. It is by entertaining the legitimacy of the claims and perspectives of others, by imaginatively taking the reality of the other inside ourselves and seeing how it feels to be that other in these circumstances. This applies to the experience of being connected to family and ethnic roots, to friends, to the environment, and to the civic community. This dynamic of empathy provides one clue to developing the quality of connectedness in an educational setting, a dynamic that involves both understanding and feeling, a kind of sympathetic knowing (Starratt, 1969).

Green, however, roots his foundation for moral education in the formation of a conscience of *membership*. If there is to be a strong sense of a public, a sense of a shared life together, a sense of concern for the common good, then citizens must learn to be bound by a strong sense of membership. Membership brings certain rights, but it also brings responsibilities. As was mentioned above, there is a strong sense of individualism within American culture. Often that sense ignores the notion of an "us;" it is more about *my* rights. Green rightfully insists that in our moral education, we continually position ethical obligations as connected both to individuals and to the group. If it were a good thing for John Doe to do such and such, would it not be a good thing for *us* in similar circumstances to do also? If something pertains to membership, ought it not to pertain to *our* membership? This issue will arise in later chapters concerning one's sense of moral identity, as well as concerning the moral character of learning.

Transcendence

Transcendence is a term that might frighten some people off. For some it signifies an attempt to climb above our humanity, to leave it behind in a journey toward some higher, more spiritual form of life. This seems to be the Platonic ideal, where the philosopher ascends through a process of spiritual purification and mental abstraction to grasp the eternal form, The Good. I am not using the term in this sense. Rather, it has for me three levels of meaning, one dealing with the reach for excellence, the other with the turning of one's life toward something or someone else, and the third with achieving something heroic.

On the first level, transcendence means going beyond the ordinary, beyond what is considered average. In this sense, it means striving for and achieving a level of excellence that exceeds anything one has ever done before. The standard of excellence will be relative both to the type of activity involved (playing the violin, or high jumping, or writing poetry) as well as the person involved (a physically uncoordinated person, a mature professional athlete, a sight-challenged person).

Transcendence on this level means a struggle to stretch the limits placed upon us by nature, to create a purer sound, to leap against gravity's pull, to see clear through to the essence of a feeling and capture it just so in the perfect metaphor. It is the struggle for the perfection of a human talent, and it is a struggle precisely because the possibilities of reaching that perfection, let alone of sustaining it, are limited by self-doubt and our very ordinariness as human beings (Nussbaum, 1990).

On another level, transcendence means going beyond self-absorption (which the search for excellence can sometimes promote) to engaging our lives with other people, whether to share their life journey with them, or to work with them towards some goal that benefits a group or society in some way or other. Transcendence in this sense also means going beyond the ordinary. By the very ordinary nature of our social existence, we have to make room for others in our lives. People often intrude at times when we wish they wouldn't, but we respond to them with polite tact, and go back to our project as soon as their intrusion is over. We learn to accommodate others, sometimes cheerfully, sometimes reluctantly. This is what minimal or ordinary social relations require. Transcending this level of social relations means taking on the burdens of others, caring for them, putting ourselves in their place—not once a month, but very often, if not habitually. It means anticipating their needs, surprising them with thoughtful gifts. It means finding our fulfillment in easing the burdens of others, making them laugh, helping them finish a project. This form of transcendence is clearly a foundation for the exercise of the ethic of care.

It also means being able to invest one's energies in a collective activity with others that serves some valued purpose beyond self-interest. That form of transcendence involves becoming a part of something larger than one's own life. Through that involvement one moves beyond an exclusive concern for one's own survival and necessities of life to an effort to serve a larger common good. That common good invests the actions of the individual with higher value, with higher moral quality.

As involvement with others becomes more total, it moves toward the third level of transcendence, which is what I call the heroic. One can invest one's energies in other people and in a cause—up to a point. At some point, people say to themselves, "OK that's enough for now. Now it's time for my life, my interests, my leisure and recreation." The more total involvement is the willingness to sacrifice some of what most people would say were one's legitimate rights to "time off," "time for oneself." Teachers who consistently stay late and arrive early in order to help out youngsters having difficulty with their school work, or just plain difficulty with life; social workers who consistently go the extra mile for their clients in getting them needed assistance; doctors who continue to spend quality time with their patients, listening to their anxieties; public officials who treat ordinary citizens with as much respect and courtesy as they do the "important people"; store managers who spend countless hours devising ways to improve staff morale and customer service—these are people who transcend the ordinary and embrace heroic ideals of making a difference in people's lives. The recognition of some of the great heroes, like Mother Theresa or Vaclav Havel, with public awards like the Nobel Prize does not belittle the significance of the more everyday expressions of heroism.

Heroism, like transcendence, is often misunderstood. Heroes, it is thought, are those rare exceptions to the rule of self-interest, to the norm of mediocrity. While it is true that heroes are outnumbered by the less-than-heroic, the desire for heroism is a common human trait. From our early childhood years onward, we ask, "What is the value of my life?" We demand to be recognized, as Ernest Becker (1971, p. 76) points out, "as an object of primary value in the universe. Nothing less." Becker recognizes this as a desire to be, in one way or another, a heroic contributor to the human journey, and that nothing less will satisfy us.

Our interpretation of what constitutes heroic action is, of course, mediated by our culture and subcultures through the symbolic values it attaches to some achievements. An Olympic gold medal, a scholarship to Oxford University, an Oscar-winning performance are all culturally significant, heroic activities. On a smaller stage, the neighborhood dominoes champion walks around his turf with heroic stride, for, in that ambiance, he is somebody to be reckoned with.

By claiming transcendence as a basic human quality we recognize that it is foundational to human moral striving. If this quality is not developed during youth and young adulthood, then a mature ethical life is simply not possible. Again, Green (1985) is helpful here in pointing to an educational source for nurturing this sense of transcendence, namely the great writers of imaginative literature. In conversations with these poets of the heroic, these prophets and utopians, youngsters are exposed to the images of possibilities for human life. By exposure to stories of great human striving, their own heroic aspirations are kindled; these exemplars provide models for possible imitation. Biographies of great leaders in history bring reality perspectives to frame the more utopian idealism of imagination. The point Green makes is important, however: our transcendent aspirations are nurtured in and through the heroic imagination.

When transcendence is joined with the qualities of autonomy and connectedness, we begin to see how the three qualities complement and feed each other in the building of a rich and integral human life. Being autonomous only makes sense when one's autonomy can be in relation to other autonomous persons, when the uniqueness and wealth of each person can be mutually appreciated and celebrated. Connectedness means that one is connected to someone or something different from oneself. Hence it requires an empathetic embrace of what is different for the autonomous actor to make and sustain the connection. Community enables the autonomous individual to belong to something larger; it gives the individual roots in both the past and the present. However the community is not automatically self-sustaining, but is sustained by autonomous individuals who transcend self-interest in order to promote the common good, who join with other individuals to recreate the community by offering satisfying and mutually fulfilling services for one another, services of protection and support, care and help, joint action on a common project, celebration of a common heritage, honoring a community tradition by connecting one's own story to the larger story of the community. This give-and-take of life in the community simultaneously depends on and feeds the heroic imagination of individuals whose action, in turn, gives new life to the community.

Although we speak of these three foundational qualities of an ethical person in a somewhat abstract way, we don't want to think of them as a list of virtues that we set out to acquire. We are speaking of an ethical *person* who has a unity and integrity, whose actions reveal qualities that shine out as from a diamond. These qualities of an ethical person, however, do not fall from the sky. They are developed in action, through choices that are acted upon. These qualities are never achieved as an acquisition. They are always to be found in the action of specific persons in this moment, in these circumstances, with these people, and hence never perfectly or fully expressed. They are achieved only in the doing and in the doing-constantly-repeated (Meilaender, 1984).

What I have described above is more like an ideal type of person. This person rarely if ever exists in perfect form. Most of the time human beings reflect imperfect efforts in the direction of truly autonomous, connected and transcending actions. The ideal type, however, serves a purpose. It points to an ideal we try to reach. It also provides a guide for those who would educate toward ethical living. By providing opportunities for youngsters to exercise autonomy, connectedness, and transcendence, educators enable youngsters to experience the fulfillment and satisfaction of the way of being human. They learn the lesson that living ethically is the fulfillment of their human nature.

If these qualities are foundational in a developing ethical person, then an ethical school will be concerned to nurture those qualities and discourage the development of their opposite qualities. Hence, teachers need to reflect on how they can use the everyday activities of youngsters in their classroom and other areas around the school to nurture these qualities. Of course, youngsters develop in recognizable patterns, so that what might be appropriate for a ten-year-old may not be appropriate for a sixteen-year-old. How one nurtures the sense of transcendence in kindergarten would differ from an approach taken in seventh grade. The three qualities can be supported in every grade, however, in ways that are suitable for the children, but it would be a mistake to expect all the children to manifest these qualities in the same way. Sex, race, culture, and class will all nuance the child's expression of autonomy, connectedness, and transcendence. Class-bound and ethnocentric teachers will have difficulty with such varied expressions. The sensitive teacher will observe the different expressions and listen to youngsters explain their behavior. Over time such teachers will be able to promote these qualities within an appropriate range of plurality and diversity.

This chapter has explored the human qualities that form a foundation for ethical maturity. Recognizing that young people in school are in those formative years before adulthood, before they will be held accountable by the community to act ethically, we can see how the nurturing of these qualities in young people begin to prepare them for the responsibilities of adulthood. Teachers should be expected to model these qualities in their professional practice. The academic, social and civic curriculum of the school should engage the development of these qualities. Moreover, the school as public institution should exhibit adult ethical standards. These standards would be considered as general ethical standards expected of adults in their everyday lives. In the next chapter we will look at some of the schools of thought that deal with what might be considered general ethics, the ethics of adult daily living. The cultivation of an ethical school involves the adults in the school in teaching these general ethical principles by example. As we will see in the next chapter, there are some disputes among scholars of ethics about what constitutes the core or essential ethical concerns of general ethics. Educators attempting to cultivate an ethical school should come to some agreements about how to frame ethical questions so as to deal with ethical issues that arise in the daily practice of conducting schools.

References

Augros, R.M. & Stanciu, G.N. (1987). *The new biology: Discovering the wisdom in nature.* Boston: New Science Library.
Bateson, G. (1979). *Steps to an ecology of mind.* New York: Ballantine Books.
Becker, E. (1968). *The structure of evil.* New York: The Free Press.
Becker, E. (1971). *The birth and death of meaning* (2nd ed.). New York: The Free Press.
Belinkey, M.F., Clinchy, B.M., Goldberg, N.R., & Tarule, J.M. (1986). *Women's ways of knowing: The development of self, voice, and mind.* New York: Basic Books.
Bellah, R.N., Madsen, R., Sullivan, W.M., Swidler, A, & Tipton, S.M. (1985). *Habits of the heart: Individualism and commitment in American life.* Berkeley, CA: University of California Press.
Buber, M. (1958). *I and thou* (2nd. ed.). Trans by R. G. Smith. New York: Scribners.
Chatwin, B. (1987). *Songlines.* New York: Penguin Books.
Dewey, J. (1927). *The public and its problems.* New York: Henry Holt Company.
Gilligan, C. (1982). *In a different voice: Psychological theory and women's development.* Cambridge, MA: Harvard University Press.
Goffman, E. (1959). *The presentation of self in everyday life.* Garden City, NY: Doubleday.
Green, T.F. (1985). The formation of conscience in an age of technology. American Journal of Education, 93 (1), pp. 1–38.
Hallowell, E.M. (1999). *Connect.* New York: Pantheon Books.
Hollway, W. (2006). *The capacity to care: Gender and ethical subjectivity.* London: Routledge.
Johnson, (1983). *He: Understanding masculine psychology.* San Francissco: Harper & Row.
Jordan:J. et al. (1991). *Women's growth in connection: Writings from the Stone Center.* New York: Guilford Press.
Macy, J. (1990). The ecological self: Postmodern ground for rightful action. In Griffin, D.R. (Ed.), *Sacred interconnections: Post-modern spirituality*, political economy and art.
McKibben, W. (2010). *Earth: Making a life on a tough new planet.* New York: Time Books.
Meilaender, G.C. (1984). *The theory and practice of virtue.* NotreDame, IN: University of Notre Dame Press.
Nussbaum, M. (1990). *Transcending humanity. Love's knowledge: Essays on philosophy and literature.* New York: Oxford University Press.
Pearson, C. (19860). *The hero within us: Six archetypes we live by.* San Francisco: Harper & Row.
Scheler, M. (1957). *The nature of sympathy.* London: Toutledge & Kegan Paul.
Shils, E. (1981). *Tradition.* Chicago: University of Chicago Press.
Sichtermann, B. (1986). *Femininity: The politics of the personal.* Trans. by John Whitlam. Minneapolis, MN: University of Minnesota Press.
Starratt, R.J. (1969). The individual and the educated imagination: An essay in curriculum theory. Unpublished doctoral dissertation. Department of Educational Administration. University of Illinois, Champaign/Urbana, IL.
Sullivan, W.M. (1982). *Reconstructing public philosophy.* Berkeley, CA: University of California Press.

CHAPTER NINE

The moral dimension of human resource development

Introduction

This chapter attempts to map out a framework for understanding the moral dimension of human resource development in education. While acknowledging the usefulness of both the more traditional ethical analyses of educational administration (Strike, Haller, & Soltis, 1998; Maxcy, 2002; Nash, 2002), and more recent attempts to open up more synthetic and late modern perspectives (Starratt, 1991; Haynes, 1998; Furman, 2003; Shapiro & Stefkovich, 2001), this chapter attempts to name a deeper substratum of moral issues at the core of the educating process which call forth specific, proactive, moral responses from human resource leaders. Working with a more focused attention to the specific ethics of the professional practice of educating in a formal schooling context—that is, beyond the use of general ethical frameworks of justice, care, and critique—enables the development of a vocabulary and a series of analytic lenses for human resource developers to name their experiences as they face the moral challenges of leadership within the present context of their schools.

The virtues of human resource leadership in education

In the field of ethics, one school of thought prefers to focus on ethical virtues rather than on ethical principles or ethical rules (Hursthouse, 1999; Walker & Ivanhoe, 2007). Virtue ethics focus more on the seeking of a moral good rather than avoiding a moral evil. Frequently, the virtue is the positive side of the negative activity prohibited by a rule: the virtue of honesty or truth-telling is the positive side of the negative activity of lying. This chapter will emphasize specific virtues of moral leadership within the profession of formal education, rather than the abstract principles intended to regulate ethical violations.

In the field of ethics, one finds a distinction between general ethics and applied, professional ethics. General ethics as it would be found in education deals more with the ethics of everyday life as that gets played out in the lives of most people in whatever context they find themselves. In the context of schools, general ethics involves issues around fairness, truth telling, respect, equity, negotiating conflict and misunderstandings, and correcting structural injustices embedded in the organizational arrangements of the school. Employing frameworks from the ethics of justice, care, and critique enables educators to name those general moral issues that face people in all walks of life and in all professions (Starratt, 1991). Applied or professional ethics has much more to do with the ethics of the profession *as a profession*. Part of professional ethics is about preventing harm in the practice of the profession. Often codes of professional ethics state what professionals should not do in their practice of their profession. Part of that ethics is about promoting the "good" essential to the practice of the profession. Medical ethics is concerned with promoting the good of its professional practice, which is physical health. Business ethics is supposed to be concerned with promoting the public and individual good involved in trade, commerce, and contracts. What is the good that the profession of education is supposed to pursue, promote, support? It is the good of learning. And what is the good of learning? It is the good of discovering, naming, constructing oneself as one is formally and systematically introduced to the natural, cultural, and social worlds that constitute one's public "situatedness," as well as learning the rights and responsibilities of being a member of those worlds. The good of learning implies coming to understand how and why to participate as citizens of those worlds. Moral educational leadership then means the proactive pursuit, cultivation, and support of those goods of learning in and for a humane community and polity. Those goods are intrinsic to the practice of formal education (Starratt, 2007).

Scholars have done a reasonably good job of describing the general ethics of educational leadership (e.g., Strike, Haller, & Soltis, 1998; Nash, 2002), but not a good enough job of describing what the proactive pursuit of those goods of learning might look like. Involved in that proactive pursuit one practices the virtues associated with the professional practice of educating. Those virtues of the practice of educating reflect leadership virtues. Here we focus on three that seem especially pertinent to the professional work of formal schooling: authenticity, presence, and responsibility (Starratt, 2004). We have already introduced the virtue of responsibility and the virtue of authenticity in much of what has preceded, but a brief recapitulation may serve to clarify our focus.

The virtue of authenticity

As we have seen in earlier chapters, authenticity is a necessary virtue for teachers to practice in their professional lives. Authenticity implies being true to oneself, owning oneself in one's professional practice, in one's working relationships. When others are in the presence of authentic people, they sense that these people speak themselves truly—that is, they are as they appear to be; there is little contrivance about them; they are relatively transparent and not afraid to be so. By and large, when they are with people, others are comfortable being authentic themselves.

The virtue of authenticity implies that being authentic is a good in itself; authentic people are more human than inauthentic people. Inauthentic people somehow have not reached a level of maturity in their humanness that authentic people have. Being authentic does not mean being perfect; rather, it means owning and accepting oneself with whatever talents and whatever limitations and imperfections one has. It also means being "upfront" in one's relationships, being present to the other person, being *there* in the now of the moment.

Being authentic in one's social and professional roles also implies a good in itself. Being an authentic father, an authentic neighbor usually implies being a good father, a good neighbor—again, not necessarily perfect, but one whose efforts, despite shortcomings, are sincere and well meaning. In one's profession or career, one can function authentically or inauthentically. One can be a careless auto mechanic or building inspector whose work lacks certain skills and understanding necessary to do reliable work. When these are joined to an attitude of not caring, of not taking pride in the work, then others will remark, "He's not a *real* mechanic." "She's a *bogus* building inspector." Likewise with the profession of teaching—some are recognized as authentic teachers, others as inauthentic. In teaching, being an authentic teacher involves the following competencies: a good understanding of the material being taught, a professional mastery of a variety of pedagogical strategies, as well as caring relationships with learners. Much the same holds for educational administrators: some have the capacities for administrative educational work which, when suffused with their personal authenticity, enables a veteran teacher to say, "Now that's what I call a *good* administrator; she knows what she's doing, she understands the complexities and demands of the classroom, she really listens to our stories, and doesn't promise what she can't deliver." Clearly, there are connections between authenticity in one's personal life and in one's professional life. However, authenticity in one's work requires levels of job-related competencies beyond those expected in private life.

One's sense of authenticity as a professional, however, is not a static, uniform thing. As we saw in chapter 2, one's sense of oneself changes as one moves through various life-cycle challenges, leaving one with new challenges to integrate earlier stages into more mature expressions of trust, autonomy, initiative, industry, identity, and so forth. As one grows as a teacher or administrator, one recognizes that the challenge of generativity in that professional role involves taking on new initiatives, acquiring new skills and understanding through various initiatives of trial and error on the job, industrious application in graduate programs and professional seminars, and developing one's professional identity within the challenges of accountability for responding to state mandates and policies.

Thus, one's own sense of being an authentic educator sometimes is called into question as one continues to respond to new challenges. One has to be able to look at oneself in the mirror every day and take stock of how much more there is to learn, how better to respond to the remains of yesterday's crisis, how to reach the person who always seems to disagree with the direction the school is moving in. As Richard Elmore suggests, a good human resource leader does not pronounce judgment on the work accomplished, but always asks, "What more remains to be attended to in this work?" (Elmore, 2008).

In this sense, one can never take one's authenticity for granted. It is always something to be validated in each day's adventures. Furthermore, one is not always happy with the day's performance of oneself; for the authentic person, that leads to greater self-knowledge and becomes tomorrow's challenge. For authentic educators, the challenge of authenticity is not so much about boosting one's self-esteem; rather it is about *attending authentically to the good* of the communal work of teaching and learning. The authentic educator lives with the daily challenge of effecting that good, despite institutional and personal limitations.

The authentic human resource developer, then, is a person who supports, stimulates, and activates the human resources that those in their charge bring to the work of learning. Through authentic involvement in promoting the good of their work, the human resource administrator practices the leadership virtue of authenticity. Reflecting back on the earlier chapters, we can now understand that the involvement in all the earlier dimensions of human resource development (human, organizational, professional, political) has a moral side to it. Through the practice of the virtue of authenticity, the human resource administrator enriches and deepens the work in the other dimensions of the work.

The practice of the virtue of presence in human resource leadership

The virtue of presence requires a somewhat lengthier treatment since it involves a vocabulary seldom used in the literature about education, or, indeed, in the literature about ethics. As we will see, it is both a psychological disposition as well as a virtue acquired through moral discipline.

Being fully present means being wide awake to what's in front of us. It could be another person, a passage in a book, a memorandum one is composing to the staff, a flower on one's desk. Being present is like inviting a person or an event to communicate or reveal something of itself. We cannot be present to the other if the other is not present to us; the other's presence must somehow say, this is who I am, this is what I am feeling about this situation, this is the part of me that I want you to really consider right now.

Being present means taking the other inside ourselves, looking at the other really closely, listening to the tone of the other, the body language of the other. This being present is also an unspoken message to the other that one is there, attending to the other's message, responding to the other from one's own spontaneous authenticity. Being present means coming down from the balcony where one was indifferently watching others' performance, and engaging them now with a full attention and risking the spontaneity of the moment to say something unrehearsed, something that *responds* to the authenticity of the other from your own authenticity.

This way of being present does not mean that one disregards the organizational context that colors every situation. Nor does it ignore the organizational roles one is called upon to act out. It does mean, nevertheless, that it is an exchange between human beings whose lives spill over beyond the boundaries of the organization and the organizational roles they play. The risk of spontaneous exchange does not assume that the exchange is free from all boundaries. Rather, the exchange tacitly acknowledges those organizational boundaries as well as societal cultural boundaries, but seeks within those constraints something genuine, something authentic between two human beings. What their meeting enacts, while subjected to the artifice of all social exchange, is a human work, something that provides some kind of support and satisfaction, along with dignity and honor.

People are present both as who they are and the roles they perform; they are present to the other in the ways they read the language, posture, gesture of the other as signaling what is going on inside. Professional people, whether architects, lawyers, doctors, sociologists, grammarians, literary critics, psychologists, biochemists, mathematicians, and airport security personnel, are trained to be present to the insides of things. They see the surface and discern the inner structures, processes, histories, aspirations and values. In fact, being present is a form of knowing (Polanyi, 1966). It is also a form of disclosing, of invitation, of communication and communion. Being present disposes one to act in response to the other, due to the knowledge communicated by mutual presence of one to the other.

We are present to something as who we are. If we are bigoted, we are present to something whose presence for us is already distorted by our bigotry. We are also present with our human history. Sometimes that presence involves ineradicable memories of sexual abuse in childhood, sometimes memories of a childhood in a loving family, sometimes memories of a lifetime of discrimination. How the other is present to us depends on our predisposition to be present to the other in a certain way, and our predisposition to allow the other to be present to us.

Does this being more fully present require something of us? It certainly does. It requires us to remove ourselves from occupying the center of the universe. It requires a certain self-displacement, letting others enter our space, monitoring our tendency to judge on first impressions, listening attentively to what the person is trying to or needs to say, and then actively engaging that person in authentic conversation. Such proactive presence flows out of some tacit awareness that this is the way humans are supposed to treat one another, that this way of relating to one another is something that sets humans apart from everything else in the universe. Our presence contributes to and enhances the human and natural energy in our surroundings.

There is a negative ethical obligation to presence and a positive proactive ethical obligation to presence. That is, we are under an implicit moral imperative to be present to the people and things around us. Being half-present may very easily be the cause of harm to another, whether we are driving a car, making a joke, making love, keeping accounts, or teaching. We have a negative obligation to avoid being half-present. There is also a proactive sense in which being present is expected of us if we are to be authentic and if we are to be responsible. Being present enables, indeed, encourages us to be authentic and to be responsible. Our presence activates our authenticity and the authenticity of others. That is why this kind of presence is a virtue: it produces good.

There are three ways of being present that suggest an ethical dynamic for educational leaders as human resource developers: an affirming presence, a critical presence, and an enabling presence.

Affirming presence

Affirming presence involves foregrounding an attitude of unconditional regard for the person or persons you are working with. It means that you acknowledge them as they present themselves, not as you would like them to be, or not to be. It means not only holding them interiorly in high regard, but also explicitly telling them that in a variety of ways. More than anything, the message will be picked up quite clearly in the leader's actions. Those actions will communicate the following unequivocal messages: Each and every person enjoys an intrinsic dignity and worth; we expect people to reach out and help one another here; we believe that every person has an abundance of talents and good ideas and, given some encouragement, will enrich the life of the community.

The work of learning provides the underlying institutional context for an affirming presence. The school is a public institution serving the community with a mission of educating all children to the best of their ability. Thus, the affirming presence of the human resource leader is an affirmation in the context of the common commitment of the community to work together to promote a quality learning environment for all of the students. Within that mission, teachers, counselors, students, parents, nurses, social workers, custodians, secretaries, bus drivers, cafeteria workers, and others bring their human talents and skills to the work of that mission. The work of learning, however, is not engaged by robots, each performing in a pre-programmed function. Learners are human beings engaged in very risky work, the daily work of overcoming ignorance and confusion and obsolete understandings. It is risky work because, in the process, fragile human beings are potentially exposed to embarrassment, ridicule, and humiliation in the public forum of the classroom as they struggle to grasp what the teacher and the curriculum is asking of them. For teachers still mastering their craft, there is the risky business of looking like a bungler in front of the principal visiting their classroom. The institutional context of the work of learning, which itself carries intrinsically moral overtones (Starratt, 2003), requires an institutionally grounded ethical demand for an affirming presence. In order for the work of learning as a *human work* to flourish, it demands an affirming presence.

Within such an educating community, everyone is affirmed; the metaphor of family is invoked; celebrations of achievement are visible all around the school; photographs of teams of teachers and teams of students involved in a variety of projects adorn the school bulletin boards. When people in the school are in the presence of one another, even on bad days, there is clear evidence of respect, humor, sharing of ideas and criticisms, shouted greetings, plenty of "thank you," "good work!" and "we need to talk about that."

Almost always, the affirming presence of the human resource leader generates an affirming presence among the staff and students. However, the affirming leader will also attempt to build in structures and processes and rituals within the school week, month, or semester for the community to express affirmation for one another and for the continuing development of a strong sense of community. Sometimes that involves a more formally structured process for communicating with parents; sometimes a student forum for airing grievances and seeking reconciliation among conflicted groups within the school; sometimes a series of sharing sessions with the teachers' union officers; sometimes a faculty musical comedy depicting the foibles of the adults in the school. However those rituals are expressed, one thing will be constant: the affirming presence of leaders throughout the building, greeting others, encouraging, cheerleading, supporting, and consoling.

Enabling presence

A second form of ethical presence flows from the affirming form of ethical presence. Through enabling presence one responds to the possibilities and the predicaments of the other, and explores the enabling aspects of situations and arrangements. An enabling presence starts with the premise: I can't do it alone; you can't do it alone; but together *we* can do it. An enabling presence signifies that one brings oneself fully into the situation with the other person. Again, the institutional setting of the school with all its limitations as well as potential, its constraints and its capacities contextualizes every situation.

Sometimes that enabling presence is predominantly a listening presence in which a teacher or parent needs to explain a problem or propose an idea that could be adopted by the school. In that case, an enabling presence communicates both a respect for the other, as well as a confidence that the other already may have the answer they are seeking, but needs to explore its dimensions more explicitly. An enabling presence also has to trust the good judgment of the other in the process of letting them try out something that is quite new to the school. The enabling leader also communicates a mutual taking of responsibility for the risks involved, and therefore the need to surround new ideas with the appropriate safeguards and institutional supports.

In other circumstances, an enabling presence might be more proactive, encouraging teachers to look at various examples of research-grounded best practices that might be adapted to their own teaching-learning environments. Some administrators' enabling presence leads to a more institutionalized practice of teacher-leadership committees, where teachers are supported in their efforts to establish project teams of peers who will explore new technologies of instruction, new assessment techniques, and the development of in-house rubrics for looking at student work. Taking it further, some administrators' enabling presence will encourage groups of students to develop their own initiatives around peer tutoring, new aspects of student government, or student-led ways to resolve conflicts among the student body.

This kind of enabling presence is concerned with capacity-building. In the national emphasis on school improvement and accountability, capacity-building appears at the top of administrators' agenda (Adams & Kirst, 1999, Elmore, 2008). Capacity-building, however, is not simply a bureaucratic matter of policy implementation. It is also a matter of deep conviction about the ways human beings ought to be present to one another, and about bringing that conviction into the institutional setting of the school whether or not the state policy makers think it is a good idea.

The leader's enabling presence takes account of the institutional mission and the institutional constraints and possibilities of schools. An enabling presence, however, also brings an affirming presence, a spirit of openness to others, a welcoming of people as who they are: a mix of talents and interests, of hopes and fears, of strengths and fragilities. What is possible for the school, for teachers, and for students will be constrained by institutional policies and resources, to be sure; but those constraints can be trans formed into possibilities, and those possibilities enlarged, by the creativity and talent of the teachers and students who feel affirmed.

The leader's enabling presence will have to attend to building specific capacities among the teachers, given the agenda of school reform. Those capacities include the developing of greater diagnostic sensitivity to how children learn and do not learn; a greater attentiveness to the so-called low achieving students in order to unlock their learning potential and to provide those institutional supports they need in order to improve; a more careful calibration of school rubrics for assessment; a more diversified approach to teaching reflective thinking and creativity; a more careful familiarity with diverse cultures in order to bring insights from those cultures into the classroom to enrich the learning of all.

On the other hand, the leader's enabling presence should also encourage a much greater development of the creativity of each teacher to enliven his or her classroom for learning. Even the so-called school improvement capacity-building lists can be carried out in the same deadening classroom pedagogies. To be sure, teachers are not in the entertainment business. But classrooms definitely need an enormous infusion of imagination, humor, and adventure to enliven the learning process. Rationality is a good thing, but humans are not simply logic machines. They need to perceive the underlying drama in life, the beauty and the pathos, the mystery and the complexity of the world in order to be attracted to studying the world. Teachers who bring an enabling presence into the classroom will explore with their students how to make the classroom learning come alive. They won't be satisfied with one new teaching strategy. They will keep coming back until the classrooms bubble over with excitement and enthusiasm. That enthusiasm will be fed by teachers and students exploring how to apply their learning to issues and concerns of the local community.

Leaders with an enabling presence will develop what is known as a spirit of efficacy among the teachers and students (Ashton & Webb, 1986). That spirit signifies that teachers, both individually and collectively, grow to believe that there is no student that they cannot reach in some significant way or other, that there is no pedagogical problem that they cannot find reasonable solutions to, when they collectively put their minds and imaginations to work. A spirit of efficacy is not a Pollyannaish claim of omnipotence; rather, it is a pragmatic understanding that every situation can be improved, not to perfection of course, but increasingly improved over time. Similarly, the enabling presence of administrators and teachers can lead students to develop an increasing attitude of efficacy, of "I can do this" or "we can do this." This is not to deny the reality of temporary failure. But the efficacious attitude toward learning expects to learn from failure and to make improvements the next time around.

By contrast, the administrator who is half-present to teachers and students comes to accept average performance as good enough, to be satisfied that the school is performing well if the teachers are at the front of the room and the students are in their seats, there are no fights in the cafeteria, and the football team wins some of their games. The half-present administrator fails to see how much time is being wasted every day, students' time being wasted by boring classes, teachers' time being wasted filling out forms and attending meetings where teaching and learning are trivialized into bits and pieces. The half-present administrator fails to see the enormous potential residing in every teacher and every student, a potential that is anesthetized every day by school routines that ensure a modicum of control and a minimum of commitment to the work of learning. The enabling administrator brings an enormous reservoir of hope and expectation to encounters with teachers and students, asking questions like, "Is that all you expect of the students?" "Is that all you expect from going to school?" "Is that all we expect of ourselves?" Those questions suggest that sometimes an enabling presence becomes a critical presence.

Critical presence

Critical presence is a form of presence that calls attention to expectations regarding the work. Critical presence, therefore, need not be negative. Critical presence also calls attention to a good performance, very much like the theater critic will do in reviewing a good acting performance. Teachers and students need to know that their work meets and exceeds expected standards. Human resource leaders will be generous in their commendations of good work, letting teachers and students know that they are present to quality performances.

The opposite side of a good performance, however, is a mediocre or poor performance, and the human resource leader does not shrink from identifying what appear to be problematic parts to the performance. In being critically present in this way, however, the human resource leader will be sensitive to the person's human need for self-esteem, and encourage the teacher or student to reflectively evaluate those weak parts of the performance, more by asking questions than by pronouncing judgments.

Another aspect of critical presence involves interpersonal misunderstandings and conflicts. A critical presence in an encounter with the other can work in two directions—in a critical appraisal of oneself as the cause of a blockage to authentic communication because of some real or perceived harm to the other; or in a critical appraisal of something in the other's presence that blocks a mutual ability to communicate authentically. Critical presence attempts to name the problem that stands between the two parties. Naming of the problem, however, should not be one-sided. Both parties have to be present to the other, to listen to each other present its case, and then see what the situation asks of both.

Critical presence should not be a haphazard occurrence. It should be an enduring predisposition that acknowledges ahead of time the reality of messes that humans make—interpersonal, institutional, and policy messes. Critical presence is not based on cynicism, but rather on compassion and hope for the human condition. It is based on compassion for a humanity that aspires to high ideals, yet whose fragility and vulnerability lead to overestimating possibilities or to shrinking back in fear of the risks involved. It is based on hope, for humans have demonstrated time and again a resilience that transforms oppressive situations into a courageous response of the human spirit to create new possibilities. Finally, it is based on an enduring sense of responsibility to make the core work of the school—teaching and learning—work for the benefit of young people.

Another crucial aspect of critical presence involves a critique of structural arrangements in the school that privilege some and disadvantage others. Examples of such structural arrangements include a one-size-fits-all set of textbooks; a one-size fits-all daily class schedule, weekly schedule, semester schedule, and assessments; a one-size-fits-all opportunity to learn the material that will be tested. These arrangements guarantee a predictable percentage of academic "failures," those who are euphemistically labeled "underperforming," and a predictable percentage of successful students whose home education mostly accounts for their readiness to succeed in school (Coleman, 1966).

Human resource leaders, critically present to these structural arrangements, work to provide differentiated instruction, use a variety of curriculum materials, provide various time frames for learning, try to connect the learning tasks to life experiences of the learner, establish collaborative learning groups, create collaboration with parents and caregivers to support learning at home (Starratt, 2003). Critical presence to disadvantaging conditions at the school leads to a proactive taking of responsibility to counteract and to change those conditions.

The virtue of responsibility in human resource leadership

We want to remind ourselves that we are speaking of the virtue of responsibility within the perspective of applied ethics, that is, the ethics that pertain to the profession of education. As such, the ethical virtue of responsibility relentlessly urges the professional to promote the moral good of learning: the development of the fullest humanity of the individual learner. The virtue of responsibility can be understood in both a negative sense and a positive sense. From the negative perspective, a human resource leader would be responsible to prevent or correct anything in the school that would impede the learning process. Often, educational administrators believe that they have fulfilled their moral responsibilities when they have provided for adequate safety and security measures in the school, when the students and teachers can go about their daily routines without fear of violence or other disruptions due to breakdowns in the functioning of the school facilities. Other administrators would add that their professional and moral responsibilities also include providing for an equal opportunity for all students to use the resources provided by the school (such as library facilities, computers, science labs).

Under stricter accountability policies in the United States, educators are now asked to assume even greater responsibility, namely, the responsibility to see that all students achieve passing grades on state administered tests. From this perspective, human resource administrators have specific responsibilities to hire and develop teachers who know the material in the curriculum in sufficient depth so as to understand the multiple applications of the curriculum standards towards which the state tests are targeted. Furthermore, these teachers are expected to scaffold learning activities to enable learners to translate the subject matter into terminology and examples that their younger, less mature minds and imaginations can comprehend. Thus, one can begin to discern that there is a moral responsibility of the human resource administrator, precisely as an educator, to hire competent teachers, and to monitor and cultivate the development of their practice of teaching (Sergiovanni & Starratt, 2006).

The moral responsibility of the human resource leader, however, goes farther than that. It involves a proactive moral responsibility to see that the learning achieved by learners in the school is itself authentic learning, namely "real" learning, not make-believe, superficial learning. Learning becomes real when it blossoms into an insightful connection to the intelligibility of a piece of the world—when the world speaks back to the learner, when the learner can say, "So *this* is what you are; so *this* is how you work; so *this* is why I should pay attention to you; so *this* is what you have to say to me." Involved in that insight is the insight, at least tacit into her or himself as being in *this* kind of intelligible relationship to *this* piece of the world. Educators captured by a sense of responsibility to nurture the good of learning will not stop trying to nudge the learner into insight until the learner looks up with a glow in her face and triumphantly announces, "I get it! I see what you've been trying to get me to see." This is the moral good which the responsible educator proactively promotes (Starratt, 1998, 2007).

The activity of attempting to learn should respect the integrity of what one is seeking to know. The learner should not approach the study of something superficially or carelessly, for that violates the intrinsic integrity of what is being studied. If the learner consciously misrepresents what he is supposed to have learned, then there is a violation not only of the integrity of what one is studying, but also the integrity of the learning process itself. This is most obvious in the case of an ideological reduction of facts to one dogmatic, or self-promoting interpretation—as may be found in politics, accounting, and warfare. The more subtle case involves the impersonal representation of someone else's right answers to test questions where one has no personal investment in the knowledge one is regurgitating.

Educators who fail to insist on the integrity of knowledge with their students can be accused of a kind of ethical laxity. Those who simply gear the work of teaching and learning to the achievement of high scores on tests, with little or no regard for the lasting meaning and significance of the subject matter, are teaching at best a superficial pursuit of knowledge and at worst a meretricious mistreatment of knowledge which empties the pursuit of knowledge of all but a crassly functional and self-serving purpose. That is to encourage a continuous violation of the integrity of learning and is, as such, a prostitution of the learning process. As that metaphor implies, the student is taught to feign learning to please those in authority—teachers, parents, politicians—in exchange for the coin of the realm in schools, namely, grades.

Human resource leaders also need to attend to this ethical enactment of responsibility. It is their responsibility to see that the teaching and learning going on in the classroom does not violate the content and process of learning, that learning and teaching is indeed of a high level of ethical enactment. That means a commitment through the hiring, evaluation and professional development procedures that (a) teachers will know well the curriculum they are expected to teach; (b) they will know how to communicate that curriculum in a variety of ways that enable youngsters to comprehend and appreciate many facets of what they are studying; (c) they will know their students well, and therefore can scaffold the learning tasks to respond to the background, interests, and prior experience of their students; and (d) they will insist that students take away from their learning important life lessons that will shape how they look upon the natural, cultural, and social worlds, and appreciate their own human adventure more deeply because of their studies. By cultivating these aspects of teaching and learning throughout the school, human resource leaders will be fully enacting the virtue of responsibility as educators.

Another perspective on the moral dimension of human resource leadership has to do, as was implied in chapter four, with their actual and potential influence on the organizational structures and processes of the school. The human resource leader, with a focus on improving the conditions of work for the primary human resources in the school—the learners—has access to the levers of organizational decisions concerning structures and processes that affect the core work of teaching and learning. These structures and processes are not ethically neutral. They either promote the integrity of the core work of the school—authentic learning—or they curtail or block the integrity of authentic learning. Often they do both at the same time. That is, they work to the advantage of some students, and to the disadvantage of other students.

Teacher evaluation schemes are another example of how many schools use a one-size-fits-all process to reward some teachers and to intimidate or frustrate others (Danielson & McGreal, 2000; Sergiovanni & Starratt, 2002). Some teacher evaluation schemes sustain intimidating power relationships that routinely issue negative or paternalistic judgments from superiors. Veteran teachers and administrators are resigned to the evaluation process as a burdensome bureaucratic task. One problem with many evaluation schemes is that they are such a colossal waste of time for everyone involved. Danielson and McGreal present, by contrast, a comprehensive teacher evaluation system that attempts to actually benefit both teachers and students. Their system is particularly sensitive to the ethical treatment of allegedly ineffective teachers by imposing obligations on the school system to show that it has done its part in providing generous remediation support to the teachers so classified.

The subtle bias in the various classifications of some children as special education children (Hehir, 2002), the tracking of students into dead end, low expectation programs (Oakes, 1985), the scheduling of the "best" teachers in honors classes and the least experienced teachers into the lowest performing classes—the list of organizational arrangements that disadvantage students in schools can go on and on. These are human inventions, not arrangements of divine decree. They can be changed by educational administrators so that more and more students have a better chance in schools. Human resource administrators who refuse to risk changing the organizational structures and processes in schools might be accused of ethical laziness in the face of the evidence of how these arrangements discriminate against some or, indeed, most of the students.

Human resource leaders want to transform the school as an organization of rules and regulations and roles into a much more intentional self-governing community. In such a community, initiative and an interactive spontaneity will infuse bureaucratic procedures with human and professional values. Such idealism does not ignore the need for organizational supports and boundaries. This leadership is compassionate and expects messes, but uses the mess as a learning opportunity rather than a self-righteous occasion for punishment.

At this level, the human resource leader has to be much more proactive than reactive. The human resource leader now focuses less on what should be avoided or prohibited and more about the ideals that should be sought, more on actively creating enhanced opportunities for human fulfillment of teachers and students through the work they co-produce. This is a distinctive, value-added moral leadership. It is a dimension that is often ignored in scholarly treatments of human resource administration in education. This kind of moral human resource leadership enhances the resources of a community of teachers and learners who are transforming the mundane work of learning into something that engages the deeper meanings behind the drama of the human adventure, meanings that implicate them in that adventure.

Summary

This chapter has conducted an exploration of important moral virtues of human resource leaders. We can see how these virtues challenge the human maturity of leaders, and at the same time how those virtues invite a reciprocal response from those in their charge. The exercise of these virtues in the professional work of these leaders reveals the human significance, indeed the beauty of adult human interaction to which that work can aspire. The impact of these kinds of adult models on the young learners can be especially profound. The kind of community that can be formed by a culture of authenticity, presence, and responsibility can itself be a form of teaching that the young learners absorb and imitate in their own relationships. The constant, formative examples of leaders throughout the system enacting these virtues, when combined with their influence on the professional development of their colleagues, and linking those two dimensions to the visionary focus of the leadership team presents a powerful model of this different kind of leadership.

References

Adams, J.E. & Kirst, M.W. (1999). New demands and concepts for educational accountability: Striving for results in an era of excellence. In J. Murphy & K. Seashore Louis (Eds.), *Handbook of research on educational administration* (pp. 463–489). San Francisco: Jossey-Bass.
Ashton, P.T. & Webb, R.B. (1986). *Making a Difference: Teachers' sense of efficacy and student achievement*. New York: Longman.
Coleman, J.S. (1966). *Equality of Educational Opportunity*. Washington, DC: Office of Education, National Center for Educational Statistics.
Danielson, C. & McGreal, T.L. (2000). *Teacher evaluation: To enhance professional practice*. Alexandria, VA: Association for Supervision and Curriculum Development.
Elmore, R. F. (2008). Improving the instructional core. Retrieved from http://www.iowa.gov/educate/ecpd//index.php?option=com_docman&task=doc_details&gid=15&Itemid99999999
Furman, G. (2003). What is leadership for? *UCEA Review*, 55(1), 1–6.
Haynes, F. (1998). *The ethical school*. London: Routledge.
Hehir, T. (2002). Eliminating abelism in education. *Harvard Educational Review*, 72, (1), 1–32.
Hursthouse, R. (1999). *On virtue ethics*. Oxford, England: Oxford University Press.
Maxcy, S.J. (2002). *Ethics of school leadership*. Lanham, MD: Scarecrow Press.
Nash, R.J. (2002). *"Real World" ethics; Frameworks for educators and human service professionals*. (second edition). New York: Teachers College Press.
Oakes, J. (1985). *Keeping track: How schools structure inequality*. New Haven, CT: Yale University Press.
Polanyi, M. (1966). *The tacit dimension*. Garden City, NY: Doubleday.
Sergiovanni, T.J. & Starratt, R.J. (2006). *Supervision: A redefinition* (eighth edition). New York: McGraw-Hill.
Shapiro, J.P. & Stefkovich, J.A. (2001). *Ethical leadership and decision making in education*. Mahwah, NJ: Erlbaum.
Starratt, R.J. (1991). Building an ethical school: A theory for practice in educational leadership. *Educational Administration Quarterly* 27(2), 195–202.
Starratt, R.J. (1998). Grounding moral educational leadership in the morality of teaching and learning. *Leading and Managing*, 4(4), 243–255.
Starratt, R.J. (2003). Opportunity to learn and the accountability agenda. *Phi Delta Kappan*, 58(4), 298–303.
Starratt, R.J. (2004). *Ethical leadership*. San Francisco: Jossey-Bass.
Starratt, R.J. (2007). Leading a community of learners: Learning to be moral by engaging the morality of learning. *Educational Management, Administration, and Leadership* 35(2), 165–183.
Strike, K.A., Haller, E.J., & Soltis, J.F. (1998). *The ethics of school administration*. New York: Teachers College Press.
Walker, R.L. & Ivanhoe, P.J. (Eds.). (2007). *Working virtue: Virtue ethics and contemporary moral problems*. New York: Oxford University Press.

CHAPTER TEN

The ethics of teaching

Delineating the professional ethics of teaching

General ethics in education is more concerned with the ethics of everyday life as that gets played out in the institutional context of schools and involves issues around fairness, truth telling, respect, equity, conflict, misunderstandings, and loyalties. Most case studies in the literature on ethics in teaching, or in educational administration (Strike, Haller, & Soltis, 1998; Zaretsky, 2005; Langlois & Lapointe, 2004) deal with ethics in education from this position. Professional ethics has much more to do with the ethics of the profession of educating. Part of that special ethics is about preventing harm in the process of educating; but part of that ethics is about promoting the good involved in the practice of educating (Shapiro & Stefkovich, 2001).

Just as medical ethics is concerned with promoting the good of its professional practice, which is physical health; just as business ethics is supposed to be concerned with promoting the public and individual good involved in trade, commerce, and contracts, just so one would expect educational ethics to be grounded in the particular good involved in teaching and learning. What is that good that education is supposed to pursue, promote, support? Shapiro and Stefkovich (2001) advance that that particular good is "the best interests of the child." I want to specify that in schools, the best interests of the child is the good to be found in learning—not any old kind of learning, but in a deep and broad learning that enables the child to accelerate the process of self-understanding and agency in relation to the natural, the cultural, and the social worlds. The good of learning involves the good of discovering, naming, constructing oneself as one is introduced to the natural, cultural and social worlds that constitute one's public "situatedness." The good of learning involves, as well, learning to enact one's life as an agent as least as much as a patient, that is, to participate as a member of those worlds. The ethics of teaching then comes to focus very intentionally on the *proactive* pursuit, cultivation, and support of those goods of learning in and for a democratic community and polity.

The current scholarship on ethics in education has done a reasonably good job of describing the general ethics of teaching in and administering schools but not a good enough job of describing what the proactive pursuit of those *special goods of learning* might look like. Lacking that clearer focus on the proactive pursuit of those goods of learning, the profession of teaching fails to grasp that their core work—not the work that surrounds that core work like communicating with parents, avoiding racism or religious prejudice in the classroom, collaboratively setting up the ground-rules that will govern classroom behavior, but the core work of the complex and intricate craft of teaching—is moral work. The general ethics of justice, care, and critique (Starratt, 1991) provide guidance for how to respond to students, colleagues, parents, policy makers, and the public at large ethically while going about the core work of their profession. General ethics, however, do not provide sufficient ethical insight into the specialized professional work of teaching, a work whose moral character is intimately tied into cultivating the moral character of learning.

The ethics of teaching is bound up with the ethics of learning

Teaching is the practice of a profession; that profession professes to stimulate and cultivate and sustain learning in its deep and broad sense (Hargreaves & Fink, 2006; Nixon et al., 1996; Sizer, 1996; Wood, 1998). As Macintyre observes,

> What is distinctive of a practice is in part the way in which conceptions of the relevant goods and ends which the technical skills serve—and every practice does require the exercise of technical skills—are transformed and enriched by these extensions of human powers and by that regard for its own internal goods which are partially definitive of each particular practice or type of practice. (1981, p. 180)

The good of learning, then, can be asserted as the good which the technical skills of teaching serve and which are transformed and enriched by the extension of human powers which learning produces.

The activity of learning, however, is itself a large generalization. What is the special good of the learning that takes place in schools, a good so important that societies everywhere throughout history have attended to its preservation? It is the good of learning, in an organized way (frequently referred to as the scope and sequence of the curriculum) the accumulated wisdom of the tribe or nation about how the world of nature works, how the social world works, how the cultural/religious world works. That learning involves learning about who one is by how one belongs to the biophysical, social, cultural, and religious worlds, about the rights and responsibilities of membership in these worlds. In societies that separate religion from the education of the young in secular subjects, religious education is left to families and those religious communities they belong to. School learnings constitute such an important good for both the individual young person, the community of young persons, and the adult society, that they are usually placed under the direction of persons who have made a special effort to systematize, or organize that knowledge in its basic intelligibility, who, in short, practice the profession of education. The assumption behind this formalized process of teaching and learning is that through it, the new generation of members will be able to participate as full adults in carrying on and renewing the life of the community.

The heart and soul of the ethics of teaching is to be found in the cultivation of learning in pupils. The word cultivation involves a metaphor taken from the work of agri-culture. It suggests that the teacher is somewhat like the gardener who aerates the soil, provides supports for the shrubs and plants to hold on to, prunes them, waters them and weeds the soil around them. The metaphor also implies that it is the plant that does the real work, namely the growing. The gardener supports and encourages that work, but the plant does the growing. Teaching does not do the work of learning; the student does that work. The metaphor suggests as well that the teacher is a culturing resource and model, providing critical appraisal of the learners' work the way cultural critics would, relating the students' work to criteria of style and grace, logic and clarity, robustness and sophistication, simplicity and integrity.

When we speak of teaching as cultivating learning, we also mean engaging something larger than skills and information. We mean that teaching cultivates literacy, cultivates character, cultivates taste, cultivates civic dispositions; cultivates generous understandings of the processes and patterns in nature, in social life, in cultural life; cultivates ideals, cultivates a sense of community, cultivates responsibilities.

Knowledge as independent, dependent, and interior

Tom Sergiovanni (2001) suggests helpful distinctions between assumptions about knowledge. He suggests that some teachers think about *knowledge as standing above the learner*; some think of the *learner as standing above the knowledge*; still others think of *knowledge as something inside the learner*. When we think of the content knowledge of the curriculum the teacher is supposed to know, we can view it from each of those assumptions and see the implications for their professional development that flow from each assumption.

Content knowledge, for example, about Shakespeare or about genetic biology can be thought of as something standing above the teacher. It is knowledge "out there"; it is knowledge standing on its own, in books, in libraries, in the research findings of scholars. The job of the teacher is to absorb it as it is, with its scientific or aesthetic conceptual apparatus, its definitions, its research methodology, its canonical grammar, so to speak. Once the teacher has absorbed, mastered, accumulated all this objective content knowledge, the teacher shapes this knowledge into a digestible and manageable logic called the school curriculum (or has this done by a textbook publisher) for the learners to master, absorb, accumulate. The students' expression of that mastery is revealed in the students' ability to get the right answers on the test, which supposedly reflect that content area as it is "out there," uncontaminated by students' subjective interpretations and cultural applications. We see this somewhat reflected in the "Teaching for Understanding Curriculum" (Wiske, 1998), with its categories of dimensions of understanding (knowledge, method, purpose, and forms) and levels of understanding (naïve, novice, apprentice, and master) implying the gradual mastery of an academic discipline.

For others, content knowledge still remains outside the learner, standing on its own, a true reflection of some aspect of reality. The teacher, however, as the professional educator, stands above this knowledge and decides to use it in a variety of ways, sometimes in a cross disciplinary lesson ("King Henry and the Working Class," "Shakespeare's Sense of Science"), sometimes in a thematically organized unit ("Patriotism in Shakespeare, in Rupert Brooke, in Margaret Thatcher") and sometimes as a stand-alone lesson ("An analysis of the *Merchant of Venice*"). The teacher as the professional educator knows which pieces to pick and choose for certain grade levels: DNA in dinosaurs for second graders, in insects for fifth graders, in microbes for tenth graders. Learners will follow the same approach to these content areas of biology: definitions, methodology for studying genetics, identification of genetic reproductive patterns, evolutionary genetic variations, and so forth, but in more simplified form for the earlier years.

The third assumption about content knowledge is that though the content knowledge might be stimulated from the canon-ized knowledge "out there," it doesn't remain out there. It becomes the learner's knowledge; it enters into the learner's understanding of her or himself; it situates the learner in the natural, cultural, or social world, it is inside the learner; it becomes a part of her. The learner may continue to feed and enrich that inside knowledge with further study of other knowledge sources. These learners see themselves inside the realities being studied, and see these realities inside themselves. There is a dialogue between the knower and the known. The intelligibility of the known enhances the intelligibility of the knower. In naming the known, the knower is implicated in a relationship of responsibility to the known, a responsibility to name it truly, accurately, in its clear, at least for the moment, meaning. But that meaning does not stand totally outside the knower. The meaning of the known is also *what it means to me*, not in a whimsical, arbitrary way, but in a way that implicates me in the relationship to the known and in the integrity of announcing what it means to me. Thus, the knowledge gained through the learning process is *necessarily* personal, at least *partly* subjective, while at the same time capable of being presented in its public sense.

From this third perspective—and this is the perspective on learning that ties it to the intrinsically moral character of learning—everything within the biophysical, the cultural, the social worlds has within it some form of intelligence, whether that is found in its genetic or cellular intelligence, the intelligence of a human artifact, the intelligible patterns of human association. That intelligibility may have been discovered by someone else and enunciated in a theory, an interpretation, a formula. Nevertheless, in coming to know some aspect of reality, the knower has to come to know that reality in some kind of personal appropriation of that reality's intelligibility. Otherwise, all the knower would know is the formula, the theory in its verbal or mathematical expression, but not apprehend the reality those expressions pointed to. The knowledge would be of the name, but not of the reality behind the name. Without that dialogue with reality, mediated through language, theoretical frameworks, or formulae, then the intelligibility of that reality does not engage the intelligibility of the knower, for it does not illuminate any relationship with the knower's reality. The knower needs to understand that relationship if the knowledge is to mean something to the knower. Otherwise, what is the point of learning anything?

What we have said about the learner taking knowledge inside of him or herself in a dialogue between intelligences applies equally to the teacher who, before becoming a teacher, has to go through the same process of learning. Thus, "Shakespeare" is not only a corpus of poems and plays that sits on a library shelf, a body of work the teacher has read, memorized, analyzed, critiqued, perhaps even played a part in a production of Shakespeare is now inside the teacher. Romeo, Lear, Falstaff, Richard, Hamlet, Ophelia, Cleopatra, Lady Macbeth have entered the teacher's soul, have set up a dialogue with her identity, have opened doors to the intimate chambers of the human heart and the human beast. Those characters speak to the heroic, as well as to the devious, defensive, and silly impulses of human beings. Through these characters the teacher recognizes aspects of him or herself. He also recognizes how many of these dramatic characters have become stereotypes for recognizing and naming those traits in others. They stand for the breadth and depth of human possibility, as well as for the tragic predicaments humans face.

When that teacher teaches the "content knowledge" of Shakespeare, that content knowledge can now emerge in its transformative power. Teaching Shakespeare now becomes an opportunity to help Shakespeare speak to the humanity of the learners, and thereby increase their self-knowledge and their knowledge of the heroic, the foolish, and the darker side of human nature.

Similarly, for the biology teacher, the content knowledge of genetics works its way inside. It helps the teacher understand her/himself more profoundly as a living organism in nature. A personal appropriation of genetic biology establishes a dialogue between the intelligibility of the double helix and the intelligibility of the teacher's biological inheritance. That dialogue also reveals how science enables nature to understand itself, and enables humans to understand the "mind of nature" (Augros & Stanciu, 1987; Bateson, 1979a; Eiseley, 1962; Prigogine & Stengers, 1984; Zohar & Marshall, 1994). Such knowledge places the knower in a new relationship to the worm that contains most of the genetic material that humans possess. Such knowledge places the knower in touch with an enormous history, an "immense journey" (Eiseley, 1957), of terrestrial life which has creatively and patiently struggled through day after day after day, year after year after year, century after century after century, millennium after millennium after millennium until it had finally figured out how to think for itself, then think about itself, then think about its thinking, and, finally, think about what it wanted to do with itself (Seilstad, 1989). This knowledge reveals the knower to him/herself in a profoundly transformative way.

This kind of personalized knowledge of genetic biology—attained only after considerable study and reflection—now prepares the teacher to facilitate at least the beginning of a dialogue between DNA and the learner's mind, imagination and soul. This dialogue will lead to multiple additional dialogues with DNA in worms, insects, flowers canaries, gerbils, sheep dogs, classmates, even Shakespeare and his circus parade of heroes and heroines, villains, knaves, and fools. Perhaps the English and the biology teacher might hold a seminar on the Shakespearean variations of DNA.

One might imagine that these three approaches to curriculum knowledge might reflect a progression from the first-year teacher, to the post-tenure teacher, to the mature teacher. In some teachers' development that may be the pattern. Yet, others may begin with the more mature fascination with knowledge of the world and of themselves that their discipline provides. Even these kind of beginners, however, will need to deepen their understanding of their discipline as well as broaden their pedagogical repertoire to facilitate a captivating dialogue with that world for all of their students.

The cultivation of this kind of learning lies at the heart of the teacher's professional work. It is the special good which the practice of teaching promotes. In learning about the worlds of culture, society, and nature, the learner is learning what membership in those worlds means and how his or her own best interests bisect with those memberships. This analysis of learning may be brought to a larger synthesis by referring to the types of learning enunciated by the committee that formulated the vision of learning needed by all citizens in a global society (Delors et al., 1996).

In their report to the United Nations Educational, Scientific, and Cultural Organization (UNESCO), the authors foresaw that learning conceived as building a storehouse of static knowledge would not prepare the young for all the changes, challenges, and opportunities of the Twenty-first Century interdependent world. They proposed, rather, a larger view of continuous learning which schools should attend to: Learning to know; learning to do; learning to be; and learning to live together. To this vision of learning, Hargreaves and Fink (2006) add a fifth: Learning to live sustainably. The school's curriculum should stimulate these five kinds of learning as it exposes learners to the natural, cultural and social worlds in which they are assuming membership. As they learn how to learn, how to do, how to be, how to live together, how to live sustainably in the three worlds of nature, culture, and society, they will be taking inside themselves the lessons those worlds teach, creating a dialogue out of which they will continue to construct themselves as bio-physical persons, as cultural persons, as social persons. Thus will the learning process be transformative as it "extends the reach of human capabilities" (Macintyre, 1981) to embrace and enact those goods found in the learning process.

As teachers attempt to engage learners in this deep and broad kind of learning, we can see how their practice calls them to model the very kinds of learning that they hold out for their students. In the process of teaching, teachers have to learn and model how to learn, how to do, how to be, how to live together, and how to live sustainably.

A model of the ethical practice of teaching

The following model attempts to capture the intrinsically moral character of teaching and learning, and, in the process to illuminate the practice of teaching at its best, as virtuous practice. The model presumes that learning is dialogical as the previous chapter and the above commentary was intended to demonstrate. The model assumes that teaching is also dialogical. Teaching flows from the teacher's dialogue with the curriculum material, and also from the teacher's dialogue with the learner before, during, and after the learning episode. With knowledge of both the students and the particular curriculum unit actively present in the teacher's mind and imagination, the teacher constructs a variety of learning activities that will bring the students into lively conversation with a piece of the curriculum unit. The model is illustrated in Figure 10.1.

The first order of business in a teaching learning situation is for the teacher to establish a working relationship with the learners. That relationship has first to build up some trust between the teacher and the learners. The learners need to know that the teacher is interested in them, cares for and respects them as human beings with huge potentials. The learners need to see the teacher as an authentic person, not as some distant, cardboard authority figure, but someone who can laugh and cry, someone who is consistent and reliable, someone who tells the truth.

144 *The ethics of teaching*

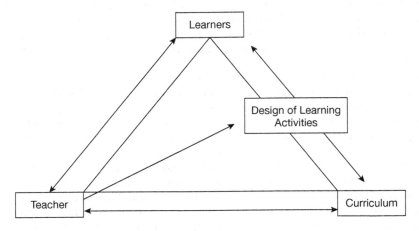

Figure 10.1 Model of relationships within the ethics of teaching.

The teacher has to try to get to know the learners as well as possible. Figure 10.2 attempts to outline the knowledge that results from that dialogue with the learners. That dialogue helps teachers know the learners' individual interests, hobbies, career interests, academic strengths and shortcomings, fears and uncertainties, family background and home context. At the start of the school year, the teachers should assess each student's readiness for the work expected of them: their reading levels, their study skills, their social skills, their cultural background and how that can be called upon in various learning assignments. This knowledge enables the teacher to differentiate her instruction to target the interests, talents, and deficiencies of various students in the class.

The task has grown more demanding in the last twenty-five years or so as schools have mainstreamed students with handicapping conditions ranging from physical disabilities such as blindness or deafness, to mental disabilities such as Down's syndrome, to learning difficulties such as dyslexia or attention deficit disorder, to emotional disabilities. With students identified with special learning needs, teachers have to be much more attentive and knowledgeable as they seek to uncover the ways students may effectively engage the curriculum. In many schools, teachers will be assisted by special education teachers and teacher aides who can work as a team to design appropriate learning activities more suited to particular students' abilities.

For the primary school teachers establishing a dialogue with the learners in the class is a relatively manageable task. For secondary and middle school teachers who normally teach one discipline in many classrooms during the day, getting to know over one hundred students very well is a daunting task. Some schools try to lessen the burden by having two or three teachers from the different subject areas teach the same learners for two or three successive years. That extended time frame enables those teachers to share their knowledge of that group of students and to share ideas on how to capture their interest in the curriculum and to overcome learning problems they might be having in several subject areas. That arrangement

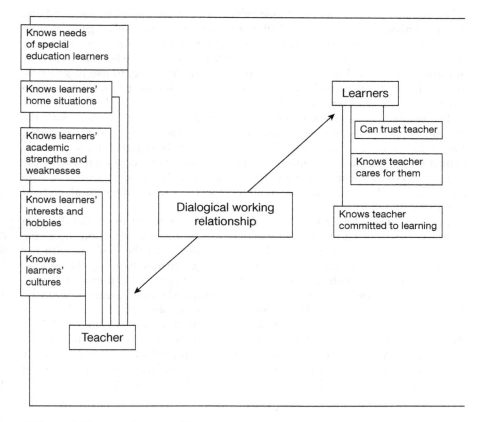

Figure 10.2 First leg of the model: Teacher's working relationship with learners.

also provides opportunities for cross-disciplinary learning activities as well as for student peer coaching.

The second leg of the triangle concerns the teacher's knowledge of the curriculum. As indicated earlier, that knowledge can be relatively superficial and naïve, as simply external knowledge of an academic area to be mastered and reproduced for assessment exercises, or it can be personalized knowledge that continues to reveal the knower's relationship to the natural, cultural, or social world. Primary teachers have a life-long agenda here, for they may know one or two academic areas reasonably well, but have a very limited mastery of several others. They have to continually listen to the curriculum content talk back to them, to show a side of its intelligibility that will be useful for students to discover, that will in turn talk back to the students and help them see more deeply how they are connected to the natural, cultural, and social worlds.

One of the challenges for primary teachers is to translate their adult understanding of the subject matter into the design of learning activities that can appeal to the minds and imaginations and feelings of their young learners, while at the same time being true to the integrity of their own understandings. This translation

146 *The ethics of teaching*

of the teachers' understandings of their subject matter into appealing and clarifying learning activities is, of course, a challenge for teachers at all levels. Again, because of the diversity within classrooms, much of this translation will have to be more and more customized to fit various groups of learners. Here is where the five kinds of learning mentioned above (learning to know, to do, to be, to live together, to live sustainably) may provide an enlarged imaginative landscape for the teacher to construct a variety of learning activities.

The teacher's dialogue with the curriculum will always take place with the students standing in the picture, with the teacher asking of the subject matter, "What do you have to say to these learners that might be of particular importance to their lives? How do you connect to them? How might they connect to you? How do you help them understand something about themselves that adds value to who they are? How do you re-place, re-mind these learners within the natural, cultural or social worlds?"

These questions lead naturally to the third leg of the triangle, the dialogue between the students and the subject matter. The teacher's work on this leg of the triangle involves her bringing together her knowledge of the students with her knowledge of the curriculum and designing learning activities that bring the students into active dialogue with the subject matter. Those activities can involve games, puzzles, memory tricks, projects, problems, reading and writing exercises, dramatic performances, story-telling, dance, experiments with color, shape, sounds, movements, measurement exercises, songs, debates, jigsaw exercises—whatever will bring the learners into some kind of experience with the subject matter. As the learners become more familiar and more comfortable with the subject matter, the teacher will inevitably involve the learners in reflective questions about how they are making sense of the material, and how the material is talking back to them.

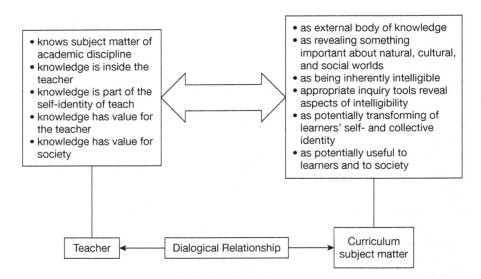

Figure 10.3 Second leg of the model: Teacher's dialogical relationship with curriculum subject matter.

The important part of any pedagogical scheme is to bring the knowledge from outside to inside the learner. The teacher should insist on the learner being responsible to the knowledge they are personally appropriating and constructing. That means naming what they know carefully and truthfully, not attempting to inflate their knowledge beyond what it is, not making believe that they know something when they don't. The learners should constantly be encouraged to name what they know as far as they know it, even if that knowledge is expressed tentatively, in a hunch or a guess. Such responses as "It seems to me that this story is about making friends, about the risk of making a friend, because when you tell stuff to your friend that you wouldn't tell to anyone else because they might think you're weird, you hope your friend will still accept you." The response indicates a learner attempting to articulate some truth about the nature of friendship, especially as the learner may have experienced it in her or his own life. The teacher might follow up with the question: "And when a friend accepts what you tell about your self as ok, how does that make you feel?" The question invites the student to generate additional learnings about friendship, not from a book, but from a dialogue with his own experience of friendship. But the teacher can also refer back to the story and ask whether the story provides confirming evidence that friendship is risky but worth the risk. The question requires the student to take elements of the story further inside to probe what his answer will be.

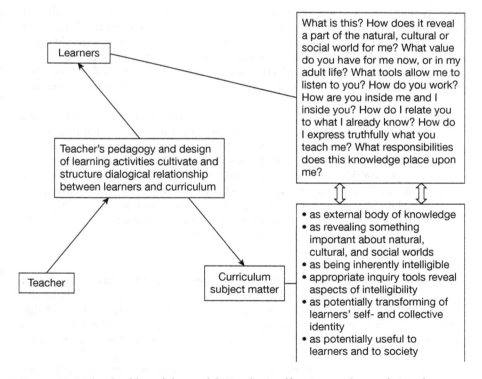

Figure 10.4 The third leg of the model: Teacher's efficacious pedagogy brings learners into dialogue with the curriculum.

No matter what the academic subject matter, the teacher can always encourage this movement from outside knowledge to inside knowledge, bringing the learner into dialogue with that knowledge and how that knowledge might be in relationship to the learner, what that knowledge helps the learner to understand about her or himself or about the world in which they exercise their membership. This kind of learning process always intentionally raises the questions, "What's the point of learning this stuff? What does it have to do with us? Why is it important? What is its value for us?" Requiring the learners to answer those questions as truthfully as they can occasions that ongoing dialogue with knowledge that makes it personally significant. The teacher, however, will not necessarily require these dialogues between the learner and the subject matter every day, because sometimes the focus of the lesson will be relatively narrow or it may not lend itself to that kind of reflective learning. Often, such deep, internalizing of the learning is more appropriate toward the end of a larger unit of the curriculum.

Implications of the model for teachers' growth

Teachers will always be refining their pedagogical skills and strategies. One of the obvious reasons behind professional development programs is precisely to support improvement of their pedagogical skills and strategies. Often these programs, however, provide a kind of cookbook menu of exercises, a new bag of tricks to hook students into learning the material, without being grounded in any kind of deeper purpose than it helps learners prepare for exams. What this third leg of the triangle provides is that deeper rationale to the learning process which should guide and shape all of the pedagogical skills and strategies the teacher employs.

Let us listen to a teacher's reflection on her individually devised professional development project to target her pedagogy towards the perceived needs of students.

> The most beneficial aspect of the process was probably the initial planning of it ... thinking about it even before the implementing ... thinking in my own mind what I could do with my particular group of students and my unique situation ... what would be one thing that I could really work on and concentrate on this year that would impact them. And I think even if I'd only done a small segment of what I'd planned, I think it would have been worthwhile because it made me look at what the needs might be within my students that I could have a personal impact on within the school year. It made me take a look at myself and at my teaching and what I could work on.
> (Adams, 2004, p. 113)

In passing it might be helpful to observe how this teacher was not using an officially prescribed technique based on research studies (knowledge above the teacher), but was calling on the knowledge gained from experience, the knowledge inside her, to construct new approaches to her teaching. The tone of her reflections represents a deep commitment to her students, and to a dialogical working relationship with them, thus indicating professional growth on both the first and the third leg of the model outlined above. In honoring these interests, the teacher practices the good of the teaching profession. While the results are seldom perfect, a community of teachers' continuous practice of attending to these interests cumulatively over twelve or thirteen years produces the "good" of a reasonably well-educated person who is ready to take charge of her or his life, participate responsibly in public life, take on full membership in the worlds of nature, society, and culture.

The model can easily be incorporated in the work of cultivating an ethical school. It suggests that teachers need to continuously improve their dialogical knowledge on all three legs of the triangle. For some teachers that might mean a year or two additional learning about special needs children and how better to respond to them. For other teachers that might mean a year or two devoted to a greater personal understanding of the science embedded in the curriculum he or she teaches. For still others, it may mean a year working in a new team to develop appropriate rubrics for assessing student work. For teachers feeling the intense pressure to map their teaching to the state curriculum standards, that may mean developing a personal understanding of the knowledge required by the standards in order to reconstruct his or her teaching in such a way that students can encounter that material in a dialogical learning process and engage in the five kinds of learning within that dialogue.

Virtues that facilitate the ethical work of teaching

Virtues are ways of engaging the good that one is seeking. They are ways of achieving those internal goods which extend our human reach toward becoming more fully human. An earlier inquiry into the virtues that seems intrinsically tied to the work of educating and leading a process of educating proposed three virtues that seemed especially important in realizing the goods of learning and teaching: the virtue of presence, the virtue of authenticity, and the virtue of responsibility (Starratt, 2004). The final part of this chapter explores—all too briefly—how those virtues hold up when placed against the moral landscape of learning and teaching we have been considering.

The virtue of presence

One has to be present to the material or topic under study. Presence implies a dialogical relationship between the learner and the material under study. As with two persons, their mutual presence to each other makes a relationship possible, a relationship bonded by telling and listening. Each person listens to the other's words, taking them in, and with the words, taking the other person inside as one interprets what the other's words mean. The listener then responds to the other, presenting in the response both the listener's interpretation of what the other has said, and also how the listener responds from his or her perspective or feelings to what the other has said. Thus the dialogue goes back and forth with each person disclosing more of themselves and taking in richer and fuller understandings of the other. If one of the parties to the dialogue becomes distracted and fails to be fully attentive to the other person then the mutuality of presence is diminished, if not broken, and the integrity of the dialogue and the relationship that was developing is put in jeopardy

The practice of the virtue of presence in the process of learning is something that itself is learned. Some teachers will explicitly teach it under the guise of study skills, or creating a readiness set at the beginning of class. There are ways of getting the learners' attention, motivating them to focus and concentrate in anticipation of learning something of personal value to them. As the lesson progresses, teachers increase the learner's attention by posing new questions, "If x is thus and so, what does that imply for y?" or "What does this situation suggest for its resolution?" "Put yourself in this character's place. How would you reply? What would you do?" The point behind the questions is to encourage the learner to listen to the intelligibility embedded in the subject matter talking back to the learner, and inviting the learner to respond with her own understanding of the issue. The teacher is suggesting ways for the learner to be present to that intelligibility and to be open to taking that inside her own personal world.

While there are many nuances to being present, three seem particularly apropos in the activity of learning: (1) affirming presence, (2) enabling presence, and (3) critical presence. Affirming presence accepts the person or the event as it is, in its ambiguity, its incompleteness, it particularity, its multidimensionality. Enabling presence is open to the possibilities of the person or event to contain or reveal something special, something of deep value and significance. Critical presence expects to find both negative and positive features in persons and events. People and events and circumstances reveal unequal relationships of power and reciprocity. Critical presence brings to light what is tacit, assumed, or presumed in situations that reflect human constructions and beliefs. All of these ways of being present to what is being studied energize the dialogue between learners and one or more of the worlds under consideration in that unit of the curriculum. Those kinds of presence of the learner to those worlds enable those worlds to illuminate how the learner is already a member of those worlds, affirming something of the learner's identity, enabling the learner to become more fully him/her self, and as critiquing inappropriate assumptions and presumptions about their mutual relationships.

A second virtue that honors the integrity of learning is authenticity. The virtue of authenticity involves human beings in their most basic moral challenge, namely the challenge to be true to themselves, to be real. The opposite of that virtue is inauthenticity, playing false, making believe one is someone other than who one is. As with presence, the virtue of authenticity is a dialogical virtue. One cannot be authentic alone locked up in a closet. One is authentic in relationship to another. Authenticity is revealed in our words and actions, in our acting out the various social and cultural roles we play. Most basically one is authentic as a human being in response to the humanity of the other. One is also authentic as a son or daughter, as a friend or lover, a father and a mother. In all of these roles, one strives to be real, not a fake or cardboard character. But the expression of our authenticity has to take into account the similar effort of others to be true to themselves as well. Authenticity supposes a kind of social contract, namely, that if I expect a certain latitude to be myself, to own my life and my choices, so too must I afford to others the latitude to chart the courses of their own lives (Taylor, 1992).

The practice of ethical teaching asks the learner that he or she acknowledge the world as it is and to recognize that the learner's integrity is connected to the learner's relationship to the physical, social, and cultural worlds he or she is studying. Those worlds invite the learner into membership. Membership, however, imposes a recognition both of the benefits, and privileges, as well as responsibilities of membership.

In other words, one's authenticity as a member of these worlds requires an understanding of the ways these worlds work. Understanding, however, does not always equal approval. Corruption in the world of politics is a familiar possibility. Recognizing that, one confronts the reality about politics as potentially corrupt, and therefore in need of critical participation. Racism is a reality in the social world. One's membership in the social world requires a critical stance toward that reality. Arrogant elitism based on class, wealth, or social standing is a feature of the cultural world. One's membership in a cultural world has to deal with the distorted stereotypes bred by that elitism. The learner pursues a way of being real, a way of expressing her or his goodness always in relationship to the realities of the worlds he or she inhabit.

The practice of the virtues of presence and authenticity in one's pedagogy imply a third virtue that seeks the goods of the learning process—the virtue of responsibility. It is a virtue exercised by teachers by being responsible to what one is teaching about in the worlds of nature, society, culture, and history. This virtue is enacted in two ways. First, in the teaching process itself, the teacher adopts an attitude of responsibility toward the material under study, whether it be the genetic code, the physics of magnets, a poem of Wordsworth, an historical account of the crusades, a novel by William Faulkner, the geography of Egypt or the geometry of architecture. These curricular elements reveal how humans have interpreted and represented aspects of the natural, the social, the cultural, and the historical worlds. The teacher has a responsibility to work with the learners to get inside the realities being represented in those curriculum units, to grasp the value or the intelligibility, or the perspective (or conflict of perspectives), or the multiple implications and applications to be drawn from those curriculum units. In other words, the teacher takes seriously her or his responsibility to bring students ever closer to the truth (and its opposites), the beauty (and its opposites), the values (and their opposites), the reasonableness (and its contradictions) illuminated by those curriculum units as well as the connections to aspects of the students' lives. The second way the virtue of responsibility is exercised by teachers is more of a proactive responsibility to the learners in one's charge to refuse to give up on their potential to learn. That sense of responsibility continually asks of the teacher to uncover the reason for students' underperformance. That sense of responsibility is a challenge to the teacher's sense of efficacy, namely, that there is no learning difficulty that she cannot find the answer to. If students are not learning, then the teacher may have to go back to the drawing board *with the student* to find out where the blockage or the misunderstandings began, or what motivations, or life connections can be uncovered, and more appropriate learning activities designed.

Teachers, moreover, should begin to link the moral character of their work to the moral character of learning. That is, they need to teach these very virtues of presence and authenticity and responsibility as virtues that cultivate the good of learning, both by explicitly developing the learners' study skills, attitudes and methods of inquiry, and implicitly in the way they, the teachers, model their approach to the study of these worlds. They should be modeling their sense of presence to the complexity, beauty, and challenges of the biophysical, cultural, and social worlds; their sense of authenticity in dialogue with the truths of these worlds; and their sense of responsibility to and for these worlds. This aspect of teachers' ethical work deserves a treatment of its own. For the moment, suffice it to say that the work will require so much more than preparing young people to paint by the numbers, or getting them to construct the right answers to someone else's questions on high stakes tests.

Summary

This chapter has attempted to expound a view of teaching as a special kind of moral activity, an activity, therefore, that needs its own special ethical analysis and its own chapter among scholarly summaries of special or professional ethics. In claiming a special view of its moral goods and the virtues that promote those goods, educational leaders can appeal to the wider public that supports the practice of teaching and benefits from it to honor the moral integrity that learning and teaching entail and request that misguided policies that distort or frustrate that integrity be amended. Furthermore, we have to remember that the special moral integrity of education, as with all other professions, will always be situated within those larger frameworks by which morality in all its special forms receives its ultimate legitimation, namely, the frameworks of the general ethics of justice, care, and critique. Those ethics not only legitimate the special concerns of different professions and practices, they are the tap roots, so to speak, which give them an enduring vitality.

Currently, the policy emphasis on curriculum standards is being driven by the assumption (along with an exclusively cognitive brand of psychology) that schools should be teaching learners to think like mathematicians, scientists, historians, literary critics (Wiske, 1998). This exclusive focus is misguided on two counts. First, as evidenced by high stakes testing protocols, it concentrates the work of the schools almost entirely, mission statements to the contrary notwithstanding, on the cognitive development of learners, to the neglect of the psycho-social development of learners, thereby sacrificing some of the most important goods of the learning process. Second, in its efforts to turn learners into mini scholars, it turns schools into university prep schools. A tiny fraction of the learners in a given nation's schools will become academic scholars. The upper years of college and graduate school will take care of preparing the scholar academicians, and the highly specialized professionals. *All* learners in our public schools, however, will become adult citizens. The focus on the goods of learning ought to be concerned primarily with learning—within and across the academic subject areas—what young people need to know as human beings, as citizens who vote, who debate public policy, who have to manage households and participate in neighborhood projects, who have to learn to live with and learn from people and groups who are different in many ways from them, and contribute to the common weal in their careers and leisure activities. As a foundation for that kind of citizenship, schools need to promote through the academic subject areas, co-curriculars, and student support services, what young people need to learn to become intelligent, responsible, self-fulfilled, healthy, other-connected, compassionate, and mature human beings who can participate, contribute, and find fulfillment in various dimensions of democratic public life. That should be the ultimate moral good pursued by the profession of education in the nation's public schools.

References

Adams, P. (2004). Supporting teachers' professional development. In P.E. Holland (Ed.), *Beyond measure: Neglected elements of accountability* (pp. 101–132). Larchmont, NY: Eye on Education.

Augros, R.M. & Stanciu, G.N. (1987). *The new biology: Discovering the wisdom in nature.* Boston: New Science Library.

Bateson, G. (1979). *Mind and nature: A necessary unity.* New York: E.P. Dutton.

Delors, J. et al. (1996). Learning: *The treasure within.—Report to UNESCO of the International Commission on Education for the Twenty-first Century.* Paris: United Nations Educational, Scientific, and Cultural Organization.

Eiseley, L. (1962). *The mind as nature.* New York: Charles Scribner & Sons.

Hargreaves, A. Fink, D. (2006). *Sustainable leadership.* San Francisco: Jossey-Bass.

Langlois, L. & Lapointe, C. (2004). Ethical leadership in linguistic minority settings: Adding new colors to the patchwork. Paper delivered at the annual conference of the University Council of Educational Administration, Montreal, November 11–13.

Macintyre, A. (1981). *After virtue.* Notre Dame, IN: University of Notre Dame Press.

Nixon, et al. (1996). *Encouraging learning: Toward a theory of the learning school.* London: Open University Press.

Prigogene, I. & Stengers, I. (1984). *Order out of chaos: Man's new dialogue with nature.* New York: Bantam Books.

Seilstad, G.A. (1989). *At the heart of the web: The inevitable genesis of intelligent life.* New York: Harcourt Brace.

Sergiovanni, T.J. (2001). *The principalship: A reflective practice perspective.* Boston: Allyn & Bacon.

Shapiro, J. P. & Stefkovich, J.A. (2001). *Ethical leadership and decision making in education: Applying theoretical perspectives to complex dilemmas.* Mahwah, NJ: Lawrence Erlbaum.

Starratt, R.J. (1991). Building an ethical school: A theory for practice in educational leadership. Educational Administration Quarterly, 27 (2), 185–202.

Strike, K. A., Haller, E.J. & Soltis, J.F. (1998). *The ethics of school administration (2nd ed.).* New York: Teachers College Press.

Taylor, C. (1992). *The ethics of authenticity.* Cambridge, MA: Harvard University Press.

Wiske, M.S. (Ed.) (1998). *Teaching for understanding: Linking research with practice.* San Francisco: Jossey-Bass.

Wood, G.H. (1998). *A time to learn.* New York: Dutton.

Zaretsky, L. (2005). Enacting democratic ethical educational leadership: Moving beyond the talk. Paper delivered at the annual conference of the University Council of Educational Administration, Nashville, Tennessee, November 11–14.

Zohar, D. & Marshall, I. (1994). *The quantum society: Mind, physics, and a new social vision.* London: Harper Collins.

CHAPTER ELEVEN

Cultivating a mature community

New understandings for re-imagining community

We begin the 21st century with the tensions between individualism and communitarianism as an apparently unresolved and irreconcilable problem. Some would have us go back to the premodern notion of community, in which individuality and autonomy were absorbed in a communal identity (MacIntyre, 1981). Others continue to pose the freedom of the individual as the bedrock of our national identity. Rather than demanding an either/or solution to the tension, our challenge is to create an ecology of community that promotes the richest form of individual human life within the richest form of community life (Becker, 1967). We are closer now to understanding community in a large enough sense to fashion such an ecology. Advances in the natural and human sciences ground new understandings of the symbiotic interconnection of all natural systems on the planet (Lovelock, 1979), a growing understanding of the reflexivity of cultural systems in their own complexification (McCarthy, 1996), and a new awareness of the continuum of intelligence in its tacit or inchoate state in subatomic physics and in its increasingly more obvious presence from lower to higher life forms to its flowering in human systems of understanding (Bateson, 1979; Bohm, 1981; Ferris, 1988; Swimme & Berry, 1992; Zohar & Marshall, 1994). These understandings provide the building blocks for constructing a richer understanding of community.

This challenge in our schools is a reflection of the challenge facing our society at large—namely, the creation of richer forms of community life within civil society. As we said earlier, this does not require wholesale rejection of the achievements of modernity or an anarchy of isolated critical enclaves (whether from the right or left) in a revolution against the excesses of modernity (MacIntyre, 1981). It is impossible to return to a premodern state of affairs, attractive as Aristotelianism appears (Taylor, 1989). We can only move forward, learning the lessons that both Aristotle and history teach us. This journey requires, however, a transformation of our limited understanding of both the individual and the community.

Communities of mature individuals

Achieving or performing community is only partially realized at best. It involves a struggle. Why? Because we, although incomplete as individuals, want to be the center of attention, respect, admiration, and control. We desperately need, as Giddens (1984) suggested, a sense of ontological security—a sense that the world is not going to snuff out our life in the next moment or the next day. We want to be secure in our basic physical needs for food and shelter. We want the world to be predictable. For the world to be predictable, we must somehow, even if only in our fantasy, control it. We must arrange it to suit our needs. One way we do this is by inventing science. Science, we think, places us in the driver's seat. Knowledge of nature enables us to control it.

We also need to feel secure in our social world. We are always checking that social world to see how it is responding to us. The tape at the back of my head is always running: "How do I look? Am I saying the right thing? Am I being noticed? Are these people friendly or unfriendly, attentive to me or bored with me?" I must control my social world because that world is what defines me. It can disapprove of my actions and punish me by redefining me as stupid, dumb, crazy, or bad (Goffman, 1959).

The pulls toward self-sufficiency and self-gratification are strong. They are some of the survival instincts we inherit by being a child of nature and the cosmos. The universe appears indifferent to our needs and desires, unforgiving of our excesses, and capricious in inflicting the calamities that fall on us from nature. My life can be snuffed out in an instant by an earthquake, destroyed by a mosquito, ruined by a drought, or made miserable by a bacterial invasion. The universe does not weep over my demise or misfortune. Some humans never make it past the first 3 weeks of life; some are born with severe physical or mental disabilities. Nature appears to respect only one law: adapt or disappear. Dysfunctional species disappear. Add to the impersonal disinterest of the universe and the struggle for survival of all life forms a social environment of competition for scarce resources (whether those resources are oil, money, or a mother's attention), and we begin to recognize the depth of the survival instinct and its roots in the human psyche. This instinct, embedded in the genetic material of our chromosomes and the quantum mechanics of our nervous system, prompts an aggressive self-interest.

Yet there is a second instinct that is more mature and therefore more intelligent and more human: the instinct toward connection, toward an other, whether that other is a spouse, companion, extended family, clan, or nation. This instinct is a more intelligent and creative development of the survival instinct. It is an instinct carried in the learning of atomic, chemical, and organic structures: connect, bond, unite, and become stronger through complexification. Complexification leads to increased adaptability and creativity for new forms of self-reproduction. That bonding at the inorganic and organic levels grows toward the reflexive self-awareness of attraction.

This dynamic of attraction, connectivity, complexification, stabilization in a new form, and then new transformation through new connections is indeed the most basic law of the universe. As life-forms within the universe, we experience that law in the depth of our being. It leads us to seek connections in order to live and, indeed, to be human. We only come to experience our humanity through our connection to other humans—at first with parents, then with siblings and relatives, and then with the kids next door. These connections shape us, feed our sense of who we are. We do not enter into relationships as fully formed individuals. Rather, our relationships continuously nourish and form us.

We need to be connected to other human beings as much as we need food to stay alive. Thus, we enter the dynamic of being attracted by other people by their wit, talent, good humor, and honesty. We reciprocate by attempting to make ourselves attractive by showing forth socially appealing qualities. From that reflexive self-awareness of attraction grows the creativity of making oneself more attractive (the bright colors of some flowers, the fantastic plumage of some birds and their complex birdsong, the daily makeup and weightlifting, and the wearing of perfume, designer clothing, and even university degrees).

At the higher levels of social bonding, one encounters various forms of love: symbolic expressions of cherishing that are expressed in language, touching, and gestures (the gruff handshake between two tradesmen; the cradling of infants in their mothers' arms; the entwining of lovers; the placing of a flower on the grave of a dear friend).

At more general levels of bonding, there is a more expansive awareness and experience of love. The sociology of everyday life, the sociology of the professions, feminist studies, biographies, and popular history, help us appreciate how much one depends on the gratuitous generosity of countless people whose work makes social life possible (the farmers who produce the food, the builders who build the shelters, the planners who anticipate the complex needs of a modern city, and the countless men and women who attend to the daily maintaining of transportation, communication, financial, health, and education systems). Added to their fidelity in maintaining the infrastructure of society are the efforts of scholars and artists to probe the mysteries and complexities of the natural, human, and social worlds. They tease out and express the meaningfulness of life and its underlying beauty and terror.

Although the social world we live in is far from perfect, it is this social life that feeds us—that nourishes our sense of our individual and social identities. This social world can be seen as a gift that is gratuitously given to us. There grows a gradual appreciation that deeply embedded in the ambiguity and muddiness of social life is a massive, incoherent, yet clearly spoken collective act of love. All the effort that goes into making sociocultural life (as opposed to the self-seeking efforts of those who manipulate social arrangements to their own benefit at the expense of others) in the present, and even more so during the past centuries of struggle, can be seen as a gratuitous act of love.

We celebrate this collective act of love by remembering the public heroes of the past: The young men and women who gave their lives in battle to defend the country's future; the founding fathers and mothers of the republic; the states-people, inventors, artists, and saints whose achievements and creations continue to shape our sense of ourselves. Beyond the public heroes is the mass of humanity, whose daily performance of their work in factories and farms, universities and government offices, hospitals and homes, sustained the sociocultural fabric of past generations. These are the ordinary heroes of human history whose biographies were written in the hearts of friends and families, but who never made it into the official histories of their times. However, their lives as well as the lives of public heroes express a self-giving, a struggle on behalf of human destiny and human dignity against the forces that would destroy us. We live off this inheritance; their self-giving enriches us. They provide us examples of how we might repay the gift by adding the gift of our own lives' work to it, whether that involves raising children whose experience of love enables them to reproduce that love in their adult lives, fidelity to the highest quality of our craft, or the search for a new medicine, a new symphony, or a new world order.

At these higher levels of awareness of social bonding, one becomes increasingly aware of the gratuitous gift of nature in all its variety, complexity, inventiveness, and sheer abundance. Our bodies are extraordinary creations, the result of millions of years of patient experiment. We are the result of the efforts of cosmic dust reaching for the dream of life, the struggle of life to become more and more in charge of itself, and the amazing flowering of atoms into human intelligence over eons of cosmic time. Whether our religious beliefs posit a transcendent God or Creator, or whether we leave the existence of some divine force outside of or above the universe as an open question, we are still confronted with the awesomeness of the existence of life and its almost infinite variety as a natural miracle.

As we saw in chapter 3, the sciences continue to discover the enormous intricacy of the structures and processes of life forms and the interpenetration and mutuality among levels of life systems, from the biochemistry of DNA to the neurochemistry of consciousness to the social ecology of cultural rituals that create and sustain meaning. What this inheritance points to is a universe that is ultimately benign despite its apparent indifference to dead-end experiments and despite the chaos and randomness embedded in its very intelligibility. This awareness of a benign universe—a mothering universe, if you will—leads to thankfulness for this patient, mutely eloquent, self-giving process that has given birth to us and to a planet in which we find a home and all the ingredients for a full and rich life. It also leads to a sense of responsible membership in a community of life, so that the gift becomes enriched not diminished by my history, by our history.

The individual's response to community

Through this growing awareness of being bonded to and gifted by successive levels of community, we see how love generates love—how our affective, cognitive, and personal participation in community reveals to us deeper and richer insights into love as the center of these communities. Therefore, love is a response to community—a reciprocal gift of life to the welfare of the natural, social, and human communities we inhabit. In that giving, we more fully realize the meaning, identity, and purpose of our lives as human beings (MacMurray, 1970).

From this vantage point, we understand the instinct for individual survival as immature, small-minded, and self-defeating. We also see how immature communities are (tribes, cities, states, nations) that close in on themselves, mistakenly believing all other communities to be inferior to them in strength, intelligence, cultural achievement, or nobility, seeing all other communities as threats to their hegemony or simply to their survival. The more mature community embraces the community of humanity, the community of life, and the community of being, and finds through that bonding an increased wisdom and strength that are the seeds of its own transformation.

The struggle for a mature community

That is the game, epic, metanarrative, tragicomedy that is played out in everyday life. The instinct for individual self-survival pulls us in one direction; the instinct for connectedness and complexification, the attraction to loving relationships, pulls us in another. Sometimes the two instincts become confused. Often the two pulls are entangled in the same choices and actions. Sometimes one is used to rationalize the other ("The arms race is necessary for world peace"; "We need more prisons to promote the security of the community"; "A healthy economy requires an unemployment rate of 6%").

When we speak about cultivating community, we are not imagining a sugar-coated, utopian reality. Rather, we are speaking of attempting to build an environment where the pulls and tugs between these two instincts provide the very stuff of the social learning agenda—an environment that is noisy; conflicted; filled with ambiguity; muddied by the traditional vices of anger, lust, envy, contentiousness, and greed; and yet encourages trust, openness, loyalty, integrity, generosity, courage, and love as responses. Nevertheless, this struggle for a community goes on within larger communities where the selfish influences of individualism control vast resources of institutional and political power. The influence of this power will not evanesce simply by our wishing it to. Neibuhr (1932) criticized this naivete when he observed:

> ... most ... social scientists ... seem to imagine that men of power will immediately check their expectations and pretensions in society as soon as they have been appraised by the social scientists that their actions are anti-social. (p. xvii)

Neither can those who cultivate such a community stand above the struggle in paternalistic self-righteousness. They enter the struggle as wounded healers, as humans who experience and openly acknowledge the pulling and tugging of the two instincts in themselves. In concert with teachers, parents, and students, cultivators of community engage in the struggle and pain of calling forth the larger, more generous, more mature instincts.

The issue of citizenship

The concept of this more mature community requires a rethinking of our notions about citizenship and concomitantly of our notions about education for citizenship (Kymlicka & Norman, 1993). Previously, citizenship was seen as a role made up of limited activities required of isolated individuals who shared responsibility for the social contract. Remember that the individual was seen as the primary unit of society. The duties of the citizen, then, were to see that the social contract was maintained and the justice envisioned in this contract was upheld (a justice, primarily of legal protections of private property and constitutional rights and of legal punishments for violators of private property broadly conceived). The upholding of the social contract was achieved through participating in the election of those who would support the social contract thus understood. Because the common good was identified with the freedom of individuals to pursue their own self-interests (limited by the rule not to interfere with the legitimate interests of others), it was assumed that the state (and other do-gooders) would not interfere with the natural course of events that would result from everyone pursuing their own self-interests because that would naturally result in the best arrangements for everyone.

There would be room for charity to be extended to the destitute and mentally incapacitated, of course, but that was a matter of personal choice, not of social policy. Because citizens were only minimally a community, and much more a collection of private individuals with rights that pertained to them as individuals, being *civil* to one another meant extending the minimal signs of a superficial goodwill toward the other.

In contrast, citizenship can be understood in terms of building up the community—proactive activities that create fellow feeling among people. For example, the proactive citizen gives time and work to a serious discussion of possible solutions to widespread poverty or to the search for a better public educational system. Within the general culture, however, these activities are not seen as normal citizen activities. On the contrary, the individualist would proclaim that one's work, time, and energy belong to oneself and are to be used for one's own betterment. Everybody is responsible for looking after themselves. We should not take that responsibility away from people. If we start that, before we know it those do-gooders will be interfering in our private affairs.

Such a view of citizenship, as the minimum public participation needed to keep the social contract functioning, is based on the faulty premise of the individual as the primary unit of society. As we are coming to understand better, the primacy of the individual over the community or of the community over the individual is a false dualism. It does not have to be an either/or, win/lose relationship. We are coming to understand that communities are stronger and richer when they are made up of individuals of diverse talents and potentials. Likewise, we see that individuals are stronger and richer when they are bonded into networks of people who offer different perspectives on life, when they complement their own talents with the community's cornucopia of other talents, when they associate with others who stretch them beyond the limits of their isolated perspectives. We are also beginning to understand that individuals are sustained at every level by love—the explicit love of family, friends, spouse, and children, and the tacit love behind the generous gift of the work that sustains social and human life made by countless others in everyday life. We are starting to understand that this love, when expressed both explicitly and inchoately, creates community and gives it continuity, consistency, and value.

In this view of community, the individual is enriched simply by membership in the cultural, economic, and political life of the community and finds even greater fulfillment in responding to the community (now in the person of a beloved friend, now in the person of neighbors, now in the form of a voluntary association, now in the form of his or her career) with loving service. Through that loving service, the community is enriched and, reflexively, the individual re-creates/performs him or herself. The individual becomes a more expansive being, a more complete being by being more closely bonded to a member or group in the community or to the community itself. Through engagement with the community, the individual ceases being isolated, alone, and unconnected to anyone or anything.

Civil libertarians argue, however, that the individual has the right to choose to be alone; that every person enjoys a fundamental freedom to isolation from community involvement, the freedom to be selfish, the freedom to go off in the woods, like Thoreau, and thumb his nose at the community. This is indeed a constitutionally protected freedom. Sometimes a separation from the community for psychological, moral, or political reasons is necessary for a while. Such isolation from the community, however, especially on a permanent basis, has never been seen as a desirable state of affairs for humans. Most civil libertarians, while maintaining the right of the recluse to live that way, think of such behavior as odd and eccentric. Even in prisons, solitary confinement is seen as one of the most punitive sanctions against a person who has already been removed from normal social relations.

The normal life of humans is found in community. Even when Thoreau removed himself from his human community, he sought a deep communion with nature. He studied the rhythms, patterns, and eccentricities of nature and grounded his own identity within the web of nature's life. Perceiving the gift of nature to humans, he gave nature back to us in his writings, thus connecting us to our natural community of life.

An expansive view of citizenship

Citizenship should be a proactive involvement in the life of the community—an activity that seeks to give back to the community what the community has already given to the individual: life, talents, capabilities, energy, and love. Citizenship can take as many forms as there are relationships in the community (volunteering on a neighborhood child-care committee, serving on a faculty grievance committee, working in a clothing factory, designing a new highway bridge). In this regard, I differ with Levin (1990), who maintained that we need one kind of education for citizenship and another kind for work. Levin posited citizenship as democratic participation in the pursuit of citizens' rights (note the echo of classical liberalism). The role of worker, according to Levin, requires quite a different set of attitudes—namely, obedience to the owner or foreman, the surrendering of our rights of free speech, free assembly, and so on to the authority of the employer. Our work and our relationship with fellow workers is carefully spelled out in the contract whereby we sell our labor to the owner—a contract far different from the social contract we enjoy as citizens.

On the contrary, work can be another way of exercising citizenship. I am not simply working for an employer, I am also working for the clients of the company, the customers. Through my work, I join with the others in my company and those countless other citizens who help make the institutions of society work. The products or services I render contribute to the well-being of my society. Furthermore, if the products I produce or sell were to harm or disadvantage society (e.g., unsafe automobiles, defectively tested medicines, environmentally contaminating chemicals), I have an obligation as a citizen to speak up to my employer. If the employer refuses to respond, then I am obliged to go to the proper authorities and report it.

Another way of thinking about citizenship is to imagine the individual citizen, when he or she is proactively engaged with others, as being the community in microcosm. By this I mean that in all my relationships I should be acting out the ideals and values of the community. Acting as a *good citizen* means pursuing in all my relationships those ideals that my community stands for—at least in the minimum observance of those customs of civility, traditions of etiquette, minimal rules of social exchange, and legal requirements. If I were representing my neighborhood at some regional gathering, I would want the other participants to see me as a good representative of my neighborhood, not as someone who flaunted all the values my neighborhood stands for. That is why members of teams who represent their country at the Olympic competitions are held to exacting standards of sportsmanship and social behavior. For that moment and in that place, they *are* Italy, China, France, or Brazil. The kind of citizenship we need to promote is not a self-centered focus on my rights as a member of such and such a community, but rather a citizenship that stands for the values and ideals of his or her community. This, of course, assumes that citizens know what their communities stand for and have come to cherish those values and ideals. When this happens, the individual becomes, in microcosm, the community in action, serving itself, knowing itself, healing itself, and celebrating its nobility and its destiny. The individual, in his or her immediate circle of family, neighbors, and coworkers, becomes the community seeking a fuller expression of itself.

Education in this kind of citizenship involves a discussion of the kinds of meanings embedded in the community's understanding of itself. It also involves the practice of those ideals and values in specific and concrete ways within the school setting. Teachers can devise learning activities that require exploration and performance, within the school itself, of justice, caring, democratic processes, nonviolent negotiation of conflict, debate on public policy, sharing of talent for the building up of community, and so forth. Unacceptable behavior is seen not so much as breaking a rule imposed by the administration, but as failing to live up to a value that is cherished by the community. This response to deviant behaviors, when reinforced over years of schooling, changes the youngster's perception of the ground for moral action away from thinking of the obligation imposed on him as an isolated individual to obey this abstract rule or principle, and toward thinking of his connection to his community and how that behavior enhances or diminishes the community's life. We move from a kind of Kantian abstract ethics of duty to an ethic of citizenship, of proactive participation in the life of the community.

Preparation for citizenship is still one of the mainstream, traditional purposes of public education. That purpose is served not only by civics courses dealing with the structures and processes of government, but also by exposing youngsters to the arena of public policy—its formation and implementation in laws and regulations; exposing them to the major issues contested in public debate: ecological preservation; alternative energy sources; full civil rights for various groups disadvantaged by social and political structures; government regulation of global corporations; international agreements on investments in global economic and technological infrastructures; ownership of the airways, the oceans, the rainforests, the Internet; international responses to terrorist organizations; genetic engineering of food, livestock, medicine, human organs; immigration rights and responsibilities, to name a few. Many of these public policy issues can contextualize the academic curriculum content, thereby ensuring a greater student interest in these topics.

The purpose of preparation for citizenship has traditionally included learning to live with people whose class, race, religion, and ethnic background differs from one's own. Although traditional assumptions about schools serving a melting pot function have been shown to be naive, the deeper dream of *e pluribus unum* still remains a social and political ideal that schools are supposed to serve (Whitson & Stanley, 1996). Given the stridency of identity politics in the present, schools can no longer assume that minimum social harmony between antagonistic groups happen automatically simply by placing these groups under the same roof for 7 hours a day; they have to work at making it happen—indeed, strenuously work at making it happen. As Goodlad (1996) reminded us, schools need to teach the rudiments of political democracy, but they also need to teach social democracy and, beyond those two, the democracy of the spirit. That kind of teaching requires attention to building community at the school for its own sake, as a good in its own right, as an essential learning experience for young people growing up under conditions of late modernity when the identity of the individual and the formation of community have to be reinvented. Education for a productive life remains a primary purpose of schooling, to be sure, but it must share the stage with education in and for community.

Self-governance

One of the fundamental questions facing the individual as well as the community is "How shall I/we govern myself/ourselves?" This question covers a whole host of decisions, from how one controls the schedule of digestive relief, to how one gets a fair share of the family platter of macaroni, to how a school makes out a class schedule, to how a family makes out a monthly budget, to how I respond when an opposing player in the neighborhood basketball game knocks me down from behind. In the formation and building of community within a school, the processes by which a community governs itself, and the corresponding processes whereby individuals govern themselves, are crucial.

I am not referring to the drawing up of a student book of rights, nor of a faculty/parents bill of rights (although that may eventually be treated in a much larger and continuous development of processes of self-government). The formation and building of community should start with questions: What kind of a community do we want to be? What do we value most about the prospect of our life together in this school? When a new class comes into our school, what do we want them to know about us as a community? What do we want to be thought of by people in the wider community?

Discussions of these questions bring to the surface the values that members of the school community hold sacred. These values are articulated in stories (precision of philosophical definition is not the goal of these discussions) that provide typical examples of behaviors that reflect those values. These discussions (which should include parents and school board members as well as students and teachers) should produce the choice of two or three central values by which the community wishes to distinguish its life. The school may want to adopt a motto or coat of arms expressing these values. These values can be embossed on a school flag, pins, or emblems, and written into a school song or school pledge. All these symbolic representations become ways for the community to remind itself what it stands for. Membership in the community brings with it general obligations to enact those values in the daily course of the school week or school year. School awards for outstanding contributions to the living out of those values can become a semester or end-of-year occasion.

Encouragement of a generalized, proactive exercise of membership is far more important in the activity of self-governance than a book of rules and prohibitions. The community governs itself by pursuing those human ideals that make living in that community desirable and humanly fulfilling. In reality, the interpretation of these values as justifying or rationalizing certain behaviors is a daily process of negotiation. There will be a pull toward self-centered behaviors. There will be normal misunderstandings between people and arguments that tear at the fabric of the community. It is the community's daily work and responsibility to heal divisions, provide space for differences of opinion, and allow for a plurality of cultural expressions while calling the members to honor and pursue those common human values that unite them.

Besides the honoring of central values that unite the community, there is a need for explicit policies and procedures for handling grievances, arbitrating disputes, and setting community goals. This, of course, requires constituting a body or group that has the authority to set the general frameworks by which the community conducts its business (calendars, budgets, work schedules, delegation of responsibilities, standing committees, etc.). This authority within the school is exercised in conjunction with the authorities of the local community and state who have jurisdiction over aspects of school life. Hence, if the school establishes a student court, that court's jurisdiction needs to be defined in reference to the civil law as well as the internal procedures of deciding disputes within the school. For example, the student court may have something to say to a student who is caught selling drugs within the school, but it also has to recognize the civil jurisdictions of law enforcement agencies in the larger community over such illegal behavior. The school may have an internal budget committee, but that committee has to function within the resources and limitations set by local and state agencies. The school budget committee may have little discretion, for example, in limiting expenditures for children with special needs.

Involving the school community or representative committees of the community in *administrative* decisions helps cement ownership of the practical decisions necessary to run its affairs. Whenever possible, however, these decisions should be related to those large values by which the community wishes to govern itself and not simply to the technical values of efficiency and expediency. Self-governance involves self-administration, but it is not to be equated with it. Governance involves not simply the administration of scarce resources or restricting of unacceptable behavior; it also involves those proactive choices that go beyond expediency to reach out in more generous ways to our fellows—not so much in the pursuit of some abstract virtue, but simply out of a caring for the person, a desire to share a part of our life more fully with that person or persons.

A community governs itself proactively by seeing to the necessary services required of all or some members of the community. These services include the communication of news and public opinion, assistance to disabled members, health and sanitation services, commercial services, and so on. In the school community, every person should be involved in some kind of service activity. This might involve working on the student newspaper, putting out the daily bulletins and announcements, serving as big brothers or big sisters to underclass students, serving as peer tutors, working with maintenance crews on special cleanup projects, serving on peer conflict-resolution teams, or working on the student court. These service activities can be cycled periodically so that students experience serving the community in a variety of ways.

Service activities that reach outside the school into the larger community can be options for the older children as well. Every child should learn the lesson that their quality participation is needed by the community. That lesson, repeated over 8 to 12 years of schooling, can create a life-long habit of community participation.

Self-governing is about self-control, to be sure, but it is also about channeling one's actions in a certain direction, and that channeling may be narrow or expansive. Governance may involve a choice to go beyond what administrative guidelines suggest to the more generous choice of self-giving. Hence, a teacher may follow administrative guidelines in providing her class with crayons and colored paper from general supplies. She may also pay out of her own pocket for a pair of eyeglasses for a child in her class whose family cannot afford them. A school may provide administratively for cooperative learning arrangements; a group of students may decide to govern themselves in a way that, besides following the administrative arrangements for cooperative learning, sets up an after-school tutoring service for younger students who are having academic difficulties or an after-school enrichment program for children whose parents are working. They govern themselves just as surely by choosing to go beyond the normal administrative arrangements of the school as by complying with those normal administrative arrangements. In that case, they are exercising their rights to help others.

Under the influence of modernity's ideology of individualism, our culture does not see that kind of proactive building up of community as part of the democratic process. That is because deeply embedded in our notion of democracy is the notion of possessive individualism, which uses democratic procedures to protect this possession, this property of *my life*, by which I stand apart from the community of other separate property owners, by which standing apart I exercise my basic freedoms. Freedom is not seen as the freedom to share my life and possessions with others; it is seen as freedom from other people, from their interference with my life, from their intruding on my living my life the way I want to live it. The rights of free speech, assembly, and owning property, however, can also be understood as necessary rights for building community, as necessary to a form of proactive citizenship on behalf of a democratic community.

Community as curriculum

While promoting the ideal of a mature community, educators must also work with youngsters—perhaps the majority of teenagers—who experience the social world as fragmented, impersonal, transitory, and untrustworthy. As Delanty (2000) suggested, following the leads of Castoriadis (1987) and Maffesoli (1996), community is imaginary, not in the sense of pure fancy, but as a projected state of affairs that has affective influence on people or groups that are contemplating cooperating together. We speak of the European Community. Europe is clearly a collection of distinct nation-states whose history reveals more conflict than cooperation. By referring to the larger construct of *community*, these nation-states suspend their differences to invent a greater reality. European Society will not do; it must be European Community. Community implies solidarity, a togetherness around common interests, *trust* that members will hold to their agreements, and *autonomy* on the part of the members responsibly acting in the social world (Delanty, 2000). Community does not smother differences. Here community relies on and prospers due to differences. Similarly, we speak of the *university community*. That community is made up of diverse academic departments who guard their territory and integrity quite passionately, although within those departments there are fierce disagreements over research methodologies and theoretical interpretations. Nonetheless, there is a solidarity around the pursuit of understanding—a trust that each scholar pursues that understanding according to legitimate methods and an honoring of the individual scholar's autonomy to conduct the search.

These guiding principles of community—solidarity, trust, autonomy—can provide the scaffolding for cultivating community at school. Cultivating community means that it is always something out in front of us, something that each day we construct, however fallible and messy. In appealing to their sense of community, we invite youngsters to work toward it.

The curriculum of community is not one course or a cluster of courses. Rather it is a sequence of multiple learning activities spread out over the whole K–12 curriculum. Some of these learning activities take place in the classroom through deliberations of how the class will comport itself; some are explicitly connected to learnings in the academic subjects such as geography, history, literature, science, world languages, and art; some take place on the playground, in the cafeteria, or on the school bus; some might be learned in group communication exercises run by the guidance department or homeroom teachers; some may be learned in school-sponsored special events for grandparents and parents. The curriculum of community is likewise taught by the establishment and maintenance of a school honor code, by the establishment of and frequent reference to schoolwide core values, by the daily engagement of student conflict-resolution teams, in activities conducted by the student government and student court, in school-sponsored community service activities, through big-brother, big-sister arrangements, through peer tutoring programs, through the dramatization of student issues in dramas, musical comedies, and artistic displays, and through special assemblies where civic community issues are deliberated. The curriculum of community is explicitly taught in all the co-curricular activities of the school as well, through the exercise of teamwork and contributing to a sense of pride in the school.

Much of the curriculum of community grows out of the community issues students bring to school, such as conflicts over cultural expressions of pride, identity, attitudes toward authority; perceived inequalities in the way different groups are treated; learning styles; relationships with teachers; perceived humiliations in classrooms and corridors; explicit bullying, intimidation, disrespect, stereotyping, insults, name-calling; student property and theft; parental involvement; and student privacy and record keeping.

By and large, adults in the school tend to make all the decisions about what should be done or not done about these issues. As a result, students have little or no voice in how the school regulates behavior around these issues. Furthermore, students are thereby prevented from involvement with shaping the values by which they might preserve and protect public and private spaces in the school. Their only cultural activity within the school is more or less compliance with adult-imposed regulations or more or less resistance to these regulations. They have no voice in shaping their learning environment. Adults complain that youngsters in school never think of anyone else but themselves while they deny them the opportunity to think about their mutual responsibilities to one another.

The building and sustaining of community will have to deal with the messy side of community as well as its more uplifting side. Thus, students will need to learn how to disagree, resolve misunderstandings, settle disputes nonviolently, and repair broken relationships. They will also have to work to overcome prejudices they have learned at home, how to place their own interests aside to help someone else. That is hard work, learned only over multiple experiences in a solicitous and supportive environment. This work needs structured and programmatic support. It needs teachers to provide the scaffolding for students to move from what they know to what they do not know. It needs teachers who take student mistakes as opportunities to learn, rather than opportunities to punish.

School leaders concerned to build community as one of the primary curricula of the school would encourage students, first and foremost, to compose the curriculum of community—to name those learnings that are important and essential to them. As that curriculum was being composed, the adults in the school could be invited to join with the students to explore some planned sequence of proactive learning experiences that would engage that curriculum. Following those discussions, students could draw up a list of learning activities that older students might teach to younger students. Adults in the school might develop their own collective notebook of actual and potential learning activities, perhaps arranged in some developmental sequence—activities that could make up the curriculum of community that they agree will be taught by everyone in the school, including the students, support staff, cafeteria workers, and custodians, applying those learnings consistently in the various interactions among children at various grade levels. Every year, faculty, staff, students, and parents could add new suggestions to the notebook of learning activities.

Obviously, this curriculum would be constructed over several years by the educators, students, and staff at the school with the help of parents and district professionals. It would grow out of a commitment to make the school a humane and socially nurturing environment in which the pursuit of academic learning would go hand in hand with social learning. The curriculum would build on the basic experiences of people being present to one another, learning to trust one another, to talk to one another and share stories. It would progress to more intentional and explicit focus on the active establishment and maintenance of a culture and of structures that support community.

The curriculum of community flows from understanding community in late modernity as a complex, multidimensional, fluid, contested, and pragmatic phenomenon. It is built on and sustained by relationships of interpersonal mutuality (Kerr, 1996), a mutual presence to a shared common work or activity (Boyte & Kari, 1996), shared responsibilities and rights of membership, and mutual commitments of loyalty. This curriculum recognizes that community has to be actively constructed every day by the members of that community because the agreements of today may sew the disagreements of tomorrow. It also recognizes that a contemporary community inescapably involves diversity and the politics of identity, and so it builds in structures and processes to negotiate and honor difference, to find common ground, as well as time and space for a variety of interests. In all this, it insists on processes of deliberation. Finally, this curriculum explicitly attends to the institutionalization of communal self-governance, thereby sewing the seeds for more adult participation in a democratic community.

Summary

We have seen how administering community involves a refashioning of the term into a richer, more expansive idea. This more expansive idea of community is called for as we enter the 21st century with its concepts of the global village and a planetary community of life. It is an idea of community that is called for not only by the critique of individualism, but by the growing contributions of women scholars, scholars from our increasingly multicultural citizenry, the many scientists who provide a new view of the planet and the cosmos. Once again, we see that the message of the first chapter has been underscored. Educational administration is not for the fainthearted. It is not for those who cannot sustain the intellectual effort to understand, study, and attempt to verbalize a sense of community that is still being formed within our culture. It is also not for authoritarians or rugged individualists. Rather, it is for those who have the courage to make a career in a profession that is finding its way in a time of transition, the courage to forge a vision of schooling that honors a mature sense of community and educates youngsters in its imperfect realization. This curriculum cannot be ignored on the excuse that there is already too much academic material to be mastered in an already crowded school year. Mastering that academic agenda without preparing youngsters for participating in a new kind of community renders that academic learning problematic, if not dangerous. That is why we have to look at the cultivation of meaning and the cultivation of community as inescapably intertwined.

Activities

1. In your journal, describe how democracy is understood and taught in your school or school district.
2. Generate five schoolwide activities that could be initiated within a month in your school that would increase your school's sense of community.
3. In your study group, brainstorm administrative initiatives that would improve the sense of community at schools.
4. The author presents some fanciful ideas about the individual belonging to a variety of communities—cultural, national, natural, and cosmic to which a response of bonding and participation, rather than withdrawal and protective isolation, is the more mature response. In your study group, discuss how strongly the cultural understanding and ideology of individualism might inhibit your own school embracing this expanded sense of community.
5. In your own words, prepare a statement on the school as a self-governing community. Present this statement to your faculty for their response and commentary.

References

Bateson, G. (1979). *Mind and nature: A necessary unity.* New York: E. P. Dutton.
Becker, E. (1967). *Beyond alienation: A philosophy of education for the crisis of democracy.* New York: The Free Press.
Bohm, D. (1981). *Wholeness and the implicate order.* London: Routledge & Kegan Paul.
Boyte, H. C., & Kari, N. N. (1996). *Building America: The democratic promise of public work.* Philadelphia: Temple University Press.

Castoriadis, C. (1987). *The imaginary institution of society*. Cambridge: Polity Press.
Delanty, G. (2000). *Modernity and postmodernity*. London: Sage.
Ferris, T. (1988). *Coming of age in the Milky Way*. New York: Doubleday Anchor Books.
Giddens, A. (1984). *The constitution of society*. Berkeley, CA: University of California Press.
Goffman, I. (1959). *The presentation of self in everyday life*. Garden City, NY: Doubleday Anchor Books.
Goodlad, J. I. (1996). Democracy, education, and community. In R. Soder (Ed.), *Democracy, education, and the schools* (pp. 87–124). San Francisco: Jossey-Bass.
Kerr, D. H. (1996). Democracy, nurturance, and community. In R. Soder (Ed.), *Democracy, education, and the schools* (pp. 37–68). San Francisco: Jossey-Bass.
Kymlicka, W., & Norman, W. (1993). Return of the citizen: A survey of recent work on citizenship theory. *Ethics, 104*, 352–381.
Levin, H. M. (1990). Political socialization for workplace democracy. In O. Ichilov (Ed.), *Political socialization, citizenship, education, and democracy* (pp. 158–176). New York: Teachers College Press.
Lovelock, J. (1979). *Gaia: A new look at life on earth*. Oxford: Oxford University Press.
MacIntyre, A. (1981). *After virtue: A study in moral theory*. Notre Dame, IN: University of Notre Dame Press.
MacMurray, J. (1970). *Persons in relation*. London: Faber.
Mafessoli, M. (1996). *The contemplation of the world*. Minneapolis, MN: University of Minnesota Press.
McCarthy, E. D. (1996). *Knowledge as culture: The new sociology of knowledge*. London: Routledge.
Neibuhr, R. (1932). *Moral man and immoral society*. New York: Charles Scribner's Sons.
Swimme, B., & Berry, T. (1992). *The universe story*. San Francisco: Jossey-Bass.
Taylor, C. (1989). *Sources of the self: The making of the modern identity*. Cambridge, MA: Harvard University Press.
Whitson, J. A., & Stanley, W. B. (1996). "Re-minding" education for democracy. In W. C. Parker (Ed.), *Educating the democratic mind* (pp. 309–336). Albany, NY: State University of New York Press.
Zohar, D., & Marshall, I. (1994). *The quantum society*. London: Flamingo/HarperCollins.

CHAPTER TWELVE

The complexity of ethical living and learning

Cultivating an ethical school is never a finished task, just as living an ethical life is never a final accomplishment. Much of ethical experience is complex and saturated with ambiguity. To be sure, many ethical choices are simple and straightforward. Should I walk out of the store without paying for the merchandise? Should I falsely accuse someone of breaking the window, when I am the one who broke it? Usually, the answers to these ethical questions pose no problems. But other situations may not be so clear. If we put ourselves in a student's place, we would have to struggle with many of their questions. How should I treat a bully who is picking on my older brother? How should I respond to the demands of a drunken parent? How should I respond to a police officer who uses an ethnic slur when addressing me? How do I respond to my best friend who wants to copy my homework? How do I respond when my classmates are scapegoating a student I don't like? How do I respond to a reckless driver who pulls out of a side street just in front of me, without even slowing down at the stop sign? How do I respond to another person who shoves me against the lockers in the school corridor? How do I respond when I see some of my friends making fun of a handicapped person? For many young people, the complexities of social life—when their own identities are only in the process of being formed, and their loyalties uncertain—leave them morally conflicted or uncertain. Not a few adults face similar uncertainties as they confront ethical choices.

It is relatively easy to speak in generalities of autonomy, connectedness, and transcendence, as well as justice, caring, and critique. In lived experience, however, circumstances often pose two or three apparently valid interpretations of what comprises autonomy, connectedness and transcendence. In other circumstances, our connectedness may be to two people to whom we owe allegiance, but only one of whom can be served by our decision, while the other is harmed by our decision.

In any given ethical decision we often find layers of motives, some of which are self-serving, some of which are more altruistic. Most situations in our lives involve ambiguities, ironies, and paradoxes. We are seldom all aligned in one direction toward virtue. Self-deception and rationalization constantly intrude, often at a subliminal level that avoids detection until someone else points it out to us. For persons of integrity, living ethically usually involves struggle and conflict; even the virtuous have their moments of weariness and discouragement, when the easy way out is chosen over the more ethically "correct" response.

Cultivating an ethical school will demand that teachers always communicate that they care about the moral tone of the school community. That caring, however, will always have to be mixed with sensitivity to the difficulty that even mature adults, let alone children and adolescents, have with consistently living an ethical life. Teachers will have to set limits, but the limits should be imposed with love and compassion. The ethical school will exhibit "tough love" at times; at other times it will exhibit unconditional love; it should teach students how to forgive themselves and each other. It should also acknowledge that ethical values are expressed in a variety of ways, and be aware that sometimes students will express their values in unpredictable and unconventional ways. The ethical school, while standing for ethical values, also has to avoid the self-righteousness of the ethical know-it-all, admitting that in some instances certainty eludes us all.

For the ethical school to succeed, all the members will need constantly to remind themselves that this is a human enterprise. As such, they should expect mistakes and imperfections. They will have to remind themselves that human beings are flawed and inconsistent, that despite their best intentions, self-interest will creep in to even the most altruistic of enterprises. The effort has to be entered upon with a sense of humility and sustained with a sense of compassion; otherwise it will defeat itself by expecting too much and by becoming a prisoner of its unrealistic expectations. The community will have to remind itself constantly that one learns to become ethical perhaps more often by learning from failures than by celebrating successes.

Summary

Throughout this book I have insisted on the cultivating of the ethical character of the educating process and the need for creating multiple supports and expressions of its ethical character. Now, in this last chapter, am I allowing myself to be defeated by doubts as to its feasibility? To think so would be a misreading of the argument of this chapter. I believe that educators must continuously struggle to cultivate an ethical school; that struggle is integral to any process that deserves the name of education. In our exploration of a rationale and a process for cultivating an ethical school it is natural that high expectations would arise. Without backing down from those high expectations, it is important to realize that the experience of the ethical community will always involve the comedy and tragedy of the human situation.

Ethical education is not a simple training in the predisposition to be ethical, the lessons of which, once learned, guarantee an ethical adulthood. Ethical education is a lifelong education. It takes place simultaneously with our efforts to be human. We learn to be human in the *struggle* for integrity. Virtue is not something we achieve and then continue to possess. Virtue is always out in front of us to be achieved; it involves a perpetual doing. The human person is always incomplete. In a sense we do not create ourselves, we do ourselves. We do not make "good works"; we do good. We can't lay it out ahead of time. We can't say, now that I have developed and possess this virtue, I know how to act in this or that circumstance, in advance. The virtuous act must be continuously sought and improvised (Meilaender, 1984).

Since ethical education is a life-long experience, it should begin in school so that the process of ethical learning can become more intentionally reflective and its lessons more clearly learned. Paradoxically, we learn what it is to be human as well when we *fail* as when we succeed. In failure, we learn the hard lesson of our limits and the ambivalence of our motives, and the wonderful lesson of being forgiven by our fellows. We learn through failure the lesson of compassion, compassion for ourselves and compassion for our brothers and sisters. We discover the emptiness of a self-centered life, and the richness of a life whose connections sustain us even in our failures. In the pursuit and occasional achievement of some virtuous activity, we discover the quiet joy of enhancing someone else's life, the satisfaction of easing someone else's pain, the surprising pleasure when our honoring a relationship is acknowledged, the paradoxical fulfillment of ourselves when we give away ourselves. The learning is in the striving, not simply of the individual but in experiencing the striving of the community, where we gain our humanity in interaction with other humans who are struggling with all the heroic ambiguities of the human condition. A perfect ethical community would probably bore us to tears; we would not recognize it as a human community. A human community is a community that expresses the full range of the journey toward its fulfillment; in short a divine comedy. In school, we learn that our life, collectively and individually, is a divine comedy, but that the direction it takes is our responsibility.

Cultivating an ethical school, then, calls for great courage, a modicum of intelligence, lots of humility, humor, and compassion, and an unyielding hope in the endurance and heroism of human beings. It is a dream worthy of educators.

Reference

Meilaender, G.C. (1984). *The theory and practice of virtue*. Notre Dame, IN: University of Notre Dame Press.

INDEX

Note: Page numbers followed by 'f' refer to figures and followed by 't' refer to tables.

academic: disciplines and influence on learning 67–68; meanings of learning 61; self-image 97
Adams, P. 148
adolescents: anti-establishment postures 115; human development theory 97
affirming presence 129–130, 150
application of learning at home or in community 61
appreciation, sympathetic knowing as 17–19
assessment exercises: according to criteria of assessment rubrics 64–66; illustrating teacher's monitoring of 69–71; reflective 62, 63, 63f, 65, 70; summative 62, 65, 70–71
Australia 13
authentic learning 72–73, 75, 105–106, 108, 134–135
authenticity: connecting learning to journey toward 107–108; ethic of 108; human resource leadership 126–128; presence and 129; professional 127; of teachers 150–151
autonomy 115–117; paradox of 118–119

Begley, Paul 14
Bellah, Robert 33, 78, 119
Bickimer, David 13
Bolivia 12
Buber, Martin 86, 116

Canada 14
capacity-building 131–132
caring, ethics of 85–87; and cultural tone of school 87; integrity of human relationships 86–87

Carnoy, M. 34
Carver, F.D. 38
Catholic schools 11–12, 13
Chardin, Teilhard de 4
Chicago 12
citizenship: in contrast to social contract 158–159; expansive view of 160–162; issue of 158–160; public education a preparation for 161–162; schooling in scripts of 33–34
cognitive rape 21
community: citizenship, 158–162; cultivating see cultivating community; as curriculum 164–166; democratic 43–44, 45, 53, 138, 164; dialogue with administrators 73; as imaginary 164–165; individual's response to 157; isolation from 159–160; learning partnerships with 73–74; lesson for lifelong participation in 164; of mature individuals 154–158; membership of school 162–163; new understandings of 154; self-governance of school 162–164; tensions with individuality 33, 154, 159; understanding of ethic of justice 84, 85; values 160–161, 162–163
competition, script of 33–34, 87
connectedness 117–120; sympathetic knowing as experiencing 19–21
connection, instinct toward 155–156; struggle between survival instinct and 157–158
"conscience of membership" 120
consciousness of an educational administrator 45–47
conversations: about institutional arrangements 75–76; with external

constituencies 71–74; with internal constituencies 74–75
critical ethics 80–82, 85
critical presence 132–133, 150
Cultivating an Ethical School 14, 112
cultivating community 45, 46, 47, 66, 158, 165; work of administrators in 71, 72, 72f, 74–75, 75–76
cultivating meaning 45, 46, 47, 66; work of administrators in 71, 72, 72f, 74–75, 75–76
cultivating responsibility 45, 46, 47, 66; work of administrators in 71, 72, 72f, 74–75, 75–76
cultivation of learning 139–140
cultural values 118, 122
cultural world, situating learner in 108, 126, 135, 138, 139, 141, 143, 145, 146, 151
culture: acting ethically within 118–119; cross-cultural understanding 21–22; tone of school 87; youth 66–67
curriculum: authentic ways of connecting life of learner to 105–106; bringing learners into dialogue with 146–148, 147f; community as 164–166; conference 11; development program 12–13; from educational administrator's perspective 46–47; knowledge, approaches to 140–142; local issues included in 73–74; project for more coherent development planning 10; restoring balance of public school 13, 16–17 *see also* sympathetic knowing; science 22–23, 28, 69–70, 73; standards, relating classroom learning to district 63; of sympathetic knowing 17–23; tailored to mastering standardized tests 16; teacher's dialogic relationship with subject matter 145–146, 146f; from teacher's perspective 46
Curriculum Reconceptualists 11

Danforth Foundation 41
democracy: competing scripts of individual and community 33–34, 119, 164; curriculum support for participation in 22; Dewey on living in a 26; ideal of 117; need to teach political and social 162
democratic community 43–44, 45, 53, 138, 164
Dewey, John 7, 26, 84, 112, 117
dissertation 6–9
diversity, celebrating 21–22

drama of schooling/schooling of drama 26–37; in citizenship scripts 33–34; following rules of school 29–30; friendship 30–32; life-long choices as a result of 35; perpetuating subjugation of women 34; power relationships in schools 34–35; problems with 34–35; redefining 35–36; refusing to accept the script 30; social behavior and 29; teaching and administrative staff as players 35–36; in work script 32–33, 34

educated person, ideal of 46, 47
educational leadership: accountability for student performance 40; consciousness in 45–47; democratic community theme for school renewal 43–44; Elmore on 42; ethics of 79–80; extending perspective of center for 44–45; external constituencies, conversations with 71–74; former views of educational administration 38–40; institutional arrangement conversations 75–76; internal constituencies, conversations with 74–75; Leithwood's embracing of transformational leadership 41–42; managerial approach to 39–40; Murphy and school renewal 42–44, 53; new views of educational administration 40–41; rationality 39; recasting vocabulary and terminology 44–45; school improvement theme 43–44; in the service of school community 76; social justice theme for social renewal 43–44; university degree programs 40–41; vision behind *see* vision behind administrative leadership; work of administrators 71, 72f
ego: development outcomes 96t; identity 107; as source of understanding and agency 95, 103–105, 104f
Eiseley, Loren 8–9, 142
Elmore, Richard 42, 127, 131
Emerging Patterns of Supervision 6
Emile 21
empathy 120
enabling presence 130–132, 150
Erikson, Erik 94–107
ethic of authenticity 108
ethic of justice 83–85; community as source of 84, 85; individual as source of 83–84, 85
ethical laxity 135, 136
ethical living, complexity of 169–170
ethical person, foundation qualities of an 112–124; autonomy 115–117;

connectedness 117–120; convergence of ethical and human development 112–113; development 114, 122–123; gender differences in expression of 114; reflecting relationality of humanity 112–113; transcendence 120–122

ethical school, building an 14, 78–92; complexities of ethical choices 169–170; continual struggle 170–171; ethic of critique 80–82, 85; ethic of justice and serving individual and common good 83–85; ethics of caring 85–87; ethics of educational administration 79–80; legitimacy of combining ethical theories 88; multidimensional foundation of 88–90, 89f; nurturing foundational qualities of an ethical person 123; practicality of construct 88

ethics: applied 126; of caring 85–87; critical 80–82, 85; general 125–126, 138–139; of learning 139–140; professional 14, 126, 138–139; virtue 125

ethics of teaching 138–153; approaches to content knowledge 140–142; bound up with ethics of learning 139–140; professional 14, 138–139; virtues to facilitate 149–152

ethics of teaching model 143–148, 144f; dialogue between students and subject matter 146–148, 147f; establishing a working relationship with learners 143–145, 145f; five kinds of learning 143; implications for teachers' growth 148–149; teacher's dialogic relationship with subject matter 145–146, 146f

evaluation process, teacher 135–136

female–male relationships 117–118
five kinds of learning 143
Fordham University, New York 12–13; Masters program in Educational Leadership 13–14
formal logic 106
frames of understanding 27
Freire, Paulo 12, 80, 94
Freud, Sigmund 94, 95
friendship and schooling 30–32
future, influenced by a nation's schools 35

gender: differences in expression of foundational qualities of an ethical person 114; redefinition of masculinity and femininity 117–118; in schools 118

general ethics 125–126, 138–139
generativity stage 98
Giddens, Anthony 97, 155
grades 34
grading system 9–10
Green 118, 119–120, 122
Griffiths, D. E. 38

Harvard University, *Teaching for Understanding* project 61
heroes 121–122, 156–157
high standards 93
human development theory of Erikson 94–107; academic self-image 97; adolescents 97; cautions against simplifications 100–103; developing trust 100–101; generativity 98; infancy and childhood 96–97; intimacy 98–99; life-cycle challenges 95–99, 96t; linking school learning to life-cycle challenges 102–107; prior learning incorporated into new development challenges 100–101; psychosocial transitions through continuous life development 100f; repeating passage of earlier challenges 101–102, 101f; self-identity 97–98; and sense of authenticity 107–108; split between cognitive and psychosocial development in classrooms 108–109

human resource leadership in education 93–94, 109; affirming presence 129–130; authenticity 126–128; critical presence 132–133; enabling presence 130–132; moral responsibility 134–136; virtue of presence 128–129; virtues of 125–126

The Immense Journey 8
inauthentic learning 106, 108, 134
individualism: and democratic process 33–34, 119, 164; freedom to choose not to be part of community 159–160; tensions with communitarianism 33, 154, 159
indwelling 18–19, 20
influences on student learning 66–68
instincts: struggle between survival and connection 157–158; survival 155, 157; towards connection 155–156
institutional arrangements, conversations about 75–76
intimacy stage 98–99

Jenkins, Iredell 17, 18
Jentzi, Doris 41–42

Index

Jesuit schools: as a Principal 9–12; as a student 3–4; university research and development team serving 12–13
justice, ethic of 83–85; community as source of 84, 85; individual as source of 83–84, 85

Kant, Immanuel 83
knowledge: approaches to content 140–142; bringing from outside to inside 141–142, 146–148, 147f; integrity of 134–135; teacher's translation of 145–146, 146f
Kohlberg, Lawrence 83–84

Langlois, Lyse 14, 138
learning, cultivation of 139–140
learning, five kinds of 143
learning model 60–68; academic disciplines and influence on 67–68; creating a product 64–65; creating readiness for learning 62f, 64, 68f; design of student work beginning at end 62–63; evaluating performances according to criteria of assessment rubrics 65–66; framing student work 62–63, 62f; influences on student learning 66–68; meanings, personal, public, applied and academic 60–62; and personal life world of student 66, 67f; placing work in wider context 66, 67f; reflections on assessment exercises 66; reflective assessment 62, 63, 63f, 65, 70; scaffolding 64; summative assessment exercises 62, 65, 70–71; youth culture and influence on 66–67
learning, nature of 59–60
Leithwood, Kenneth 41–42
Levin, H. M. 160
life-cycle challenges 95–99, 96t; cautions against simplifications 100–103; linking school learning to 102–107
life-long learning 34
Lindbloom, C. E. 39
literature: on leadership, focus of 10–11; study 7–8
living by learning/learning by living 112
love: in community 156, 157, 159; ethical school exhibiting 170; life-cycle challenge 98–99

MacIntyre, A. 78, 139, 143, 154
make-believe learning 106, 108, 134
male–female relationships 117–118

managerial approach: integrating with leadership aspect of work 51–53, 52f; problems with 39–40
Masters program in school leadership 10; Fordham University 13–14
meaning making, influence of ego on process of 103–105, 104f
meanings, personal, public, applied and academic 60–62
membership 113, 150–151; "conscience of" 120; of school community 162–163
"mind" 104
moral reasoning 83–84
moral responsibility 80, 134–136, 151
morality 78, 83, 84
multidimensional ethic in a school setting 88–90, 89f
Murphy, Joseph 41, 42–44, 45, 53
myths and meanings 50–51, 50f, 52f, 54f

National Commission on Excellence in Education 34
National Commission on Excellence in Educational Administration 41
natural world: benign universe 157; situating learner in 108, 119, 126, 135, 138, 139, 141, 143, 145, 146, 151; survival instincts in 155
Neibuhr, R. 158
nonconformity 30

Onion Model of Schools 49–53; dimensions of school life 49–50, 50f; schools with integrated vision 51–53, 52f; schools without vision 51, 51f

parents: gaining autonomy from 100, 115; working with 10, 72, 76, 166
partnerships: in learning 74; with schools abroad 22
personal learning 60; application at home or in community 61; sharing in public discourse 60–61
personal life world of student 66, 67f
personal meanings 60; shared in public discourse 60–61
Peru 12
philosophy studies 4, 7
Piaget, Jean 106
Polanyi, Michael 7, 8, 18, 20, 129
poverty 12, 116
power: control in communities 158; relationships in schools 34–35; sources of 116

presence: affirming 129–130, 150; critical 132–133, 150; enabling 130–132, 150; practice in human resource leadership 128–129; virtue of, facilitating ethics of teaching 149–152
presentations to external constituencies 71–72
professional development 73, 135, 148–149; weekends 11–12
professional ethics 14, 126, 138–139
psychosocial development: neglect of learners' 152; split in schools between cognitive and 108–109
psychosocial model of learning 104f
psychosocial transitions through continuous life development 100f
public meanings of learning 60–61
Purpel, D. E. 40, 78

Rawls, John 83
readiness for learning, creating 62f, 64, 68f
reflective assessment 62, 63, 63f, 65, 70
relationality 14–15, 112–113
religious education 23, 139
report card system 9–10
responsibility, virtue of: human resource leadership 134–136; teachers 151
rocks lesson 69–71
"roles" 103
Rousseau, Jean-Jacques 21
rules of school 29–30, 32, 49, 114, 136

scaffolding 64, 68, 69, 134, 135
school renewal: accountability for 40; conversations with internal constituencies 74–75; democratic community and 43–44, 45; Elmore on 42; initiatives in 2 different schools 9; Murphy on 42–44, 53; social justice and 43, 45, 81, 83; student as worker in process of 58–60
schooling of author 2–3
science curriculum 22–23, 28, 69–70, 73
self-governance 162–164
self-identity challenge 97–98
Sergiovanni, Tom 5–6, 7, 13, 38, 78, 134, 135, 140
Shapiro, J. P. 40, 125, 138
social behavior, learning 29
social bonding 156, 157
social contract 83, 119, 150, 158–159
social justice 43, 45, 81, 83

social life 156; friendship and schooling 30–32; as problematic 81; unscripted 29
social responsibility: of educational administrator 82; sympathetic knowing as experiencing 21–23
social science 23, 28, 38, 78
social world, situating learner in 108, 126, 135, 138, 139, 141, 143, 145, 146, 151, 155, 156
special learning needs, children with 144
spirituality of teaching 11–12
standardized tests 16, 17, 23, 34, 44; administrative accountability for 40, 134; conversations with external constituencies 73; misguided assumptions 152; reinforcing use of assessment rubrics 65
Stefkovich, J. A. 125, 138
Steinbach, Rosanne 41–42
structural arrangements: ethic of critique and 80–81, 81–82, 85, 133; human resource leadership and 135; interventions to benefit all pupils 136; one-size-fits-all 133
student as worker 58–60
student courts 163
Sullivan, William 78, 83, 84, 119
summative assessment 62, 65, 70–71
survival instincts 155, 157; struggle between connection and 157–158
sympathetic knowing 17; as appreciation 17–19; as experiencing connectedness 19–21; as experiencing social responsibility 21–23

Taylor, Charles 108, 150, 154
teachers: evaluation schemes 135–136; hiring and developing good 10, 134, 135 see also ethics of teaching; ethics of teaching model
teaching career of author 4–5; as Principal of a Jesuit high school 9–12; in sixties 5
Teaching for Understanding 61
teaching, model of 68–69, 68f; rocks lesson to illustrate 69–71
team teaching initiative 9
terminology, recasting vocabulary and 44–45
Tocqueville, Alexis de 33
transactional leadership: blending with transformational leadership 53; literature focus on 10–11
transcendence 120–122; levels of 120–121

transformational leadership 41–42; blending with transactional leadership 53; literature focus on transactional rather than 10–11
trust, developing 100–101

United Nations Educational, Scientific, and Cultural Organization (UNESCO) 143
University College for Educational Administration (UCEA) 41, 42–43
university courses: accreditation requirements 40–41; Masters programs in educational leadership 10, 13–14
university studies of author 4–9; dissertation 6–9; as Sergiovanni's research assistant 5–6; serving on research and development team for Jesuit high schools 12–13

values: community 160–161, 162–163; cultural 118, 122; of school community 162
virtue ethics 125
virtue(s): of authenticity 126–128, 150–151; to cultivate good of learning 151–152; of human resource leadership in education 125–126; of presence 128–129, 149–152; of responsibility 134–136, 151; that facilitate the ethical work of teaching 149–152

vision behind administrative leadership 47–55; communal institutionalization of 53, 54f; dimensions of school life 49–50, 50f; integrating leadership and managerial sides of administrative work 51–53, 52f; Onion Model of Schools 49–53, 50f, 51f, 52f; schools with integrated vision 51–53, 52f; schools without vision 51, 51f; testing ideas in forum of public debate 55; vision statements 48–49, 51
vision statements 48–49, 51
vocabulary and terminology, recasting 44–45

Whitehead, A.N. 8, 16, 19
Wirth, A. 34
women: schools perpetuating subjugation of 34; teachers, hiring 10
work of administrators 71, 72f; external constituencies, conversations with 71–74; institutional arrangement conversations 75–76; internal constituencies, conversations with 74–75; in the service of school community 76
work, schooling in script of 32–33, 34
worker, student as 59–60
workforce, impact of high technology on 34
writings, influences on 10–15

youth culture 66–67